Intelligent Business

Teacher's Book

Pre-Intermediate
Business English

| Irene Barrall |

Pearson Education Limited
Edinburgh Gate
Harlow
Essex CM20 2JE
England
and Associated Companies throughout the world.

www.intelligent-business.org

© Pearson Education Limited 2006

The right of Irene Barrall to be identified as author of this Work has been asserted by her in accordance with the Copyright, Designs and Patents Act 1988.

All rights reserved; no part of this publication may be reproduced, stored in a retrieval system, or transmitted in any form or by any means, electronic, mechanical, photocopying, recording, or otherwise without the prior written permission of the Publishers.

First published 2006
Third impression 2008

Intelligent Business Pre-Intermediate Teachers Book for Pack
ISBN 978-0-582-84803-0

Intelligent Business Pre-Intermediate Test Master CDROM for Pack
ISBN 978-1-4058-4308-9

Intelligent Business Pre-Intermediate Teachers Book and Test Master CD-Rom Pack
ISBN 978-1-4058-4339-3

Set in Times New Roman

Printed in the UK by Ashford Colour Press

Acknowledgements

The author would like to thank Yvonne Harmer, Tony Garside, Bernie Hayden and Nikolas Barrall for their help in preparing and editing the teacher's book and Stephen Nicholl for his excellent support.

Front cover copyright images supplied by Goldcorp Inc (left), Corbis (middle) and Punchstock (Comstock) (right)
Designed by Wooden Ark Ltd (Leeds)

Contents

Page
4   **Introduction**

15   **Coursebook: Teacher's notes**
102   **Coursebook Review: Answers**
104   **Coursebook Glossary Test: Answers**
105   **Coursebook: Photocopiable resources**

           1.1:   Company activities
           2.1:   Vocabulary
           3.1:   Polite phrases and responses
           4.1:   Comparatives and superlatives questionnaire
           4.2:   Product information
           5.1:   Business plan brainstorm
           7.1:   Presentation outline (Tourism and business)
           8.1:   Notes for a CV
           9.1:   Balloon marketing
          10.1:   Card activity (infinitive, past simple, past participle)
          11.1:   Insurance quote
          12.1:   Card activity (complaints)
          13.1:   Simon's two lives
          14.1:   Creative thinking
          15.1:   Office design
          15.2:   Motivation game

118   **Skills Book: Teacher's notes**
174   **Skills Book: Photocopiable resources (in the order that they appear)**

           1.1:   Talking about jobs
           2.1:   Telephone preparation
           3.1:   Card activity (small talk)
           7.1:   Card activity (prepositions of time)
           4.1:   Describing products
           5.1:   Talk preparation
           8.1:   Card activity (places in a company)
           8.2:   Find someone who …
           9.1:   Card activity (respond to suggestions)
          10.1:   Graph grid
          11.1:   Market research questionnaire
          12.1:   Telephone phrases (complaints)
          13.1:   Agenda suggestions
          14.1:   Card activity (negotiations)
          14.2:   Negotiations outline
          15.1:   Motivational factors

185   **Photocopiable frameworks**

INTELLIGENT BUSINESS (PRE-INTERMEDIATE) TEACHER'S BOOK

Introduction

Rationale

Today, the demand for Business English is greater than ever. And with the increasingly globalised world of international business, it looks set to keep on growing. As a result, the teaching and learning of Business English is playing an increasingly important role in business studies and everyday corporate life. Although the need for Business English is the same for students at a business school as it is for employees in a company, their needs and learning circumstances are very different.

For students at a business school, the main challenge is often understanding business itself, not only the English language. Fortunately, the tertiary education environment usually provides enough classroom hours to deal with these challenges. For students studying business full time, the key is to *learn business* through the medium of the English language.

For people already active in the workplace and with some understanding of the world of business, often the challenge is finding the time to learn Business English. Furthermore, for managers with a very good business knowledge, their learning experience must reflect this understanding of business practices and reality. For these students language learning is not an academic exercise but a need to translate familiar business practices into English as quickly as possible. Here the key is to do *business* in English.

Intelligent Business is a range of Business English materials that includes components specifically designed to meet the needs of students who either need to *learn business through English* or *perform familiar business tasks in English*. These materials can be used individually or, as they share a core language and skills syllabus, can be used in a variety of combinations described later in this introduction. For an overview of all the *Intelligent Business Pre-Intermediate* components, please see Fig. 1.

As well as sharing a common demand for Business English, both institutional and corporate learning environments are experiencing an increased demand for measurability. Today, both course tutors and training managers are under increasing pressure to measure and demonstrate progress and a return on the investment in Business English learning activities. As this is most effectively done using external, standardised and globally recognised examinations, *Intelligent Business Pre-Intermediate* is benchmarked against the Cambridge Business English Certificate (BEC) Preliminary level.

Finally, any Business English materials today need to draw on authentic sources and achieve a high degree of validity in the eyes of the learners and teachers who use them. Developed in collaboration with *The Economist* magazine, *Intelligent Business* draws on this rich source of authoritative and topical articles on the business world.

INTRODUCTION

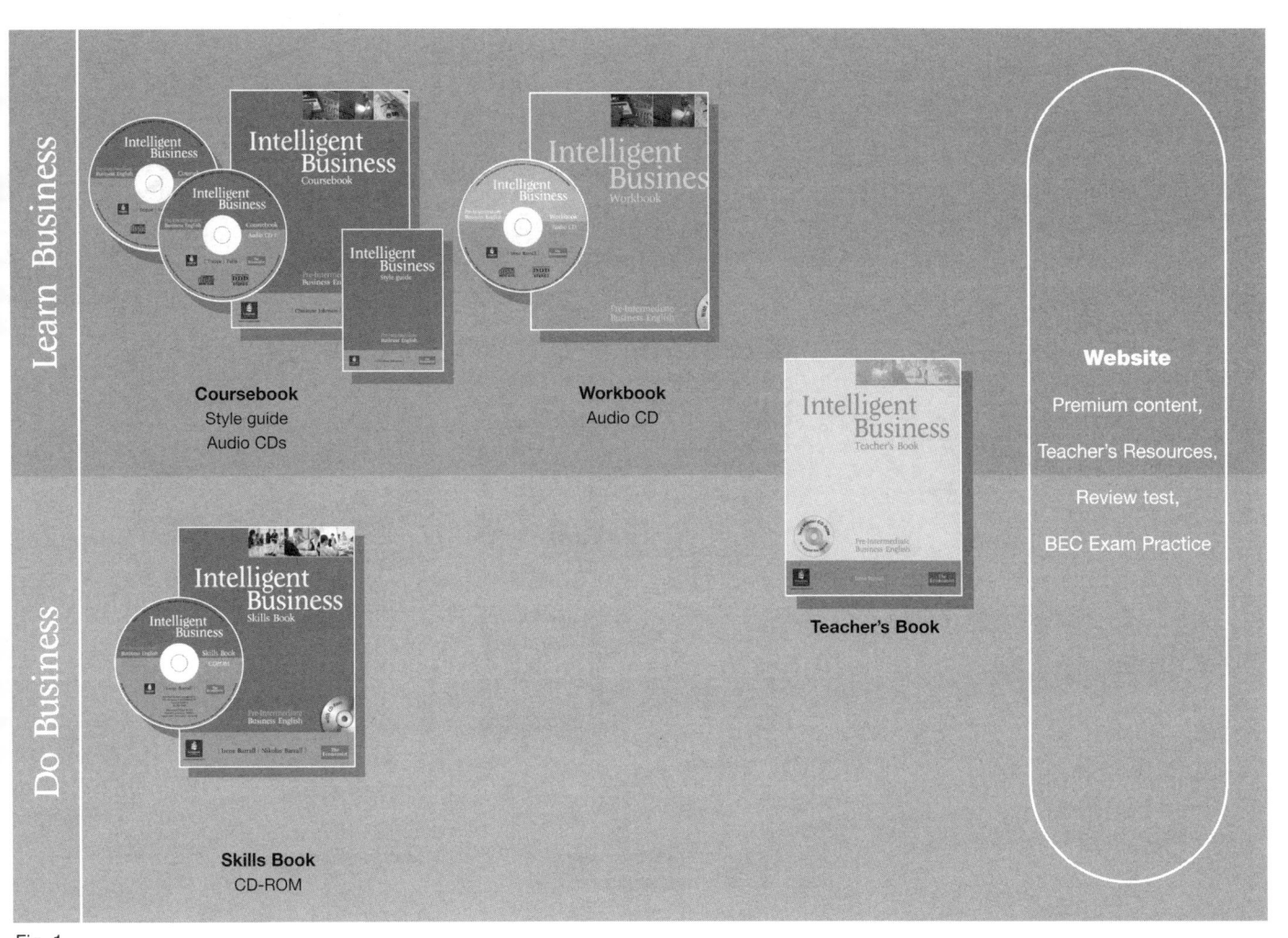

Fig. 1

- **Learn Business**
  - Coursebook — Style guide, Audio CDs
  - Workbook — Audio CD
- **Do Business**
  - Skills Book — CD-ROM
- Teacher's Book
- Website — Premium content, Teacher's Resources, Review test, BEC Exam Practice

Learn Business

Learn Business refers to the components designed to be especially accessible to learners who may not have much business experience or knowledge. These components include the *Intelligent Business* Coursebook and Workbook. The Coursebook provides 100+ hours of classroom-based teaching material divided into fifteen units. The course is built on a pre-intermediate grammar syllabus and uses plenty of authentic text to present grammar and vocabulary that is then extracted and practised in isolation. The texts are benchmarked against the word limits found at Cambridge BEC Preliminary.

The Coursebook also includes a *Career skills* syllabus that develops key communicative skills to help people within any kind of organisational – not just a corporate – environment. These communicative skills are supplemented by a *Culture at work* feature that raises students' awareness of how cultural differences can affect communication between people of different nationalities.

In addition, the Coursebook includes *Dilemma and Decision* (case study-style problem-solving activities) and regular reviews. These are designed to review the key grammar and functional language developed within the unit.

5

At the back of the book there is a grammar reference, a glossary with test and a *Style guide* – a pocket-sized 32-page booklet providing support on common forms of business correspondence such as email, letters and memos, along with general notes on organisation, style and accuracy.

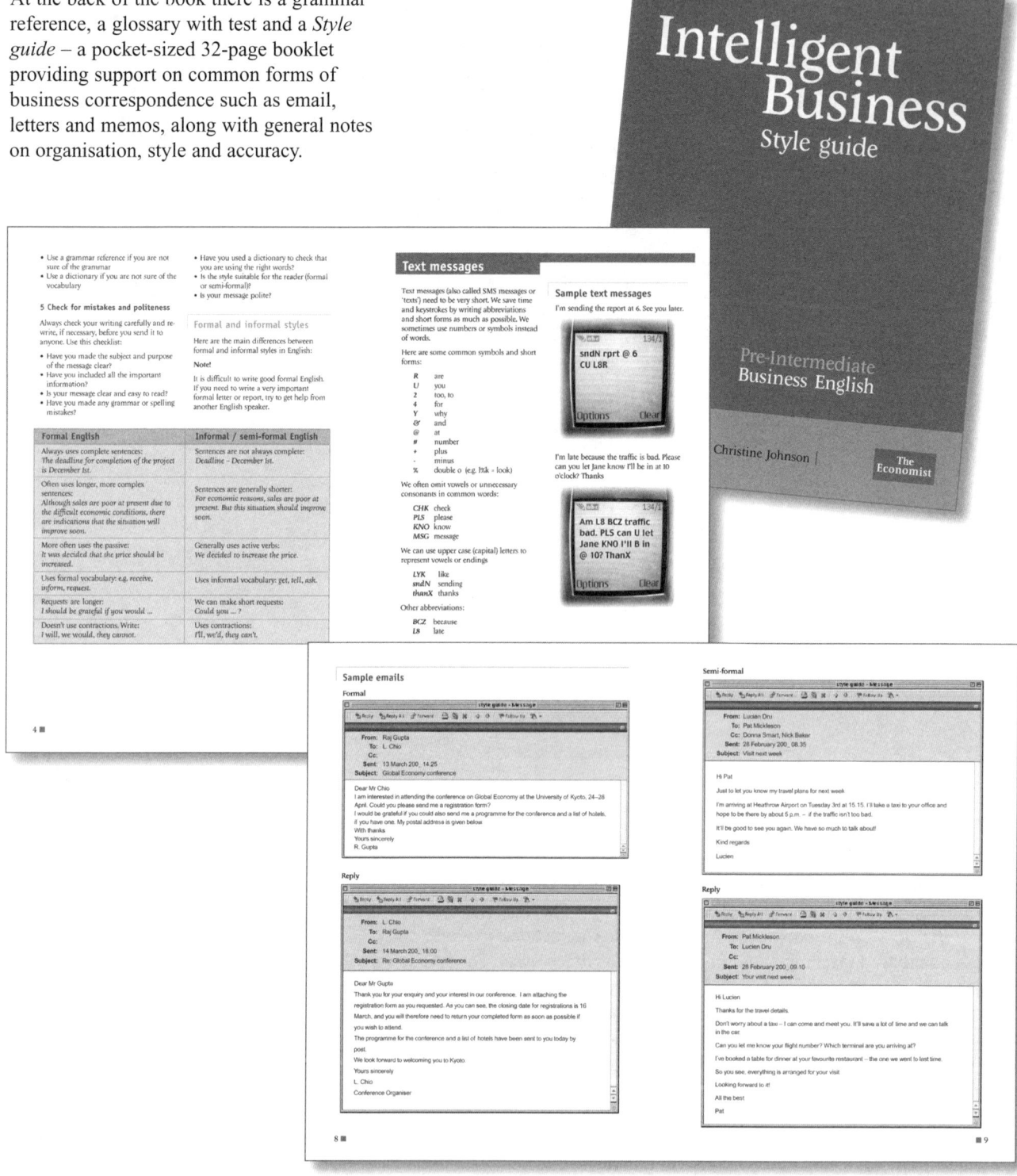

The Workbook consolidates the language of the Coursebook by providing further practice of the key grammar, vocabulary and skills found in the core *Intelligent Business Pre-Intermediate* syllabus. Throughout the Workbook there are Cambridge BEC Preliminary style tasks to familiarise students with the exam should they wish to take it. At the back of the Workbook is a complete BEC Preliminary Practice Test. Finally, the Workbook includes an audio CD containing all the Workbook listening material.

Do Business

Do Business refers to the *Intelligent Business Pre-Intermediate* Skills Book, which has been developed especially for busy employees who are on a company English language training programme. The Skills Book is a self-contained intensive Business English programme providing 30 hours of classroom-based material divided into five days of training. The course is aimed at small groups and built on a syllabus of key business skills such as presenting, socialising and taking part in meetings. The language development work focuses on the functions and communicative strategies required to perform these skills effectively. Unlike in the Coursebook, target language is presented mostly through dialogues and other listening extracts. Students then perform similar tasks and are invited to analyse their own performance. The Skills Book follows the same core syllabus as the Coursebook so the same grammar and functions appear in the equivalent units of both books.

The Skills Book has regular writing sections, a grammar reference with activities, and a *Good business practice* reference. The *Culture at work* syllabus of the Coursebook is followed and expanded upon to explain in detail how national culture can affect international business communication. There is also an interactive CD-ROM with the Skills Book that contains extra language practice and all the listening material for the book. There is also an extensive reference section for Grammar, Good business practice and Culture at work.

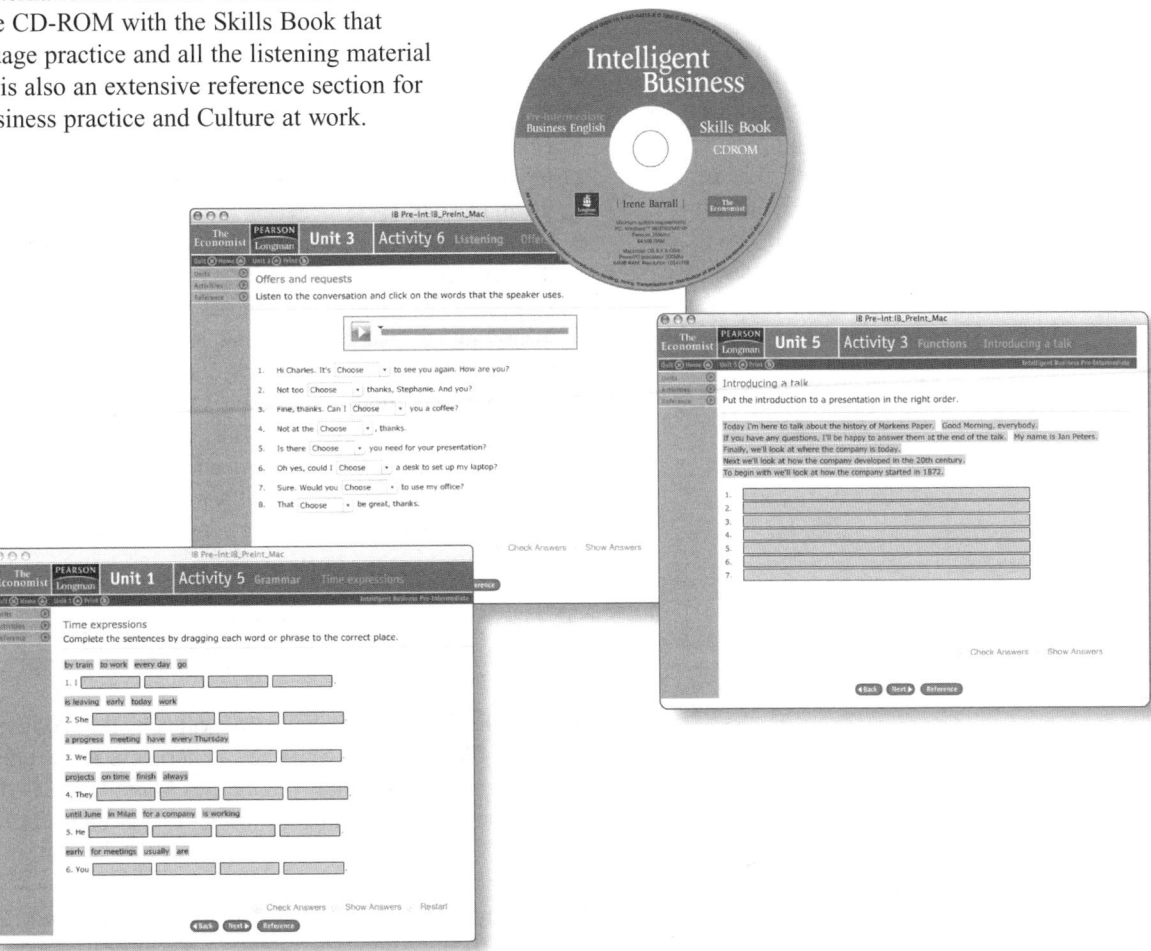

INTELLIGENT BUSINESS (PRE-INTERMEDIATE) TEACHER'S BOOK

General support

The key Learn Business and Do Business components are supported by the *Intelligent Business Pre-Intermediate* Teacher's Book covering both Coursebook and Skills Book and the *intelligent-business.org* website.

This Teacher's Book is split into two sections: the first covering the Coursebook and Workbook; and the second covering the Skills Book. Both sections provide step-by-step notes, answer key and background information, and at the end of each section there is a bank of photocopiable activities. There are also several photocopiable frameworks at the end of the book which help teachers with task preparation and feedback.

The *Intelligent Business* website is an entirely free supplement that provides resources for both learners and teachers. For learners there are review questions for each unit of the Coursebook, with which students can interactively measure their progress unit by unit. There is also the Premium Content that allows access to two free articles from the Economist.com subscription website. These articles are updated monthly. For teachers there are handy notes on ideas for making the most of authentic texts. The Teacher's Guide to Using Authentic Materials uses Economist texts to demonstrate useful teaching tips on how to exploit the Premium Content and similar articles from the press.

The Test Master CD-ROM

The Teacher's Resource Book includes a Test Master CD-ROM which provides an invaluable testing resource to accompany the course.
- The tests are based strictly on the content of the corresponding level of *Intelligent Business*, providing a fair measure of students' progress.
- An interactive menu makes it easy to find the tests you are looking for.
- Keys and audioscripts are provided to make marking the tests as straightforward as possible.
- Most tests come in A and B versions. This makes it easier for you to invigilate the test by making it harder for students to copy from each other.
- The audio files for the listening tests are conveniently located on the same CD-ROM.

Types of test

The Test Master CD-ROM contains five types of test.
- Placement Test/s
- Module Tests
- Progress Tests
- Mid Course Test
- End of Course Test

Flexible

You can print the tests out and use them as they are – or you can adapt them. You can use Microsoft® Word to edit them as you wish to suit your teaching situation, your students or your syllabus. Here are some of the things you may wish to do.
- Delete or add exercises to make the test shorter or longer.
- Delete exercises or items which relate to points which you decided to skip.
- Add in exercises to cover extra content you introduced into the course.
- Edit exercises to make them harder or easier, or to introduce key vocabulary.
- Edit the format of exercises so that they are consistent with other exams that you use.
- Personalise the content of exercises to bring them to life. For example, incorporate the names of students in the class, other teachers in the school, famous people and places from your country …
- Use the audioscripts to create extra listening exercises – for example by removing words to create gap fills, adding options to create multiple choice exercises or introducing deliberate mistakes for the students to correct.
- Add in the name and/or logo of your school at the head of the test. Finally, save your new version on your hard drive.

Using this CD-ROM

The ideal way to use this CD-ROM is to treat it as a master. Copy the tests to the hard drive of your computer and burn the audio files to CD or copy them on to cassette.
- **Test files** The installation wizard will copy the files to your hard drive.
- **Audio files** If you don't have a CD burner or if you prefer to teach with cassettes, you can simply put the Test Master CD-ROM into the CD drive of an ordinary hi-fi and copy the audio files onto a blank cassette.

Levels

Test Master CD-ROM are available for all levels of *Intelligent Business*.

The Language of Intelligent Business

All Pre-Intermediate components of *Intelligent Business* are based on the same core syllabus. The syllabus is broken down into 15 units and covers four main strands: grammar, vocabulary, functional language and cultural awareness. Although the different components emphasise different strands, they recycle and reaffirm all four key syllabus strands. Furthermore, the different components focus on different language skills in order to present the core syllabus. The Coursebook, for example, focuses on reading skills by introducing key grammar and vocabulary through authentic text, whereas the Skills Book focuses on listening skills by introducing functional language through transactional dialogues and meetings. The key productive skills of speaking and writing are covered extensively in both the Coursebook and Skills Book.

1 Grammar

The grammar content of the core syllabus is benchmarked against ALTE level 2, Common European Framework level up to B1 and Cambridge BEC Preliminary. The syllabus balances the need for grammatical accuracy required to pass exams with the need for the functional language required to develop fluency and communicative competence quickly.

Each unit of the core syllabus focuses on one grammatical structure. In grammar presentations examples of the target structure are drawn from the previous reading or listening text. The grammar is then highlighted and reviewed. It is assumed that very few students will be seeing the structures for the first time and the approach is very much one of reviewing and consolidating what has been taught before.

The main presentation of grammar is found in the Coursebook. The approach is one of review and students are often asked to demonstrate their knowledge before rules are given. After each grammar presentation there is both written and spoken practice with varying degrees of control, depending on the complexity of the grammar. The Workbook also provides plenty of self-study style grammar practice activities.

There is an extensive Grammar reference in the back of both the Coursebook and Skills Book and on the Skills Book CD-ROM. The reference covers all the grammar from the core syllabus and extends the notes provided in the classroom material. As the Skills Book focuses on fluency and communicative effectiveness, there is little explicit grammar presentation within the classroom material. However, this material follows and recycles the core syllabus and the Skills Book CD-ROM provides a wealth of interactive grammar practice. Furthermore, the Grammar reference at the back of the Skills Book also includes integrated practice activities.

2 Vocabulary

In line with the Learn Business, Do Business concept of *Intelligent Business*, vocabulary is dealt with according to the different needs of the various learners who use the course. For students needing to learn business, the vocabulary focuses on topics that describe the basic structures and functions of the business world. These include company structures, sales, marketing, HR, logistics, pay, etc. There are also topics relating to specific issues affecting today's business world such as globalisation and environmental sustainability. Key vocabulary and concepts are introduced in the keynotes, defined, used in context and tested throughout the units. Students are encouraged to activate the vocabulary through speaking and writing activities such as the Dilemma & Decision problem-solving tasks that end each unit. Furthermore, these key items are listed in the Coursebook glossary along with definitions, collocations, synonyms and alternative British and American English usage. There is also an end of glossary vocabulary test. The Workbook provides further extensive recycling and consolidation of the key vocabulary covered in the Coursebook.

For students needing to do business in English, the vocabulary focuses more on functional frameworks rather than individual topic-based items. The Skills Book *What do you say?* feature reviews communicative strategies and models effective examples through dialogues, presentations and meetings. These key phrases and frameworks are practised interactively on the CD-ROM and throughout the Skills Book classroom material.

INTELLIGENT BUSINESS (PRE-INTERMEDIATE) TEACHER'S BOOK

3 Functional language

As with the vocabulary, the functional language of the core syllabus is dealt with according to whether students need to learn or do business. For students with little experience of hard business skills such as presenting, negotiating and taking part in meetings, the Coursebook presents functional language through the *Career skills* feature. Here the language is given general relevance to anyone within an organisation, be it an academic institution or commercial company. These functions include checking information, making predictions and finding creative solutions, for example. As with the grammar, items are modelled in context, highlighted and then practised. Further practice can be found in the Workbook.

For students familiar with hard business skills, the functional language is presented in the context of traditional business skills such as negotiating and presenting. Each Career skill from the Coursebook is transferred to the Skills Book as one of three business subskills in each unit and given a more overtly in-work treatment. Telling a story, for example, becomes Present a company history. The basic functional language is drawn from the core syllabus in both cases but extended and practised more extensively in the Skills Book. As the functional language is so vital for achieving fluency and effective communicative competence, it is the key syllabus strand for the Skills Book and practised extensively throughout. The CD-ROM provides further interactive support and the Good business practice reference at the back of the Skills Book and on the CD-ROM provides further guidance on communicative strategies.

4 Cultural awareness

It is now widely accepted that simply learning a common language is no longer enough to prepare people to do business in the global market place. Equally as important as linguistic competence is the ability to understand and deal with the cultural differences that prevent mutually beneficial and rewarding long-term business relationships forming across international borders. Therefore, the final strand of the core *Intelligent Business* syllabus is cultural awareness.

In each unit a cultural aspect is explored and opposing attitudes are presented. Once more, the content is dealt with according to students' needs and world knowledge. For students learning about business, each cultural aspect is briefly glossed as part of the Career skills feature in the Coursebook. Without naming nationalities, the opposing behaviours are briefly described and students are asked to consider which attitudes are more familiar to them. They are also invited to discuss how opposing attitudes could cause confusion and possibly conflict between people from different cultures.

For students with knowledge of the working world and experience of cultural differences, the Skills Book presents the same cultural aspect as the Coursebook but explores it in far more detail. The same two opposing ends of the spectrum are considered but the differences in values, attitudes and outward behaviour are discussed in greater depth. As students consider each cultural aspect, they are encouraged to plot their own culture on a Culture profile in the Good business practice reference at the back of the Skills Book. While working through the book this will create a culture curve plotting the values and behaviour of the students' native culture. In multicultural classes the convergence and divergence of the various curves can provide further discussion and comparison. The culture reference notes are also on the CD-ROM at the back of the Skills Book.

Using Intelligent Business

As all components are built on the core 15-unit pre-intermediate syllabus, the components can be used in various combinations that will consistently cover the same core grammar, skills and cultural issues at the same time. The following combinations are suggestions only and teachers may well wish to mix the various components differently or even all together.

1 Extensive use

Extensive courses delivered over a period of several weeks or even months are usually found in either tertiary institutes or weekly in-service programmes. Such courses can require over 100 hours of material and usually have linguistic knowledge as their goal – in the form of structures and vocabulary. The duration of these courses means that students require substantial practice and regular revision to consolidate what has already been processed. A typical *Intelligent Business* learning package for such students would include the Coursebook and Workbook. The Coursebook provides a large amount of language input, formal processing of grammar and plenty of written and spoken language practice. There are also reviews every three units. All key vocabulary items that students have to process in order to work through the Coursebook are collected in the unit-for-unit glossary at the back of the Coursebook. Each item includes synonyms and common collocations to help the student activate use of vocabulary. There is also a separate Glossary Test at the end of the section to provide another tool for assessing students' assimilation of the core language of the course.

The Workbook provides further practice of the grammar, vocabulary and functional language presented in the equivalent Coursebook units. It also provides further skills work with many more Economist texts and listening exercises. There are BEC-style tasks to prepare students either for the actual Cambridge exam or for the Practice Test at the back of the Workbook. As the Practice Test recycles many of the themes and vocabulary introduced in the Coursebook, it can be used as an end-of-course assessment. The Workbook is designed as a self-study component with its own key at the back and audio CD inside the back cover.

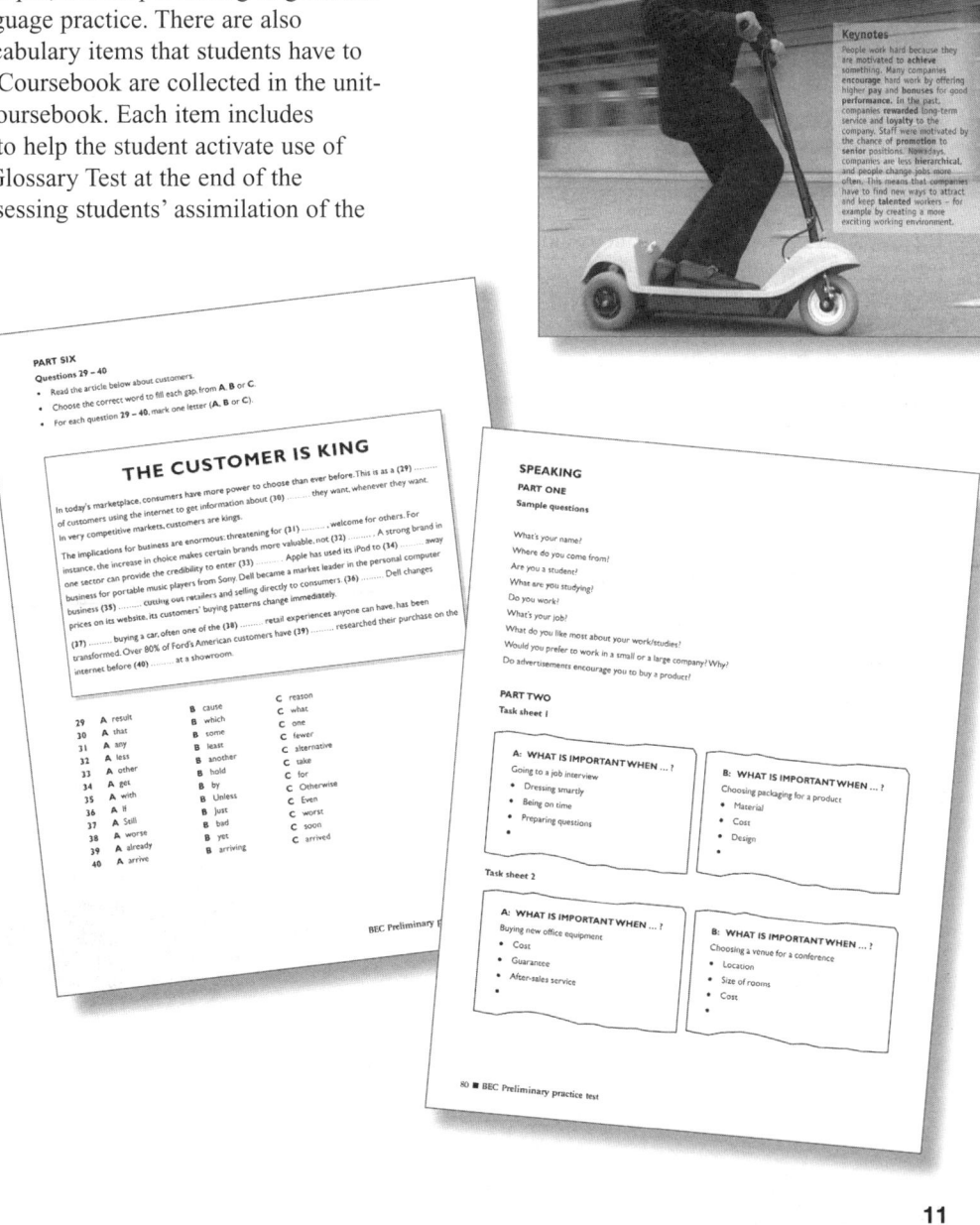

INTELLIGENT BUSINESS (PRE-INTERMEDIATE) TEACHER'S BOOK

Alternatively, if the language programme provides enough hours of classroom tuition, the Coursebook and Skills Book can be used together. As they are based on the same core syllabus and share the same 15-unit structure, the Skills Book can be used either immediately after the whole of the Coursebook or integrated on a unit-by-unit basis. The Workbook and Skills Book CD-ROM will both provide further practice and self-study.

Intelligent Business Pre-Intermediate

	Unit 3	Language	Vocabulary	Skills	Culture
Learn Business	Coursebook	Offers and requests	Synonyms Prefixes	Being polite	Being direct
	Workbook	Offers and requests	Etiquette	Being polite	
Do Business	Skills Book	Offers and requests	Offers and requests	Make polite offers and requests Make small talk	Direct and indirect requests

2 Intensive use

As already mentioned, the trend in the corporate Business English sector is for increasingly intensive tuition – but with even more pressure on measurable achievement. Typically, intensive courses are a week long and delivered to small groups or even individual managers. However, even shorter courses of 2–3 days and less are becoming more common. Many schools also provide hybrid courses where an extensive programme delivered over a period of months can have an intensive component built in where students will have a full-day of intensive tuition every so many weeks of extensive study.

The *Intelligent Business* Skills Book follows the same core 15-unit syllabus as the other components but groups them into 5 blocks of three lessons each – making it perfectly compatible with a standard 5-day intensive programme. The Writing units at the end of each block provide self-study consolidation as does the CD-ROM (with plenty of practice activities). The CD-ROM also provides an option for programming in a self-access centre component to the course. The material is aimed at small groups of up to four students but can be used individually.

As the Skills Book is very much driven by speaking activities and performance of familiar business tasks, it is essential that students receive feedback on how well they complete these tasks in English. At the end of each unit students are asked to assess their own performance in very general terms and encouraged to discuss what difficulties they experienced. The Teacher's Book also provides frameworks for assessing task performance. The teacher can use these to identify weaknesses and direct students to appropriate materials for further practice.

At the back of the Skills Book and on the CD-ROM there is an extensive grammar reference with practice activities (for students whose grammar is impeding their ability to complete the tasks successfully). The CD-ROM also includes many practice activities that target functional language.

3 Exam preparation

Although the *Intelligent Business Pre-Intermediate* Coursebook is not an exam-specific preparation text, it has been developed to meet the criteria for length and difficulty of text applied to Cambridge BEC Preliminary exam papers. There are also certain tasks that are similar to typical exam questions. The Coursebook will not prepare students in terms of exam awareness but it will give them an effective command of Business English at pre-intermediate / BEC Preliminary level.

For students wishing to take an internationally recognised Business English exam at the end of their course, the *Intelligent Business Pre-Intermediate* Workbook and intelligent.business.org website provide a variety of exam-specific material. The Workbook in particular provides plenty of practice material specifically targeted at the Cambridge BEC Preliminary exam. Each Workbook unit contains at least two BEC-style exercises and there is a complete and authentic Practice Test at the back of the book. The Listening Test is included on the audio CD.

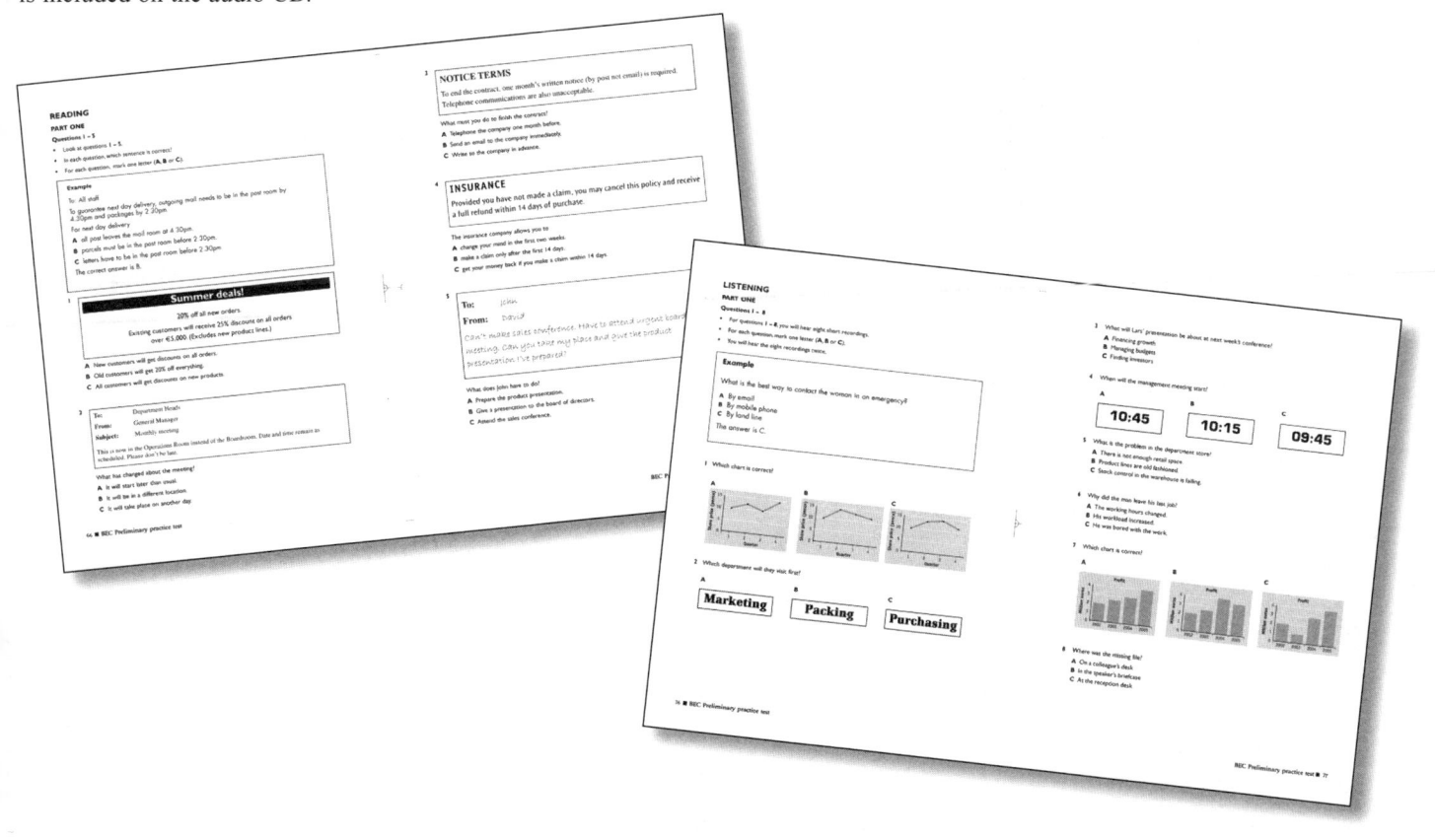

INTELLIGENT BUSINESS (PRE-INTERMEDIATE) TEACHER'S BOOK

The intelligent-business.org website provides further BEC exam practice material.

In conclusion, *Intelligent Business* provides a wealth of language learning material especially developed for a wide range of students who share the same need for Business English but whose learning environments and ways of learning are very different. As all components are based on the same core 15-unit syllabus, they can be used individually or together in a variety of combinations to suit the learner's needs without losing any consistency or continuity of language progression.

UNIT 1

Unit 1: Activities

UNIT OBJECTIVES	
Reading:	Move over game boys
Language:	Present simple and continuous
Vocabulary:	Roles and activities
	Word building
Career skills:	Explaining your job
Culture at work:	Greeting people
Dilemma & Decision:	Exporting to Mexico (email)

This unit looks at talking about a company's business activities. When we talk about a company's activities we normally describe the different areas that it is involved in. Companies can be divided into sectors – those that:
- produce goods (manufacturers)
- provide services (service providers)
- sell goods to the public (retailers)
- are involved in TV, film and publishing (media).

Some companies concentrate on one main activity, while others are involved in more than one sector. For example, General Electric (see page 8) is a multi-national company which is involved in a number of different areas such as manufacturing technological products, offering financial services and media.

It is possible to classify business activity into three sections:
- primary
- secondary
- tertiary.

Primary business activity describes extractive areas such as agriculture, mining, fishing, etc. This type of activity generally focuses on extracting and utilising resources provided by nature.

Secondary business activity includes manufacturing and construction industries (those that make, build or assemble products, e.g. car production).

Tertiary activity includes businesses that provide services (e.g. banking, public transport, consultancy, web design, etc.). Services can be divided into **direct services** that are offered directly to the general public and **commercial services**, which deal with other businesses. However, many businesses (e.g. banking) offer services which are used by the public as well as by other commercial companies.

Keynotes

Read through the keynotes with your class. Check that they understand the terms in bold. Ask questions such as: *What manufacturers/retailers can you think of? What goods do they make or what services do they provide?* Draw Ss' attention to the glossary for this unit at the back of the book.

Coursebook, Glossary, Unit 1, page 147

Preview

Focus on the company names and ask Ss if they use any of the companies listed. Ask Ss to look through the words in A (verbs) and B (nouns). Encourage Ss to use a dictionary to clarify meaning where necessary. Choose one of the companies and demonstrate the activity with the whole class, eliciting words from A and B to talk about the company's activities. Then ask Ss to work in pairs or small groups to discuss the remaining companies. Have a brief feedback session and then brainstorm more companies. Write the company names on the board as Ss call them out. Elicit information about these companies' activities with the whole class.

> **Suggested answers**
> Sony develops and manufactures electronic goods.
> Citibank offers banking services.
> Nike designs and manufactures clothing.
> AOL provides internet services.
> Wal-Mart sells food and drink.
> Toyota designs and manufactures cars.

Reading 1

Ask Ss to close books. As a lead-in, ask Ss what nationality General Electric is (American). Ask Ss to guess what business activities General Electric is involved in. Open books. Read the text with the whole class. Ask Ss to answer the questions in pairs.

> 1 media, financial services
> 2 industrial machinery, plastics
> 3 300,000
> 4 diversified

Speaking

Tell the class about a company in your country or home town. Talk about the company's main activities and tell Ss whether it specialises in one industry sector or whether it has diversified interests. Ask Ss to choose a company in their own country or town and discuss the same points with a partner.

15

> **Optional activity**
> **Photocopiable resource 1.1 (page 105)**
> Ask Ss to do more research on a company for homework. Ss can choose a company from anywhere in the world to complete the table about. Encourage Ss to choose a different company from the one they used in the speaking exercise. Give each S a copy of the worksheet and check the areas and useful phrases with them. Tell Ss that they can use the internet or any other sources to find information. For homework, Ss make notes and complete the table. During the next lesson, ask Ss to work in pairs / small groups and use their notes to talk about the company.

Reading 2 ■

Before reading the article, ask Ss to identify what the title is and how many paragraphs it has (7).

Focus Ss' attention on the title, the picture and the fact that Lynn is a woman's name, and ask Ss what they think the article is about (women making a career in the video game industry). Draw attention to the glossary on the page and remind Ss of the glossary for Unit 1 at the back of the book. Get Ss to read the first paragraph and underline an example of Frognation's activities (it creates soundtracks and designs and translates Japanese video games for the UK market) and circle an example of what Lynn Robson does in her work (creates the video games with her designers and developers). Ss read the rest of the text to find more examples.

> **Company activities**: creates soundtracks, designs and translates Japanese video games for the UK market; represents producers with great game ideas and helps them to sell their ideas to Sony or Nintendo in Tokyo; provides advice on everything from the music soundtrack and graphics to the game programming and characters
> **Lynn's activities**: runs the UK office; gives advice on what will work in both countries; gives clients in the West information about Japanese culture; helps Japanese partners present their ideas in the West

Reading 2 ■

Ask Ss to read the article again and answer the questions. Do the first one together as an example. Get Ss to compare answers with a partner before having a feedback session. You might like to ask Ss to correct any sentences that are false.

> 1 T   2 F   3 F   4 T   5 T   6 T

Speaking ■

Ask Ss to work in small groups to discuss the good and bad things about Lynn's job. On the board write the words *good* and *bad*. During feedback note Ss' suggestions under the appropriate heading. Ask Ss if they would like Lynn's job and if they would like to work for Frognation. Why? / Why not?

Speaking ■

In the same groups, Ss discuss the second question. In the feedback session for the whole class, encourage Ss to expand their answers. For example, if they do not like video games, ask why. If they do like them, ask for examples of the games that they enjoy and ask what they like about them.

Vocabulary 1

Ask Ss to match the words with the meanings (a–e). To help them, Ss could look for words 1, 3, 4 and 5 in the reading text to see how they are used in context.

> 1 e   2 a   3 d   4 b   5 c

Vocabulary 2 ■

Write the job areas (1–6) on the board and encourage Ss to suggest what to call someone who works in each area. Then ask Ss to suggest other job titles and discuss what areas each job is in. Elicit one or two of the job titles coming up in the next activity.

> 1 accountant   2 artist
> 3 banker   4 economist
> 5 engineer   6 musician

Vocabulary 2 ■

Ss can use dictionaries to help with this task. Do the first sentence together as an example.

> 1 adviser
> 2 representative
> 3 assistant
> 4 management consultant
> 5 software developer
> 6 film producer

Language check ■

Introduce the present simple and present continuous by writing the following sentences on the board:

UNIT 1

a) Lynn creates video games.
b) Lynn is meeting a client at the moment.

Check that Ss can identify the verbs used in each sentence (*create*, *meet*). Ask Ss what the tenses are called. Write a question mark at the end of each sentence and elicit the question forms (*What does Lynn create? / Does Lynn create video games? Who is Lynn meeting at the moment? / Is Lynn meeting a client at the moment?*).

Now write:

a) Lynn _____ not _____ _____ _____ .
b) Lynn _____ not _____ _____ _____ _____ _____ _____ .

Ask Ss to write the negative form of the sentences (*Lynn does not create video games / Lynn is not meeting a client at the moment*). Finally, ask Ss for the contracted forms (*doesn't/isn't*).

Ask Ss to work in pairs and match the examples with the rules. Write *be* and *work* on the board and elicit which verb is regular (*work*) and which is irregular (*be*). Check Ss know all forms of the two verbs in the present simple and present continuous. If time allows, you could ask Ss to write the negative and questions forms of sentences 1–4.

| 1 b | 2 c | 3 a | 4 d |

Coursebook, Grammar reference: Present simple and continuous, page 157

Language check 2

Ask Ss to choose the correct alternative.

| 1 simple | 2 continuous |

Practice 1

Ask Ss to choose the correct form of the verb in italics. During feedback, choose two or three examples and ask Ss to give reasons for their choice and refer to the ideas in Language check exercise 1.

1 work	2 sit
3 check	4 are attending
5 is currently changing	6 are learning
7 are staying	8 spend

Practice 2

Do the first sentence together as an example. Ask Ss to complete the text and compare answers with a partner.

1 starts	2 give
3 am giving / 'm giving	4 stay
5 are beginning	6 are refusing
7 are demanding	

Workbook, page 5

Speaking

Tell Ss about your daily or weekly routine and any special projects/events in your life at the moment. Check that Ss noticed what tense you used for each piece of information. Give Ss time to prepare by asking them to note down ideas. Ss then talk to their partner about their routines and projects/events that are happening at the moment. Circulate and check that Ss are using the tenses correctly. Note any problem areas and go over them with the whole class.

> **Optional activity**
> Ask Ss to change partners and tell their new partner information about their original partner.

Listening 1 ▮

As this is the first listening in the book, take some time to give context. Tell Ss that you will play the recordings more than once. Refer Ss to the photograph and ask questions such as: *What is the woman who is standing up doing?* (giving a presentation) *Does the audience look interested?* (yes). Ask Ss to suggest ways that international teams can communicate (phone, email, video conference). Read the introduction together. Check if Ss use emails to communicate with friends or colleagues in other countries. Ask Ss to suggest advantages and disadvantages of using emails to communicate with colleagues in different countries. Play the first part of the recording and check answers with the class.

> **Advantage:** Communication is very simple and fast.
> **Disadvantages:** There is a big risk of misunderstanding, small problems can become big problems.

Listening 1 ▮

Ask Ss to discuss their ideas in pairs.

Listening 1 ▮

Play the second part of the recording while Ss tick the points. Play it again for Ss to check, pausing to highlight the correct information.

> Tell your colleagues about yourself.
> If there is a problem, explain it carefully.
> Use polite phrases.

17

Reading 3

Ask Ss to read the two emails and, with the whole class, discuss which follows Anna Davidson's recommendations. Encourage Ss to suggest ways that email B can be improved (by making it like email A).

> Email A follows Anna's recommendations.

Writing

Discuss ways to open and close an email, encouraging Ss to give their ideas.
Possible ways to open: *Dear ... Hello ... Hi ...*
Possible ways to close: *Yours sincerely, Regards, Best wishes.*
Both the opening and closing salutations have the most formal expressions first and the least formal last. Ask Ss to write the email and compare their answer with a partner.

→ Style guide, page 6

Career skills

Ask Ss to think of situations where they may need to explain what job they do (conferences, meetings, training courses, etc.). Ask Ss to match the phrases and questions.

> 1 d   2 d   3 a   4 b   5 c   6 c

Listening 2 ▪1

Ask Ss to say what job, company and main activity they think will go together. Play the first speaker and invite answers around the class. Play the other three speakers and check answers.

> Olaf   Systems Developer   Finance house
> manages IT systems
> Rania   Project Manager   Travel company   meets clients
> Da The   Lawyer   Mobile phone company
> checks contracts
> Jaana   Accountant   Paper manufacturer
> deals with payments

Listening 2 ▪2

Play the recording again and ask Ss to note other activities that each speaker does.

> **Olaf:** He is responsible for the website and develops new systems for the future.
> **Rania:** She also finds out what clients want, prepares proposals and presents the proposals to clients.
> **Da The:** He also takes part in negotiations for new contracts with suppliers.
> **Jaana:** She checks suppliers' invoices and sends them their payments.

Listening 2 ▪3

Draw Ss' attention to the Career skills box. Ask Ss to tick the phrases they heard. Play the listening again for Ss to check.

> **Olaf:** I'm a ... I work for ... I'm responsible for
> **Rania:** I work as a ... for ... My role is to ...
> **Da The:** I'm a ... I work for ... My main role is to ...
> **Jaana:** I'm an ... I'm responsible for ...

Speaking ▪1

Pretend to be Olaf, Rania, Da The or Jaana and introduce yourself to the class. Talk about your (character's) job, company and job activities. Ask Ss to work in pairs and choose information about one of the four characters, introducing themselves to their partner.

Speaking ▪2

Take time to set up the role-play and make sure that Ss understand what they need to do. Divide Ss into pairs and ask them each to choose a different company and job to answer questions about. Ss take it in turns to ask questions a–d from the Career skills box. If your Ss are working, you could then ask Ss to ask the questions again with another partner, answering with real information about themselves.

Culture at work

Ask Ss to read the information individually and discuss in pairs or small groups. You may find it helpful to look at the Culture at work box from page 7 of the Skills Book; this is reproduced below. You may also find it helpful to refer to the relevant section on Culture at work in the teacher's notes for the Skills Book.

Formal	Informal
Some cultures treat business cards formally and with great respect. The information on the card can include the title of the person and their qualifications.	Some cultures see business cards simply as a way to exchange important personal details (name, company, contact numbers).
In some cultures the person receives the card in both hands and reads the information carefully.	The cards can be read quickly and then put in a pocket.
It is not polite to write on a card unless the person giving the cards says that it is OK.	It is OK to write additional information on the card.

→ Skills Book, Culture at work, page 7
→ Teacher's Book, page 119

UNIT 1

Dilemma

As a lead-in ask Ss: *What products or services does your country export? What countries does it export to?* Tell Ss that they are going to read about a British company called Systemax, which manufactures laboratory equipment. Focus Ss' attention on the chart and ask what countries the company exports to. Which country buys most products from Systemax? Which buys the least? Point to the title 'Exporting to Mexico' and ask where Mexico is (Central America). Read the brief with the class and clarify any unfamiliar vocabulary. Ask Ss to summarise the information in order to check comprehension. Ask Ss what three things Systemax directors need to consider.

Task 1: Divide Ss into two groups. Ask Group A to turn to page 137 and read the information about George. Group B turns to page 140 and reads the information about Linda. Each group answers the three questions that directors have to consider about the person they have information on.

Task 2: Put Ss in new groups of four to six. Half the group should contain people from Group A and half from Group B. First, the groups should tell each other the information that they have about George and Linda. The groups decide whether to give extra responsibility to George or Linda or whether to look for a third export manager. Ask each group to nominate a person to present their decision to the whole group. Encourage Ss to say why they made their decision.

Decision

Ask Ss to listen to Alistair Cross. What decision did Systemax take? (appoint Linda) What reasons does he give for the decision? (good experience of business in Spain and of Latin culture)

Write it up

Ask Ss to write an email to George or Linda offering him/her the job. You may wish to ask Ss to prepare the writing in class, complete it for homework and then compare with a partner in the next lesson before handing it in to be marked. Give each S a photocopy of the Writing preparation framework from page 188. Then use the Writing focus (Writing focus: Emails) opposite to link the use of the framework and the Style guide as Ss plan their writing. It may be helpful to use the Writing feedback framework on page 189 when marking Ss' writing.

Writing focus: Emails

1 First, decide who you are.
   (In this case, you are a director from Systemax.)

2 Every time you start to write, you need to ask yourself two questions:
   a What is the purpose of this piece of writing?
   b Who am I writing to?
   (Here Ss are writing to offer George Johnstone or Linda McCade a job.)

3 Look at the section on Emails on page 6 of the Style guide. Notice the suggested structure of an email:
   From/To/Cc/Date/Subject
   Greeting
   Message
   Closing phrase
   Name
   Start with the most important information. Put less important information in the second paragraph.
   Is this structure appropriate for this email? Plan the paragraphs you are going to divide the email into. Then brainstorm the points you might cover in each paragraph.

4 What style should the email be written in?
   (As it says in the Style guide, it is a good idea to keep emails short and use short sentences and simple language. This is an email to colleagues offering a job, so the style should be neutral/semi-formal.)

5 What words and phrases might be appropriate in your email?
   (See the Useful phrases in the Style guide.)

6 Now go ahead and write the email.

7 When you have finished, check your writing for: logical structure, clarity of ideas, accuracy of language, appropriateness of style.

Style guide, page 6
Style guide, General rules, page 3
Skills Book, Writing 2, page 32
Teacher's Book, page 138
Teacher's Book, Writing preparation framework, page 188
Teacher's Book, Writing feedback framework, page 189

Email: Suggested answer (79 words)

From: (student's name)
To: George Johnstone
Date: (today's date)
Subject: Export Manager: Mexico
Dear George
I'm writing to tell you that we would like to offer you the job of Export manager for Mexico.
We think you are the right person for this job because you are an excellent salesman and we know that you are keen to extend your area of responsibility. You already travel in your present position and it would be possible to include Mexico in your business trips when you visit the US or Canada.
Congratulations!
Regards
TC

Alternative (66 words)

Dear Linda
I'm writing to tell you that we would like to offer you the job of Export manager for Mexico.
We think you are the right person for this job because you are an excellent manager. You are very good at planning and organising your work. You also speak Spanish and French and have a lot of experience in Spanish-speaking cultures.
Congratulations!
Regards
TC

Unit 2: Data

UNIT OBJECTIVES	
Reading:	No hiding place
Language:	Countable and uncountable
Vocabulary:	Using the internet
	Quantity and number
Career skills:	Checking information
Culture at work:	Are you precise or approximate?
Dilemma & Decision:	Buy it now! (report)

This unit looks at the ways that data is collected and managed. Increased use of the internet in recent years means that more data about individuals can be collected and stored than ever before. Some of this information is used to analyse people's buying habits. Some argue that the collection of so much data about individuals can help with efficiency and improve customer service. For example, when buying goods online, a company can retain delivery details, which means that when you buy from that company again you are not required to complete your delivery address, etc. Choices that customers make mean that a company can collate information and inform customers when other similar items of interest are available. However, others are uneasy that companies and organisations are able to collect and retain so much information about individuals. They question what use the information will be put to. Some civil liberties groups argue that we live in a time of unprecedented electronic surveillance when every transaction and movement can be monitored.

Keynotes

Introduce the topic by asking Ss to suggest ways that information technology has changed the way that information is collected and stored (information technology makes it easier to collect and access information and large amounts of information can be stored). This unit is going to look at the way that information is collected and stored. Point to the title 'No privacy' and ask Ss if they think that people had more now or in the past. Now ask Ss to read the Keynotes section. Make sure that Ss understand the words in bold. Draw Ss' attention to the glossary for this unit at the back of the book.

Coursebook, Glossary, Unit 2, page 147

Preview

Draw attention to the example. Ask Ss why they think that companies and organisations might want to collect information about individuals. Elicit one or two suggestions around the class and then ask Ss to discuss the two questions in pairs.

Listening 1 **1**

Check Ss understand the information in a–c. Ask Ss to listen to the first speaker and match Amy with her job. Play the rest of the recording for Ss to match Bob and Carla with their jobs. Ask Ss which job they think sounds most interesting. Why?

1 b	2 c	3 a

Listening 1 **2**

Ask Ss to listen again and answer the questions. Get Ss to discuss their answers with a partner before checking with the whole class.

1 For when the company wants to send special offers to different groups of customers.
2 How many consumers are there in the market? Who are they? What do they want?
3 The marketing team.
4 A buyer; she tries to find the best products for the best price.
5 No – she searches for new products and suppliers.

Listening 1 **3**

Complete the first sentence together to demonstrate. Ask Ss to complete the remaining sentences individually. Listen again to check.

1 keeps
2 enters
3 browse
4 uses
5 updates

Speaking

Ask Ss in the class to read the statements aloud. Check that Ss understand the meaning. First, ask Ss to answer the questions for themselves. Then divide the class into small groups to discuss the statements and rank the things that they are most/least happy with and think are most/least necessary. Have a whole-group feedback session to compare ideas.

Reading 1

Tell Ss that they are going to read an article about data protection and the internet. Look at the headline and ask Ss to say what they think it means. From the title, do Ss think that the article will be positive or negative about internet privacy? Draw attention to the glossary and remind them of the glossary for Unit 2 at the back of the book. Ask Ss to read the article quickly and choose the sentence 1–3 that they think sums up the main idea. Ask Ss what information in the article helped them to make their choice.

3

Reading 2

Ask Ss to read the article again more slowly and carefully to answer the questions.

1 They leave cookies in their computers.
2 They can monitor mobile phone calls; collect data from electronic ticket systems and electronic access to buildings; use video cameras and tracking chips.
3 cameras that see through clothing, satellites that can recognise small objects, tracking chips
4 security against terrorists and criminals, higher productivity at work, a wider selection of products, more convenience
5 They hate the idea but don't know how to stop it.

Speaking

Check that Ss understand the questions. Ask Ss to work in groups to answer the questions. On the board write:

Governments   Individuals   Companies

Ask groups to share their ideas about how each of the above benefits from surveillance. Ask groups to compare ideas of what they think the dangers of too much surveillance might be.

Vocabulary 1 1

Ask Ss to match the words with the pictures. Go over any items that Ss are still unclear about.

1 d   2 h   3 e   4 a   5 g   6 c   7 f   8 b

Vocabulary 1 2

Ss use the words from exercise 1 to complete the text. Check answers around the class.

1 search engine   2 keyword
3 click   4 websites
5 screen   6 online shopping
7 password

Vocabulary 2 1

Focus Ss on the word box. Ask Ss to find an example of a word that means *large / a lot*. Do the same for *small / not many*. Ss complete the groups and compare their answers with a partner.

Large / a lot: huge, millions, a mountain of, substantial, wide, enormous
Small / not many: a bit of, a few, tiny, a fraction

Optional activity
To extend the activity, ask Ss to work in pairs and brainstorm things that could be described by the vocabulary words (e.g. *a bit of cake, a huge investment, millions of people*, etc.).

Vocabulary 2 2

Ask Ss to match the numerical expressions with the descriptions and check answers in pairs.

1 b   2 e   3 d   4 a   5 c

Optional activity
Ask Ss to suggest other ways of describing the size of something (e.g. *five metres high, two metres long*, etc.). Then ask Ss to suggest other ways to describe the frequency of something (*three times a month, ten times a year, every week, every other day*, etc.).

Listening 2

Ask Ss to say what they think Bob's answer to 1–7 might be. Ss listen and write the numbers they hear. Ask Ss to compare answers with a partner. Ask the class if any information was surprising.

1 4,542   2 1.5 minutes
3 2.7   4 2,430
5 1,395   6 57
7 31

UNIT 2

Listening 3

Ask Ss to practice saying the numbers. Play the recording for Ss to check. Say each number and ask Ss to repeat.

> **Optional activity**
> Dictate these words/phrases, spelling where necessary:
> *a large number*
> *a percentage*
> *a fraction*
> *a price*
> Ask Ss to write an example for each of the words/phrases and exchange papers with a partner. Ss then take turns to say the numbers on their partner's list.

Listening 4 1

Read the questions with the class and ask Ss to suggest what Sandra Ravell might say for each. Then Ss listen and answer the questions.

| 1 | managers, secretaries, students |
| 2 | If you have a good filing system, you can save a lot of time. |

Listening 4 2

Ss listen again and complete the notes. Ask Ss if they already do any of the things that Sandra suggests.

1 structure	2 categories
3 categories	4 files
5 access	6 front
7 up-to-date	8 Delete
9 Review	

Speaking

Ask Ss to talk with a partner about how they record and store new vocabulary. Discuss ideas with the whole class.

> **Optional activity**
> **Photocopiable resource 2.1 (page 106)**
> You may wish to extend the discussion and check how Ss record and revise vocabulary. Ss work in pairs / small groups. Give each S a copy of the worksheet, which shows different techniques for recording vocabulary. Check that Ss understand how these work. (In the case of 3, 4 and 5, these are on the Vocabulary record sheet on page 192, with instructions on page 185.) Ask Ss if they have tried any of the methods. Did they work? Why? / Why not? Remind Ss that it is not enough to simply record vocabulary, but that it also needs to be regularly revised. Also point out that as well as knowing the meaning of a word, it is useful to note word stress and pronunciation. After looking through all five methods, ask Ss to choose two or three words from Vocabulary 1 and 2 and use the methods to record them. Which method do they feel is most effective for them? Are particular methods suited to particular words or types of word?
> In the next lesson, and at various times throughout the course, review the vocabulary and ask Ss to report back on the methods that they used to record/revise it. You could hand out several copies of the framework on page 192 for Ss to use.

Language check 1

Look around the room and ask Ss to identify things that are countable and uncountable. It would be a good idea to include something like a glass of water to contrast: *water* (uncountable) and *a glass of water* (countable). Ask Ss if *data* is countable or uncountable (uncountable).

Do a and b with the whole class to demonstrate the activity. Ask Ss to compare answers together before checking with the whole class.

| a C | b U | c C | d C | e U |
| f U | g C | h U | i C | j C |

Coursebook, Grammar reference: Countable and uncountable, page 157

Language check 2

With the whole class, match the sentences a–j with the rules. Then ask Ss to complete the rules using *countable*, *uncountable* or *both*. Highlight the note about offers and requests.

INTELLIGENT BUSINESS (PRE-INTERMEDIATE) TEACHER'S BOOK: COURSEBOOK

1 countable nouns (sentence g)
2 countable nouns (c)
3 both (b)
4 uncountable nouns (h)
5 countable nouns (i)
6 uncountable nouns (e)
7 countable nouns (j)
8 countable nouns (a)
9 uncountable nouns (f)
10 countable nouns (d)

Optional activity
Ask Ss to call out some objects that you find in an office (stapler, files, phone, etc.). Get Ss to spend one minute offering and requesting things on the list.

Practice 1

Point out that there are two different conversations in exercise 1. Ask Ss to complete the conversations with a partner. As Ss finish, ask pairs to read the conversations aloud together.

1 some   2 any   3 some
4 any   5 a

Practice 2

Ask Ss to complete the exercise individually and then read the conversation with a partner, to check.

1 much   2 a lot of   3 a lot of   4 many

Workbook, page 10

Speaking

Give Ss time to decide what region/town/company they want to ask questions on. Ss may prefer to write the questions first. Ask Ss to take it in turns to ask and answer questions. Circulate and encourage. It would be useful to note any areas that Ss might be having problems with and go over them with the whole class.

Career skills

Books closed. Ask Ss what sort of numbers they use in their work (telephone numbers, figures, addresses). Ask Ss what they would do if they were on the phone and the other person said a number that they could not hear correctly. Note suggestions and ask Ss how they would ask the person to say the number again. Note suggestions on the board. Open

books and ask Ss to read the expressions for checking information. Compare with the phrases that the class suggested.

Together, look at the phrases for approximate numbers.

Optional activity
On the board write:
a) 6,000,126
b) 200,025
c) 2,998

First check Ss know how to say the numbers exactly. Then ask Ss how they could say the numbers approximately.
a) about/over six million
b) about/over two hundred thousand
c) just under/about three thousand

Listening 5 1

Ss are going to hear two people talking on the phone and will need to note the precise or approximate figures that they hear. Check answers around the class. Ask Ss if any of the statistics surprised them.

1 about 600 million
2 about 30 per cent
3 just under 200 million / 190.91 million
4 over 25 hours a month

Listening 5 2

Ask Ss to look again at the phrases in the Career skills box. Ss listen again and tick the phrases that they hear. You may wish to pause the recording and ask Ss to copy the intonation of the speaker as they say the phrases. Ss who are from cultures where a more direct form of communication is used may find it strange that the speaker uses *sorry* in many of the phrases for checking information. You could explain that *sorry* is being used as a polite expression rather than an apology.

Did you say … ?
Sorry, can I just check?
Can you repeat it, please?
Do you mean … ?

Speaking

Divide the class into two groups, A and B. Ask Group A to look at the information on page 21 and Group B to look at the information on page 140. Give Ss time to practise saying their figures and ask them to think about what phrases they could use to check information. After a couple of minutes, ask Ss to work in A/B pairs. Remind Ss to use phrases from the Career skills box to check information. Ask Ss to exchange information and note down their partner's answers.

Culture at work

Ask Ss to read the information and discuss the questions in pairs. Remind Ss about the phrases for approximate numbers in Career skills (*about / just under / over*). Ask if they prefer to use expressions such as these in their own language. Do Ss prefer to use phrases like these or do they prefer to give exact information? You may find it helpful to look at the Culture at work box from page 13 of the Skills Book; this is reproduced below. You may also find it useful to refer to the relevant section on Culture at work in the teacher's notes supporting the Skills Book.

Precise	Approximate
Some cultures prefer precise information. For example, if somebody is talking about data, they use exact figures. It does not matter if the information is positive or negative. The information always needs to be clear and exact.	Other cultures sometimes use approximate figures. For example, somebody might say 'sales figures increased by almost 25 per cent' when the exact figure is 21 per cent. This is sometimes used to make negative data sound more positive.

Skills Book, Culture at work, page 13

Teacher's Book, page 123

Dilemma

Ask Ss to close books. Check that Ss know what eBay is (an online auction house where members of the public buy and sell things; customers bid – say how much money they want to pay – for a product and the highest bidder wins). Ask Ss if eBay is popular in their country. Have they ever bought or sold anything on eBay or visited the site?

Open books and Ask Ss to read the Dilemma brief. Check comprehension of vocabulary they may not be familiar with (*set up operations, have access to, enter the market*). Ask questions to check that Ss understand what they have to do (*What country does eBay want to expand into? What information do they need? What is your job?*).

Task 1: Divide the class into small groups. Each group prepares a list of questions using the prompts 1–7. Point out the Useful phrases box. Circulate, checking each group's list of questions and help Ss to self-correct where necessary. As groups finish, ask them to practise saying the questions quietly.

Possible answers include:
2 Where do they usually use the internet?
3 Who uses the internet?
4 What do they use the internet for?
5 Are there any technical problems?
6 Do they use credit cards to pay for goods online?
7 Is there any competition from other online auction companies in India?

Task 2: Divide the class into two groups. Group A uses the information on page 137 to answer as many of the questions as possible from Task 1. Group B uses the information on page 140 to do the same. Move between the two groups, helping where necessary.

Task 3: Put Ss into groups of four to six. In each group, half the Ss should be from Task 2 Group A and half should be from Group B. Ss exchange information by asking the questions that they were unable to find answers for in Task 2 and answering questions that they do have information about. Remind Ss to use phrases for checking information, where necessary.

Task 4: In the same groups, Ss discuss whether they think it is a good idea to set up operations in India. Encourage groups to think of reasons why / why not. Depending on your class, you may wish to set a time limit to help Ss focus. If appropriate for your class, after a time you could open up the discussion to allow the whole class to exchange ideas. Alternatively, each group could present their ideas to another group.

Decision

Ask Ss what decision they think eBay took. Then ask Ss to listen to Deepak Gupta, an expert in e-commerce in India, talk about eBay's decision. Were Ss' ideas correct? (eBay bought Baazee, India's biggest online retailer.) Ask Ss to listen again and give reasons why eBay took this decision (buying a local company was the best way into the market). Ask Ss for their views on eBay's decision.

Write it up

Ask Ss to write a conclusion to a report giving their findings of the market research they did on India for eBay. Make sure that Ss understand that they are only writing the conclusion to the report – not the whole report. In their conclusion Ss should give the decision that their group decided on and explain the reasons for their decision. You may wish to ask Ss to prepare the writing in class, complete it for homework and then compare with a partner in the next lesson before handing it in to be marked. Give each S a photocopy of the Writing preparation framework from page 188. Then use the

INTELLIGENT BUSINESS (PRE-INTERMEDIATE) TEACHER'S BOOK: COURSEBOOK

Writing focus (Writing focus: Reports) below to link the use of the framework and the Style guide as Ss plan their writing. It may be helpful to use the Writing feedback framework on page 189 when marking Ss' writing.

Writing focus: Reports

1 First, decide who you are.
   (In this case, Ss are market researchers writing the conclusion to a market report about the decisions that their group made.)

2 Every time you start to write, you need to ask yourself two questions:
   a What is the purpose of this piece of writing?
   b Who am I writing to?
   (Here Ss are writing to eBay to help the company decide whether to set up operations in India. The purpose is to write the conclusion to their group's findings.)

3 Look at the section on Reports on page 18 of the Style guide. Notice the suggested structure of a report:
   Title
   Introduction
   Key points, in sections
   Conclusion/Summary
   Is this structure appropriate for this report? Plan the points you want to include in your conclusion.

4 What style should the report be written in?
   (As it says in the Style guide, reports for clients usually use a formal style, i.e. correct grammar and spelling, use of full sentences and no contractions. It is also a good idea to avoid informal vocabulary or phrases. The language of the report must be clear.)

5 What phrases might be appropriate in your report?
   (See the Style guide, and language for giving reasons: 'Taking all these facts into consideration, we believe that the best decision is ... because ...')

6 Now go ahead and write the conclusion to the report.

7 When you have finished, check your writing for: easy-to-follow structure, clear ideas, accurate language, appropriate style.

Report conclusion: Suggested answer (54 words)

Conclusion
Taking all these facts into consideration, we believe that the best decision is to set up operations in India because it is a growing market. At the moment, there are about 18 million people with access to the internet and this number is expected to double in the next two or three years.

- Style guide, Reports, page 18
- Style guide, General rules, page 3
- Skills Book, Writing 5, Short reports, page 74
- Teacher's Book, page 172
- Teacher's Book, Writing preparation framework, page 188
- Teacher's Book, Writing feedback framework, page 189.

Unit 3: Etiquette

UNIT OBJECTIVES	
Reading:	Office workers 'admit being rude'
Language:	Offers and requests
Vocabulary:	Synonyms
	Prefixes
Career skills:	Being polite
Culture at work:	Being direct
Dilemma & Decision:	A workplace bully (email)

This unit is about etiquette. In business situations we often have to meet new people, and first impressions are important to help relationships with new contacts get off to a good start. However, the behaviour that is considered polite may vary depending on culture. The unit also looks at the importance of manners in everyday work situations. What passes as good manners can also vary from country to country. The best advice for Ss when planning a business visit is to remind them that it is a good idea to do research into the social customs of the country that they are visiting. Modern technology means that there are now a number of areas where the rules of behaviour are evolving all the time, such as the etiquette of using mobile phones, business letters versus emails, etc. Good manners are often simply a way of showing respect. So a good guideline in these contemporary situations is to act in the same way that you would want others to act.

Keynotes

Ask Ss to look at the reactions of the people in the cartoon to the man who has just entered the room. Ask Ss to say what they think the man might be doing to upset his colleagues (he's talking on the phone while eating, is dressed untidily and has smelly sports kit in his bag). Does he look like somebody they would like to share an office with? Why? / Why not?

Get Ss to read the keynotes and check they understand the terms in bold. Draw Ss' attention to the glossary for this unit at the back of the book. To help lead in to the topics explored in the unit, you may wish to ask questions such as: *Why do you think business etiquette is important for building business relationships? Do you think it is important to be polite in work situations? Why? / Why not?*

Coursebook, Glossary, Unit 3, page 148

Preview 1

Ask Ss to work in pairs / small groups to discuss the examples of bad manners. If your class does not find discussion questions easy, you could get Ss to work individually to rank the examples in order (1 being the worst example of bad manners) before discussing with a partner/group.

Preview 2

Get Ss to work in small groups (if they worked in groups for the last exercise, ask them to change to another group). Ss make two lists: a list of good manners and a list of bad manners. Then ask groups to join with another group to compare their ideas. Did groups disagree on any examples of bad/good manners? What examples did all groups agree on?

Listening 1 — 1

Ss are going to listen to Janet Stubbs, a professor of communication, talk about politeness in the workplace. You could ask Ss to suggest what words they think she might use to complete the extract. Play the first part of the recording for Ss to fill the gaps. Ask Ss if they agree with Professor Stubbs' definition of politeness.

respect; feelings

Listening 1 — 2

Ss now listen to part two for specific information. Ask Ss to note their answers to the questions and compare with a partner. Play it again for Ss to check.

1 new contacts, customers, people from other companies, people above us in the organisational hierarchy
2 Workers are more willing to work hard, help and cooperate.

Listening 1 — 3

Ss listen to part two again and complete the extracts with words from the box. Check Ss understand the meaning of the words in the box. If the words are unfamiliar, ask them to try to work out the meaning from context before looking in a dictionary to check.

1 rules   2 status   3 hierarchy

27

Reading 1

Ask Ss to look at the title of the article. Check that Ss understand *rude*. Ask Ss to suggest examples of bad manners that they think will appear in the article. Before reading, point out the glossary and remind Ss of the glossary for Unit 3 at the back of the book. Pre-teach any other vocabulary that you think your class might need (*respond, courtesy, impact*). Ss read the article to find the information. Compare answers around the class.

> **Bad manners:** arriving late for meetings, ignoring emails, using bad language, ignoring colleagues, answering mobile phone calls during meetings, not introducing people at meetings
> **The company is trying to stop:** arriving late for meetings, answering mobile phone calls during meetings, using bad language

Reading 2

Ask Ss to read the text more closely and answer the questions. Where in the text did they find each answer? Ask Ss if they think it is a good idea for companies to invest money in training junior managers to be polite. How would companies in their country react to this sort of training?

> 1 pressure of work
> 2 distracts people, suggests that the meeting is not important
> 3 no, not as polite
> 4 investing in training
> 5 improving the working environment and relationships with others

Speaking 1

Ask Ss to discuss the questions in pairs. First, elicit suggestions for adjectives to describe how a person feels when they experience bad manners (*irritated, angry, upset, confused, unhappy, cross, surprised*, etc.).

Speaking 2

Write the two statements on the board. Ask Ss to discuss the questions in small groups and remind them to give reasons for their answers.

Vocabulary 1

Check Ss' pronunciation of the words in the box. Ask Ss to find the words in the article. Encourage Ss to work out meaning from context, where necessary. Ask Ss to complete the text using the words. Ask Ss if they think this is good advice.

> 1 invest   2 introduce   3 respond   4 ignore
> 5 admit   6 avoid   7 improve

Vocabulary 2

Check that Ss understand the meaning of *synonym*. Ask Ss to work in pairs and decide which word does not belong in each group. Check Ss' pronunciation of all the words.

> 1 stuffy   2 impact
> 3 communicate   4 rarely

Vocabulary 3 1

Ask Ss to look at the prefixes in the box. Do the first word together (*informal*) to demonstrate. Go through and check that Ss understand words 1–12. Check answers and then say the words and their opposites and ask Ss to repeat. Ask Ss to record the vocabulary in their vocabulary notebook / note cards or give each S a copy of the Vocabulary record sheet on page 192. Point out that one way to record opposites is:

formal ≠ informal
satisfied ≠ dissatisfied

> 1 informal   2 dissatisfied
> 3 dishonest   4 impolite
> 5 impractical   6 inconsiderate
> 7 unfriendly   8 inefficient
> 9 unimportant   10 disrespectful
> 11 impatient   12 inappropriate

Vocabulary 3 2

Ss use the words from exercise 1 to complete the definitions. Ask Ss to compare their answers with a partner.

> 1 dishonest   2 impatient
> 3 unfriendly   4 inefficient
> 5 inconsiderate (disrespectful) 6 dissatisfied

Optional activity

Write the remaining words with prefixes from exercise 1 on the board. Ask Ss to work in pairs and write definitions for each word. Ss join with another pair and take turns reading out a definition. The other pair has to guess the word.

Listening 2 1

Ask Ss to look at the pictures and say what city is shown in each picture. Ask what country each city is in (New York – the USA, Sydney – Australia, London – England). Ask Ss to look at questions 1–3 and predict what city each one refers to. Ss listen and note which city is being described.

1 Sydney	2 New York	3 London

Listening 2 2

Ss listen again for more detailed information. Check Ss understand the meaning of *punctuality* and *dress*. Ask Ss to compare their answers with a partner. Which of the three cities would Ss prefer to live in? Why? Now ask Ss to note information about their own town or city using the headings in the box.

Sydney: common – 8am; important not to be late; jacket and tie usually, but prefer informal clothes when weather is hot; go out for a sandwich; helps if you can talk about sport
London: people hate them; being on time for meetings is important; some wear business suits, lots wear casual clothes; sandwich and coffee; at the pub – anything
New York: start at 7am; Don't be late!; most wear suits – important to look smart; eat at desk or go to a restaurant; talk about business during lunch

Speaking

Ask Ss to discuss the questions in pairs / small groups. Ask Ss which city in Listening 2 is most like or most different to the business etiquette in their country.

Writing

Ask Ss to choose one of the cities. They are going to write an email to a friend. Refer Ss to the Style guide (page 6) or spend a short time reminding Ss of the layout and style for emails. This is an email to a friend, so Ss can use contractions and informal vocabulary. Ask Ss to make notes on what they said about their own country in the speaking exercise, and to use these to help them find differences between their city and the city they are writing about (e.g. *In Sydney people often have breakfast meetings at 8am but in Lisbon we usually …*). As Ss finish, ask them to compare emails with a partner.

Style guide, page 6

Language check

Ask Ss to work in pairs and take turns making the offers/responses and requests/responses. Ask Ss to do the two activities. Encourage Ss to suggest situations where they could use the most formal and informal expressions. Ask Ss why they think that people sometimes use other ways to say *no* (being direct is also considered in the Culture at work section). Can they think of any situations where they would prefer to use one of the indirect expressions rather than say *no* directly? It can be confusing for Ss to see expressions such as *Not just now, thanks* and *Thanks, but I don't really need one* as, at first glance, the phrases can appear to be positive. In these situations you are thanking the person for the offer, but saying 'no' to what they are offering. It might be a good idea to remind Ss that it is very important to use *please* and *thank you* when making requests and responding to offers.

1 Do you want some sugar?
   Can you phone me tomorrow?
   Not just now, thanks.
   Yes, no problem.

2 Not just now, **thanks**; I don't take sugar, **thanks**; **Thanks, but** I don't really need one; **It's a bit difficult**. I'm very busy; **I'm sorry**. I don't know this place very well.

Coursebook, Grammar reference: Modal forms, page 158

Practice 1

Ask Ss to identify which words are in italics. Then ask Ss to choose which words are most appropriate to complete the sentences. Do the first one together as an example. Ask Ss to work with a partner and take turns reading the sentences and responding.

1 Can I	2 Can I	3 Could I
4 Would you like to	5 Could I	6 Could you
7 Can you		

Listening 3

On the board write:
Can I speak to you for a moment?

Say it with falling intonation and ask if it sounds more like an order or a request (order). Then say it with rising intonation and ask the same question (request).

On the board write:
Please sit down.

Again, demonstrate how rising and falling intonation changes meaning. Encourage Ss to practise saying the two sentences with a rising and then falling intonation. Ss listen to the six phrases and decide if they have a rising or falling intonation. Ask Ss to turn to the audioscript on page 164. Get them to work with a partner and take turns saying the phrases using a rising or falling intonation while their partner guesses if they are making a request/offer or an order.

1 order	2 request	3 request
4 order	5 order	6 request

Practice 2

Ask Ss to look at the sentences individually and think of how they would refuse each request without using the word 'no'. Then ask Ss to discuss their ideas with a partner. Ss could then take turns to make the offers and requests and refuse them politely.

1 It's a bit difficult … (I go to bed at 10; I'm out this evening)
2 Thanks, but … (I don't drink beer; I don't drink alcohol); or: Not just now, thanks.
3 It's a bit difficult … (I'm very busy today; I haven't got much time)
4 Thanks, but … (I haven't got time now; I'm in a hurry)
5 Sorry, but I don't know much about it.
6 Thanks, but I don't really need one. (I can take the train; I have a taxi)

Workbook, page 13

Speaking 1

Ss are going to work in pairs and take turns asking each other for help. To demonstrate the activity, write on the board:

A I want you to stay late tonight and help me with my project.
B No!

Get Ss to practise the dialogue with a partner; encourage them to pretend to be as impolite as possible. Ask Ss to suggest ways to make it more polite, for example:

A Could you stay late tonight and help me with my project, please?
B I'm sorry, I can't tonight, I'm going to my English class.

Then ask Student A to turn to page 137 and Student B to turn to page 141. Give Ss time to read the information and prepare their requests. Circulate to check that Ss understand what they are going to do. In pairs, Ss take turns to ask each other for help and to say 'no' politely. After Ss have finished, you could have a brief feedback session and discuss what other phrases Ss could have used to make the requests and responses.

Speaking 2

Ask pairs to write two situations where people make two requests and offers, using the situation in exercise 1 as a model. Then Ss give their situations to another pair and role-play the situations that they have been given. In these role-plays you could tell Ss that they can decide whether to politely accept or refuse the offer or request.

Career skills

Ask Ss to read the information in the box and try to identify what the person is doing in each situation. For example, in *1 Can I introduce my colleague? This is Jane Duncan*, the person is introducing someone. When we are being polite we often use longer, indirect phrases (e.g. *Is it OK to smoke in here?* rather than *I want to smoke in here* or *Can I smoke here?*). This makes the request softer and less direct. Ask Ss to match the phrases with the replies. Ss can practise saying the phrases and the replies with a partner. Ask Ss to work in small groups and think of other phrases that could be used to reply to phrases 1–6. Other possible replies include:

a That's all right, you're very welcome.
b That's great, thanks. / Sorry, I'm afraid I can't.
c That's OK, it's not a problem.
d It's my pleasure.
e Nice to meet you. / How do you do?
f I'm afraid not, it's a non-smoking area.

| 1 e | 2 c | 3 a | 4 b | 5 f | 6 d |

Listening 4 1

Ss are going to listen to six short conversations where people respond politely. Get Ss to read through 1–6 before listening. Ask Ss to listen and choose the correct description in italics.

1 doesn't apologise	2 accepts
3 knows	4 can't
5 likes	6 wasn't

Listening 4 2

This time, Ss listen again and underline the phrases from the Career skills box that they hear. If you would like to spend more time practising intonation, you could play the recording again and ask Ss to identify where the speakers use rising and falling intonation. You could then ask Ss to turn to the audioscript on pages 164–165 of the Coursebook and read the conversations with a partner.

2 Would you like to … ? That would be very nice. Thank you!
3 Can I introduce … ?
4 Is it OK to … ? I'm sorry. It isn't allowed.
5 Thanks very much for … I'm glad you …
6 Thanks for … No problem.

UNIT 3

Speaking

Ask Ss to work in groups of four to six. Ss work with a partner and prepare their role-play(s) (for example, in a group of four, pairs would role-play every other situation). Then Ss role-play the situation for the rest of their group. Smaller classes can do this exercise in pairs. If Ss wish to write the role-plays first, this is fine. However, when they perform the role-play, encourage Ss not to read directly from their notes.

> **Optional activity**
> **Photocopiable resource 3.1 (page 107)**
> Photocopy and cut up the *polite phrases* and *responses* cards. Shuffle the cards and give one set to each pair/group. Ask Ss to work together and divide the cards into *polite phrases* and *responses*. Then Ss match the phrases with the most appropriate response. The activity can be extended/used to revise language by giving groups only the *polite phrases* cards. Ss take it in turns to turn a card over and say the phrase, their partner / another person in the group responds.

Culture at work

Ask Ss to read the information and discuss it in pairs / small groups. Encourage them to give examples of situations where they use direct and indirect language. You could ask Ss to try to imagine how a person from a direct culture might feel when visiting a culture that uses indirect expressions, and vice versa. Some cultures can interpret directness as being rude. People from cultures where directness is preferred may think that people from indirect cultures take a long time to get to the point, or may find the indirect ways of saying 'yes' and 'no' confusing. You may find it helpful to look at the Culture at work box from page 16 of the Skills Book; this is reproduced below. You may also find it useful to refer to the relevant section on Culture at work in the teacher's notes supporting the Skills Book.

Direct	Indirect
Use fewer words.	Use more words.
Do not always use *please* or *thank you*.	Usually use *please* or *thank you*.
Use statements more than questions for requests: *Give me the report.* not *Could I have the report?*	Often use indirect questions for requests: *Can I use your pen, please? Could you open the door, please?*

Skills Book, Culture at work, page 16

Teacher's Book, page 125

Dilemma

Ask Ss to look at the photo. Ask them to describe the expression in the woman's face. Does she look happy? Make sure that Ss understand the term *bully*. Introduce the subject by asking Ss to work in pairs / small groups and think of types of behaviour in the workplace that could be interpreted as bullying (e.g. shouting at staff/colleagues, always telling someone that they are doing a bad job, speaking to someone in a disrespectful way, sending offensive emails, etc.). Ask Ss to read the Dilemma brief. Ask Ss check questions (*What sort of company does Elizabeth work for? Did she enjoy her job in the past? Does she enjoy her job now? Why? / Why not?*) Then ask Ss to give examples of how Valma bullies Elizabeth (she finds problems with Elizabeth's work, shouts at her in front of colleagues, calls her stupid, gives her the most boring and difficult tasks and stops her going on training courses). Get Ss to look at Elizabeth's options. Are there any others? Ask what they would do in her situation.

Task 1: Ask Ss to suggest reasons why someone might be a bully. Ask Ss why it is helpful to understand why someone is a bully (because it makes it easier to find techniques to deal with bullies if you know what motivates them). Divide the class into three groups. Tell Ss that each group is going to read about a different type of bully. Group A turns to page 141, Group B turns to page 143 and Group C turns to page 144 to read the information. Circulate and check that groups understand their information.

Task 2: Put Ss into groups of three. Each group should contain one person from Groups A, B and C. Ss take turns to describe the type of bully that they read about. Encourage Ss to use language to check or clarify information where necessary. Groups then decide which type of bully matches Valma (the type Group C read about – one who is afraid of competition). Now ask the groups to decide what option they think is best for Elizabeth. Encourage Ss to give reasons why they chose their option (more than one option is possible).

Decision

Ask Ss what they think happened in real life. Then ask Ss to listen to Gary Robinson, a business psychologist, say what he thinks the best option is for Elizabeth. Ask Ss what option he recommends (talk to a senior manager). What does he say Elizabeth should do if this does not work? (leave the company) Ss listen again and note what things Gary says that Elizabeth should do to collect facts and details about the bullying (keep a diary). What can the senior manager do to help Elizabeth? (move her or Valma to another team/department)

Write it up

Ask Ss to write an email to Elizabeth to explain why they think Valma is bullying Elizabeth and suggest what she should do. This is a friendly email so Ss can use contractions and less formal vocabulary and expressions. You may wish to

INTELLIGENT BUSINESS (PRE-INTERMEDIATE) TEACHER'S BOOK: COURSEBOOK

ask Ss to prepare the writing in class, complete it for homework and then compare with a partner in the next lesson before handing it in to be marked. Give each S a photocopy of the Writing preparation framework from page 188. Then use the Writing focus (Writing focus: Emails) below to link the use of the framework and the Style guide as Ss plan their writing. It may be helpful to use the Writing feedback framework on page 189 when marking Ss' writing.

Writing focus: Emails

1 First, decide who you are.
(In this case, you are yourself.)

2 Every time you start to write, you need to ask yourself two questions:
a What is the purpose of this piece of writing?
b Who am I writing to?
(Here Ss are writing to offer Elizabeth advice about why they think Valma is bullying her and say what they think she should do.)

3 Look at the section on Emails on page 6 of the Style guide. Notice the suggested structure of an email:
From/To/Cc/Date/Subject
Greeting
Message
Closing phrase
Name
Start with the most important information and put less important information in the second paragraph.
Is this structure appropriate for this email? Plan the paragraphs you are going to divide the email into. Then brainstorm the points you might cover in each paragraph.

4 What style should the email be written in?
(As it says in the Style guide, it is a good idea to keep emails short and use short sentences and simple language. This is a friendly email so the style should be relaxed, i.e. Ss can use contractions and more informal vocabulary.)

5 What words and phrases might be appropriate in your email?
(See the Useful phrases in the Style guide.)

6 Now go ahead and write the email.

7 When you have finished, check your writing for: logical structure, clarity of ideas, accuracy of language, appropriateness of style.

- Style guide, page 6
- Style guide, General rules, page 3
- Skills Book, Writing 2, Emails, page 32

- Teacher's Book, page 138
- Teacher's Book, Writing preparation framework, page 188
- Teacher's Book, Writing feedback framework, page 189

Informal email:
Suggested answer (148 words)
From: (student's name)
To: Elizabeth
Date: (today's date)
Subject: Advice
Dear Elizabeth
I am very sorry to hear that you are unhappy at work at the moment.
I think that Valma is bullying you because she is afraid of you. You are very good at your job and Valma knows that. She is worried that you might want her job. She doesn't allow you to go on training courses because she doesn't want you to progress in your job.
I think you should talk to a senior manager about the situation. It is a good idea to get as much information as you can. For example, keep a diary and write down examples of when and where Valma bullies you. Also, speak to colleagues to ask if they can support your story. This will help you when you go and talk to the senior manager.
Good luck!
Regards

Review 1

On the next two pages of the Coursebook you will find Review 1, which reviews language, vocabulary and functional language from Units 1, 2 and 3. It can be used in a number of ways that can be adapted to suit your class, for example:

- Ss can do selected exercises for homework.
- Use in class and guide Ss to particular exercises according to their individual needs. Alternatively, if your class has similar needs, focus on exercises where they can have more practice together (Ss can work individually or in pairs).
- Use as a short progress test and review any necessary points before moving on to Unit 4.

- Coursebook Review: Answers, page 102

Unit 4: Image

UNIT OBJECTIVES	
Reading:	Fashion's favourite
Language:	Comparatives and superlatives
Vocabulary:	The fashion industry
	Word building
Career skills:	Describing products
Culture at work:	Honest or diplomatic?
Dilemma & Decision:	Volkswagen bugs (memo)

Companies aim their products at the target market that they wish to enter. For example, designer goods are aimed at the luxury market, whereas companies that want to sell to as many people as possible promote their goods on the mass market. Image is important to companies as it can affect how consumers see the company and the goods they are buying. This is why companies are willing to invest time and money building up, and guarding, their brand image. A company's image can be damaged by attracting the wrong segment of customers. The fashion house Burberry discovered this when imitations of their trademark checks started to be worn on baseball caps and bags of mass market customers, denting their exclusive image. As the reading on page 35 illustrates, the fashion world is willing to invest a huge amount of money on fashion shows which promote their label or logo. However, the fashion shows and haute couture designs are not how these companies make their money. Instead, the shows create an exclusive, luxury brand image that is then used to sell perfumes, cosmetics and accessories to the wider market.

Keynotes

Ask Ss to look at the picture on page 33. Ask what industry they think the picture is showing (the fashion industry). Where do designers usually show this sort of dress to the public? (fashion shows) Have Ss ever been to a fashion show? If so, what was it like? Check that Ss understand the meaning of 'a buzz' in the title (interest and excitement). Ask Ss to read the keynotes and check that they understand the words in bold. Draw Ss' attention to the glossary for this unit at the back of the book. Do they agree that most customers feel happier buying a famous brand than a product that they don't know? If they agree with the statement, why do they think this is?

Coursebook, Glossary, Unit 4, page 148

Optional activity

Brainstorm a variety of products that Ss have bought over the last year. Include items such as cars, computers and clothes. Ask Ss to work in small groups and discuss:
- Which products would you buy *only* if it was a well-known brand?
- Would you buy *any* of the products on the list if it did not have a recognised brand name?

Preview 1

Ask Ss to discuss the questions in pairs then share their views with the class. Make sure that Ss are clear about the difference between *cheap* and *inexpensive* (see answers). Can Ss think of any items that they have bought recently that were *value for money*? You might like to teach your Ss the phrases *It's good value for money* and *It's a bargain*.

1 luxury: expensive, high quality
2 *Inexpensive* and *cheap* can both simply mean *not expensive*. But *cheap* can also be used with a negative connotation, to imply inferior quality.
3 value for money: inexpensive, not low quality

Preview 2

Students answer the two questions on brands. Ask Ss to name the objects pictured. Can they identify the brands that each object belongs to? (phone: Nokia; pen: Bic; shoe: Gucci; bag: Louis Vuitton; car: Mercedes) Ask what Ikea sells (furniture). Choose one of the objects and ask Ss to decide if it belongs to the luxury goods group or the value for money group. Then get Ss to decide for the remaining objects.

Luxury goods: Gucci, Louis Vuitton, Mercedes
Value for money: Nokia, Bic, Ikea

Choose an object and ask Ss to use words and phrases in the box to describe the image of the brand (e.g. *A Bic pen is reliable and practical*; *Gucci shoes are fashionable and stylish*). Then ask Ss to work in pairs and do the same to describe the other objects pictured. You might like to see if Ss can think of any other words or phrases to describe each of the objects.

Speaking

Ask Ss to discuss the questions in pairs / small groups. Prompt the discussion where necessary by asking Ss to explain their ideas (*Why is/isn't fashion important to you?*).

> **Optional activity**
> Cut out a selection of pictures of products from magazines. Ask Ss to work in small groups. Give one picture to each group and ask them to write an advertisement for the product (they can use vocabulary from the preview exercises and any other words that they know). Each group then nominates a spokesperson and tries to 'sell' their product to another group.

Vocabulary 1

Ask Ss to look at the words/phrases 1–5 and suggest which industry they are often used in connection with (the fashion industry). Ask Ss to work in pairs and match the words 1–5 with the meanings a–e.

1 d	2 e	3 a	4 c	5 b

Reading 1

Ask Ss to look at the title of the article and the subheading 'The high cost of fashion shows is worth every penny to the industry'. Ask Ss why they think fashion shows are useful to the fashion industry (they advertise and promote a designer's label and brand). Check that Ss understand the meaning of 'What is the point of top-end fashion?'. Get Ss to discuss the question with a partner. Check ideas around the class. Then ask Ss to read the article and see if the writer agrees with their ideas (it creates the image of the brand). Draw Ss' attention to the glossary box and remind them of the glossary for Unit 4 at the back of the book.

Reading 2

Ask Ss to read the article again and answer the questions. Ask Ss to dictate all the prices and numbers in the article. Write the prices/numbers on the board and choose three or four prices/numbers and ask Ss what each one refers to.

1 because of the high prices ($100,000 for a dress)
2 no
3 to generate publicity (more effective than advertising)
4 It is home to the most famous brands; it has the biggest number of talented designers.
5 It is good for the economy: production, jobs, exports (8% of the country's industrial activity).
6 New York

Speaking

Ask Ss to discuss the question in pairs / small groups. Encourage Ss to give reasons for their opinions. Prompt the discussion where necessary, e.g. by asking *When you buy a designer label, are you just buying the product or are you buying the brand's image as well?*

Vocabulary 2 [1]

Ask Ss to decide if definition a or b best describes words 1–6. Do the first one together to demonstrate.

1 b	2 b	3 a	4 a	5 a	6 b

Vocabulary 2 [2]

Ask the class to name some examples of glossy magazines. Can they name any recent advertising campaigns for the fashion industry? What are the most famous fashion houses in their country? Ask Ss to work in pairs and complete the article with the words in the box. Ask check questions such as: *What fashion houses are named in the text? Who do they use in their fashion campaigns? What type of magazines do they appear in? What fashion news are newspapers interested in? Why does the fashion industry still put on fashion shows?*

1 Fashion houses	2 campaigns
3 glossy magazines	4 famous
5 wear	6 shows
7 image	8 publicity

Vocabulary 3 [1]

Check that Ss understand the terms *noun* and *adjective*. You could write on the board:
He takes beautiful photographs.

Ask Ss to identify which word is a noun (*photographs*) and which word is an adjective (*beautiful*). Ask Ss to complete the table with the missing noun or adjective. Do the first one together to demonstrate. Ask Ss to compare answers with a partner. You may wish to point out that the word *economical* also exists, but that it has a different meaning (using money or things carefully, without wasting any).

1 luxury	2 fashionable
3 industry	4 creative
5 commercial	6 economic
7 famous	8 talent

Vocabulary 3 [2]

Ask Ss to work in pairs to mark the stress in each word in the table. Focus Ss on the example and ask them to repeat the two words as you say them. You can use clapping or tapping to emphasise the stress. Write the next pair of words on the board and ask Ss to suggest where the stress should be marked. Again, encourage Ss to say the words out loud. Ss complete the table.

Listening 1

Ss listen and check their answers (you could use the audioscript on page 165 to do this). Say the words, or play each word from the recording again, and ask Ss to repeat. You could then ask Ss to take turns choosing a noun and their partner says the adjective.

luxury	luxurious
fashion	fashionable
industry	industrial
creation	creative
commerce	commercial
economy	economic
fame	famous
talent	talented

Listening 2

Check that Ss understand *lifestyle*. Ask Ss: *Do companies sell products or do they sell a lifestyle? Do the things that you buy say something about you as a person?* Point to the Ray Bans advertisement. Ask Ss to think of adjectives to describe the image that the picture is trying to promote (e.g. cool, relaxed, stylish, individual, strong, free). Ask Ss to read the questions. Then ask Ss to listen to marketing consultant, Dee Delaney, talking about how companies communicate the image of their brand. Ask Ss to compare their answers with a partner and then play the recording again for Ss to check. Ask Ss if they agree with Dee Delaney. Why? / Why not?

1 a lifestyle
2 clothes, car, mobile phone
3 strong, dynamic
4 leaders and heroes
5 men
6 relaxed, stylish

Speaking

Ask Ss to discuss the questions in groups. Ask groups to keep a note of their ideas and get each group to present their ideas to the class.

> **Optional activity**
> **Photocopiable resource 4.1 (page 108)**
> You could introduce comparatives and superlatives by asking Ss to complete the comparatives and superlatives questionnaire. Give a photocopy of the questionnaire to each S. Go through the questions and check understanding. Ask Ss to complete answers for themselves and then ask their partner the questions. Then ask Ss to compare similarities and differences in their answers.

Language check 1

Ask Ss to read the sentences and complete the table about the formation of the comparative and superlative.

1 cheaper   2 easier
3 more effective 4 less expensive
5 the biggest   6 The most famous

Language check 2

Ask Ss to say which adjectives are type A (have one syllable) and which are type C (have two or more syllables). Get them to say the comparative and superlative form of each of the adjectives.

A: high, slow, old, young
C: fashionable, beautiful, reliable, practical

Coursebook, Grammar reference: Comparatives and superlatives, page 158

Language check 3

Ask Ss to work with a partner to say the comparative and superlative forms of the adjectives *good* and *bad*.

good better best; bad worse worst

Language check 4

Ask Ss to complete the sentences using *as* or *than*.

1 as   2 than   3 as

INTELLIGENT BUSINESS (PRE-INTERMEDIATE) TEACHER'S BOOK: COURSEBOOK

Optional activity
Photocopiable resource 4.2 (page 108)
Ss work in pairs / small groups. First, Ss brainstorm products for one minute, e.g. computers, watches. Give each S a copy of the worksheet. Ask pairs/groups to choose one product from their brainstorm list. Pairs/Groups agree on three companies that make the product and note the name of the companies on the worksheet. Then Ss work individually and complete the rest of the information on the worksheet. Ss then use their notes to discuss with their partner/group the different approaches to the product that the three companies take.

Practice 1

Ss choose the words in italics to complete the sentences. Refer Ss back to the Language check to check their answers.

1 bigger	2 cheaper
3 as	4 prettier
5 the greatest	6 more talented
7 the least creative	8 worse
9 as	10 lower

Practice 2

Ask Ss what they know about Giorgio Armani. What does his company sell? (clothes, perfume, accessories) Tell them that they are going to read a text where Giorgio Armani gives his opinion about what consumers want. Ss complete the text. Check answers around the class and ask Ss what information in the text made them choose their answer. Get Ss to read the complete text again and ask check questions: *How did fashion and luxury goods companies perform last year compared to the years before?* (They performed worse than in the years before.) *What things are becoming important to customers?* (quality and value for money) *What do people expect to buy for less money?* (the latest styles).

1 worst	2 better
3 more optimistic	4 more careful
5 more important	6 harder
7 longer	8 more interested
9 newest	

Workbook, page 17

Speaking

Ask Ss to think about adjectives that they can use to describe a watch. Focus Ss on the three pictures. What materials do they think each watch is made of? Do any of the watches have special features? Give Ss a few minutes to prepare their ideas, then ask them to work with a partner to compare the watches using the adjectives in the list and any others that they want to use. Then Ss say which watch they liked best and why.

Career skills

Ask Ss what sort of catalogues or brochures they have received recently. Focus attention on the picture of a desk. Ask Ss to suggest adjectives to describe it. What kind of desk is it? (a computer desk) Do they like it? Why? / Why not? Ss read the information and then match the questions 1–7 with phrases a–h. Point out that one of the questions has two answers. Ask Ss to practise asking and answering the questions in pairs.

1 c	2 d	3 a, b	4 e	5 g	6 h	7 f

Optional activity
Ask Ss to think of an object that they have bought recently. Ss take it in turns to ask questions 1–7 and answer about their object.

Listening 3 1

Ask Ss to look at the pictures. What occupation do they think each person has? Get Ss to guess which people they think will like or dislike the desk. Ss listen and answer the question. Ask Ss what nationality they think each person is from their accent (customers 1 and 3 have British accents; customer 2 has an American accent).

No. The second customer (office designer) doesn't like the desk.

Listening 3 2

Ss listen again and tick the phrases in the Career skills box that they hear. What reasons does each customer give for liking / not liking the desk?

Customer 1: c, a, e
Customer 2: f, b
Customer 3: d, g, h

Speaking

Ss are going to take turns describing a product to each other. To prepare, choose an object in the classroom and ask Ss to help you write a description of it on the board. Does it have any special features? Does it look nice? Who are the target customers who would buy it? Do Ss like the object? Why? / Why not? Encourage Ss to use phrases from the Career skills box to help. Then ask Ss to work in pairs. Ask Student A to turn to page 137 and Student B to turn to page 141. Ss take it in turns to describe their product to their partner. Encourage Ss to ask each other questions about their opinions on the product. When they have finished, Ss check each other's charts to see if all the details are accurate.

Culture at work

Ask Ss to read the information and discuss the questions in pairs / small groups. Encourage Ss to say if they have been in a situation where they had to give their opinion about something that they did not like. You may find it helpful to look at the Culture at work box from page 22 of the Skills Book; this is reproduced below. You may also find it useful to refer to the relevant section on Culture at work in the teacher's notes supporting the Skills Book.

Diplomatic	Honest
Accept the food and eat it.	Explain that you do not like the food.
You think that it is impolite to refuse food or drink and you do not want to offend your host.	In your country, it is OK to refuse food or drink. You don't think that it is a problem to say what you like or don't like.

Skills Book, Culture at work, page 22
Teacher's Book, page 130.

Dilemma

As a lead-in, ask Ss what car manufacturers they know. Choose one or two brands and ask Ss to say which ones they prefer and why. Do any of the cars have special features? Tell them that they are going to read about a German car manufacturer. Can they name any cars that Volkswagen produce? Ss read the Dilemma brief and Ideas 1–3. Ask Ss to summarise the situation in order to check comprehension.

Task 1: Divide the class into three groups. Each group chooses one consumer group A–C. Make sure that each group looks at a different consumer group A–C. Draw Ss' attention to the Useful phrases box. Groups decide which car they think would most appeal to their consumer group. Ask groups to explain the reasons for their choice.

Task 2: Now Ss work in groups of three. Each person in the group should have looked at a different consumer group in Task 1. Ss exchange opinions about the three cars and say which one they think is best.

Decision

Ask Ss to listen to Ernst Jungbaum as he talks about the decision that VW took (they launched a sports utility vehicle and a luxury car). What reasons does he give? (they wanted to compete in the luxury market, and give their customers a car to move on to from middle-priced cars) Does the class think that VW made the right decision? Why? / Why not?

Write it up

Tell Ss that they are going to write a memo to the senior management of VW to say what product they recommend goes ahead for development. They should give their reasons why. You may wish to ask Ss to prepare the writing in class, complete it for homework and then compare with a partner in the next lesson before handing it in to be marked. Give each S a photocopy of the Writing preparation framework from page 188. Then use the Writing focus (Writing focus: Memos) below to link the use of the framework and the Style guide as Ss plan their writing. It may be helpful to use the Writing feedback framework on page 189 when marking Ss' writing.

Writing focus: Memos

1 First, decide who you are.
   (In this case, Ss work for VW in marketing.)

2 Every time you start to write, you need to ask yourself two questions:
   a What is the purpose of this piece of writing?
   b Who am I writing to?
   (Here Ss are writing to recommend which car VW should develop and give reasons why. The memo will be read by the senior management of VW.)

3 Look at the section on Memos on page 16 of the Style guide. Notice the suggested structure for a memo:
   To/From/Subject/Date
   No opening greeting necessary
   Main message
   Recommendations
   Name or initials of the writer (optional)
   Is this structure appropriate for this memo? What are you going to put on the subject line? Plan the sections you are going to divide the memo into. Then brainstorm the points you might cover in each section.

Continued on page 38

INTELLIGENT BUSINESS (PRE-INTERMEDIATE) TEACHER'S BOOK: COURSEBOOK

4 What style should the memo be written in?
(As it says in the Style guide, memos are short, official notes that will be read by people within a company. Memos are usually less formal than business letters. The language is simple and clear and the tone is normally neutral.)

5 What phrases might be appropriate for your memo?
(See the Style guide, particularly the phrases for making recommendations on page 16. See also the Useful phrases on page 40 of the Coursebook and the phrases for describing products on page 39 of the Coursebook.)

6 Now go ahead and write the memo.

7 When you have finished, check your writing for: logical structure, clarity of ideas, accuracy of language, appropriateness of style.

- Style guide, Memos, page 16
- Style guide, General rules, page 3
- Skills Book, Writing 3, Memos, page 46
- Teacher's Book, page 149
- Teacher's Book, Writing preparation framework, page 188
- Teacher's Book, Writing feedback framework, page 189

Memo: Suggested answer (82 words)
To: Senior management, Volkswagen
From: (student's name)
Subject: New Volkswagen car
Date: (today's date)
I recommend that we develop the sports utility vehicle. It is a popular choice with younger consumer groups who have a lot of money. The sports utility vehicle is more expensive than the people carrier but less expensive than the executive car. It is the best choice because it is stylish and luxurious but it also has an exciting, modern image, which is what Volkswagen wants to develop.

Unit 5: Success

UNIT OBJECTIVES	
Reading:	Passion into profit
Language:	Past simple
Vocabulary:	Opposites
	Business failure
	Collocations
Career skills:	Telling a story
Culture at work:	Telling stories
Dilemma & Decision:	Organic growth (memo)

This unit looks at factors that contribute to making a company a success or a failure. From the initial concept to getting a business off the ground and making it a success takes vision, energy and organisation. It often starts with spotting a gap in the market that existing companies are not fulfilling. Research then needs to be carried out to discover if there is a demand for the product or service being offered. One of the biggest hurdles for a start-up (new business) can be arranging the funding for their venture. The first step is to approach banks with a business plan, to see if they will agree a business loan. Another option is to start a company with a partner or partners so that the initial financial outlay is shared between two or more people. If a company is high risk, it might have difficulty attracting funding from traditional sources, so may need to approach a venture capitalist company. In return for their investment, venture capitalists would require a proportion of the new company's profits. If a person has enough funds to set up a company without requiring investors, they become the sole proprietor. This means that they will get all the profits if the company is a success but are also financially responsible for debts should the company fail. After getting it off the ground, a clear business strategy is an important factor in taking a company forward and making it a success. This includes being able to communicate the USP (unique selling point) of your company's product or service and being aware of competitors. A company also has to be able to manage change. As markets change and develop, a company must be able to react fast and change its business approach accordingly, otherwise customers will move elsewhere.

Keynotes

What do Ss think *Passion into profit* means? (turning something that you are very interested in into a business and making a profit) Ask Ss to read through the keynotes and check they understand the terms in bold. Make sure that Ss understand the difference between a *start-up* (noun) and *to start up a business* (verb). Draw Ss' attention to the glossary for this unit at the back of the book.

Coursebook, Glossary, Unit 5, page 148

Preview

Ask Ss to name some successful people that they know (these can be people they know personally or well-known people). What do each of these people do? What is it about them that makes them a success? (e.g. money, job, happiness) Ask Ss to decide which of the ideas are closest to their own definition of success. If they don't agree with any of the ideas, they can think of another example of what success means to them.

Vocabulary 1

Ask Ss to work in pairs and discuss what makes a successful company. Have a short feedback session to pool ideas. Ss work individually to complete the sentences using words/phrases from the box. Ss check their answers by listening to Jake Goldrick in Listening 1 (see below).

Listening 1 **1**

Tell Ss that sentences 1–6 in Vocabulary 1 exercise are from a talk by Jake Goldrick. Ss listen and check their answers.

1 profit	2 demand
3 control	4 market share
5 market leader	6 grow

Listening 1 **2**

This time Ss listen again more closely. Play the recording for Ss to answer the questions. Play it one more time, pausing at the appropriate points to check answers.

1 keep costs as low as possible
2 You can lose customers.
3 Companies want to grow, find new markets and new opportunities.

INTELLIGENT BUSINESS (PRE-INTERMEDIATE) TEACHER'S BOOK: COURSEBOOK

Speaking

Ask Ss to think of an example of a successful company. What makes it successful? Get Ss to work in pairs / small groups and exchange ideas. Open up the discussion to the whole class. Make a list of Ss' suggestions for what makes a successful company.

Reading 1

Focus Ss on the picture of the bottle in the text. What drink is it? (a smoothie) Do Ss know what a smoothie is? (If Ss don't know, draw attention to the glossary; also, remind Ss of the glossary for Unit 5 at the back of the book.) Have they tried a smoothie? Did they like it? Ask Ss to read through the article quickly and discuss the question with a partner.

> It's successful because the CEO saw an opportunity to market a successful US product in the UK, and because he is passionate about succeeding.

Reading 2

Ask Ss to call out all the numbers and dates in the article. Practise saying them with your class. Ss read the article again to find when events 1–4 happened.

> 1 in the early 1990s   2 in 1994
> 3 from 1994 to 1996   4 in 1996

Reading 3

Ask Ss to read the questions and check understanding. Ss read the article again more closely and answer the questions. Ask Ss to compare their answers with a partner.

> 1 They were good for the health.
> 2 They weren't available in the UK.
> 3 He sold his flat, car and investments.
> 4 The business grew quickly and they didn't have the stock to meet demand.
> 5 just under 50%
> 6 big supermarkets
> 7 His distributor went bankrupt.
> 8 No – '… you've got to have fun … You must feel really passionate about what you're doing.'

Speaking

Ask Ss to work in pairs / small groups and answer the questions. If Ss do not have an idea that they are passionate about, encourage them to think of a hobby or an area that interests them.

Optional activity
Photocopiable resource 5.1 (page 109)

You can use this activity to extend the topic of the Speaking exercise or ask Ss to complete it for homework. Give each S a copy of the worksheet. Ss think of a more detailed business idea and complete the notes. Tell Ss that the idea does not have to be serious – they can think of fun products/services. Ss then present the idea, and their partner/group decides if they want to invest in the company. Encourage Ss to explain why they do/don't want to invest.

Vocabulary 2

Ask Ss to think of words that could mean the opposite of those listed. Then Ss look through the relevant paragraphs (shown in brackets) of the text to find the opposite of the listed word.

> 1 success   2 overweight
> 3 grew   4 strength
> 5 lost

Vocabulary 3

Ask Ss if they can name any companies that have failed. What made them fail? Check Ss understand the meaning of the words/phrases in the box. Ss complete the text and compare answers with a partner. Ask Ss to suggest what Snacks 2U could have done to save the company.

> 1 sold   2 distribute
> 3 equipped   4 cool
> 5 set up   6 order
> 7 bankrupt

Vocabulary 4

Check Ss understand what a collocation is (words that go together). Ss match words from A and B to make phrases. Do the first one together to demonstrate the activity. Ask Ss to compare their collocations with a partner. Then Ss use the collocations to complete the sentences.

> 1 heads a company   2 lose money
> 3 meet demand   4 rent an apartment
> 5 have fun

Listening 2 1

Ask Ss to work in small groups to make a list of important things to do before starting a new business. You may wish to give Ss a time limit to complete the task.

Listening 2 [2]

Ss are going to listen to Alan Martin talking about five steps for setting up a business. Ask Ss to suggest what the missing words could be. Then play the recording. Ss listen and complete the chart. Depending on your class, you could play the listening again for Ss to check. Do Ss agree with the steps? Is there anything they would add?

> 1 a new product idea 2 market research
> 3 business plan   4 finance
> 5 customer base

Listening 2 [3]

Check Ss understand the questions. Ask Ss to listen again and answer.

> 1 80 per cent
> 2 usually because people don't understand the market
> 3 Is there a demand for your product or service? Who are your competitors?
> 4 focus on what you want to do; get finance
> 5 details of the type of business; goals; product or service; key selling points; how you want to run the business: staff, management, production, marketing, finance
> 6 build a customer base – you need regular customers to come back year after year

Speaking

Ss work in pairs / small groups. Ask Ss to discuss the question. If Ss need prompting, ask them to think of the ideas they discussed about what makes a company a success. What would the opposite of each idea be?

Language check [1]

Read the example sentences with the class and make sure that Ss understand the meaning. On the board write:

I rent an apartment on the beach.

Ask: *Is this happening now or in the past?* (now). Now write:

I rented an apartment on the beach.

Repeat the question (it is happening in the past). Ask Ss what letters were added to the verb to make it past simple (*-ed*). Ask Ss for ideas about how to form the negative and question forms (*I didn't rent an apartment on the beach / Did I rent an apartment on the beach?*).

Ss look at the examples and answer questions 1–3.

> 1 infinitive of the verb + *-ed*
> 2 *did* + infinitive of the verb
> 3 *didn't* + infinitive of the verb

Language check [2]

Do this with the whole class.

> finished

Language check [3]

Ask Ss to look again at the article on page 43 and underline examples of irregular verbs in the past form. Ask Ss to say the infinitive form of the verbs (*have, be, sell, find, fly, grow, begin, go, lose*). Check that Ss know both past forms of *to be* (*was, were*) and the past form of *can* (*could*).

> had, was, sold, found, flew, grew, began, went, lost

Coursebook, Grammar reference: Past simple, page 159

Language check [4]

Ask Ss to say the times, days and dates listed. Then ask Ss to work with a partner and match the prepositions in the box with the time expressions. You could get Ss to brainstorm six more times, days and dates and ask their partner to match the time expression with the correct preposition.

> 1 in   2 from ... to ...   3 on
> 4 on   5 at   6 in

Writing

Ask Ss what prepositions go with the time expressions 1–7 (*from ... to, on, in, in, in, on, in*). Draw Ss' attention to the example sentence. Ask Ss what tense the verb is in the sentence *David Willis founds Chiltern Snacks* (present simple) and in the sentence *David Willis founded Chiltern Snacks in 1996* (past simple). Point out that time expressions can be placed at the beginning or end of a sentence (e.g. *In 1996, David Willis founded Chiltern Snacks*). Check answers with the class. Then choose two or three sentences and ask Ss to put them into the negative or question form of the past simple.

INTELLIGENT BUSINESS (PRE-INTERMEDIATE) TEACHER'S BOOK: COURSEBOOK

(Note: time expressions can also come at the end of the sentence.)
1 From 1996 to 2001, he distributed crisps to local retailers by van.
2 On August 1st 2001, a customer cancelled his order because Willis didn't sell 50 gram packs.
Willis thought about starting up his own brand of crisps.
3 In December 2002, Willis started production of the first Salty Dog crisps using 50 gram packs.
4 In the first year, sales grew fast.
5 In November 2003, the first international order arrived.
6 On February 14th 2004, Willis exported the first packs to Germany.
7 In March 2004, he received enquiries from the US and China.

Workbook, page 20

Speaking

Tell the class about six key events in your life and say when each event happened. The events do not have to be in chronological order. Ask Ss to do the same with their partner.

Career skills

Ask Ss to read the information and the phrases. Check Ss understand, particularly *after* + *-ing*. Point out that *So what did I do?* is not a real question, it does not require an answer. In a story, this phrase would be used to get the audience's attention. Ask Ss if they can remember the six key events in your life that you told them about in the speaking exercise. Get the class to help you use the phrases to tell the story in a more interesting way. Give Ss time to prepare their own six key events from the speaking exercise using some of the phrases for telling a story. Ss tell the story again to their partner, using the phrases for telling a story to order the information.

Listening 3 **1**

Check that Ss understand the six events. Ask Ss to listen and number the events in the correct order.

1 graduated from university
2 joined a design company
3 lost his job
4 started his own business
5 got a big contract
6 employs 12 people

Listening 3 **2**

Ss listen again and tick the phrases from the Career skills box.

After graduating …
Two years later …
So what did I do?
To begin with …
After about a year …
Then …
After a while …
And now …

Speaking **1**

Ask Ss to prepare to tell Ben's story using their own words. They can use phrases from the Career skills box to help them. Ss work with a partner and take turns to tell their story. Afterwards, ask Ss to talk about the similarities and differences in their accounts.

Speaking **2**

This is an information-gap activity. Ss ask their partner questions to complete information about Jeff Bezos. Introduce the subject by drawing Ss' attention to the photo. Ask if they know who the man is (Jeff Bezos). Point to the amazon.com logo and ask: *What is Amazon famous for selling?* (books, although it also sells music, toys, computer games and electrical equipment) *Where does it sell its products?* (on the internet). Give Ss time to look at their information (Student A on page 47, Student B on page 141) and prepare their questions. Then get Ss to ask their partner the questions and complete the information about Jeff Bezos.

Speaking **3**

Ss work together to tell Jeff Bezos's story in the correct order.

Culture at work

Ask Ss to read the information and discuss the questions in pairs / small groups. You may find it helpful to look at the Culture at work box from page 26 of the Skills Book; this is reproduced on the following page. You may also find it useful to refer to the relevant section on Culture at work in the teacher's notes supporting the Skills Book.

UNIT 5

Fixed sequence	Flexible sequence
When talking about the history of a company or project in a presentation you structure the events into a beginning, middle and end.	When talking about the history of a company or project in a presentation you may talk about different parts of the history, out of sequence.
The background information builds towards a key piece of information.	The background information can be as important as the main story.
You get to the point quickly and keep to the facts.	You talk around the subject and jump from point to point.

Skills Book, Culture at work, page 26
Teacher's Book, page 133

Dilemma

Point to the photo of the three girls and ask what they are eating (ice cream). Ask Ss if they know what food group ice cream belongs to (dairy). Can they name any other dairy products? (e.g. milk, cheese, butter, cream) You may wish to go over any vocabulary your class might have problems with (*organic*, *subsidiary*). Ask Ss to read the brief and then summarise it to check understanding.

Task 1: Divide the class into three groups, A, B and C. Each group turns to the relevant information at the back of the book. Circulate and help where necessary.

Task 2: Ss use the information to prepare a short presentation, either working with the other Ss in their group or individually.

Task 3: Divide Ss into groups of three. Make sure that each person in the group worked in a different group in Tasks 1 and 2. Ss make their presentation.

Task 4: The class uses the information from the presentations to discuss which firm Sunshine Foods should offer to buy.

Decision

Ask Ss which decision they think the company will choose. Ss then listen to Ronald Dean, the CEO of Sunshine Foods, explaining the company's decision (to make an offer for Annie's Kitchen). Ask Ss if they think the company took the right decision. Play the recording again and ask Ss to listen for the main reason, apart from good products, why the company took the decision (owner would accept a low offer because of financial difficulties).

Write it up

Tell Ss that they are going to write a memo to the directors of Sunshine Foods to say which organic producer offers the best opportunity. They should give their reasons why. You may wish to ask Ss to prepare the writing in class, complete it for homework and then compare with a partner in the next lesson before handing it in to be marked. Give each S a photocopy of the Writing preparation framework from page 188. Then use the Writing focus (Writing focus: Memos) below to link the use of the framework and the Style guide as Ss plan their writing. It may be helpful to use the Writing feedback framework on page 189 when marking Ss' writing.

Writing focus: Memos

1 First, decide who you are.
   (In this case, Ss are themselves.)

2 Every time you start to write, you need to ask yourself two questions:
   a What is the purpose of this piece of writing?
   b Who am I writing to?
   (Here Ss are writing to recommend which organic producer offers the best opportunity and give reasons why. The memo will be read by the directors of Sunshine Foods.)

3 Look at the section on Memos on page 16 of the Style guide. Notice the suggested structure for a memo:
   To/From/Subject/Date
   No opening greeting necessary
   Main message
   Recommendations
   Name or initials of the writer (optional)
   Is this structure appropriate for this memo? What are you going to put on the subject line? Plan the sections you are going to divide the memo into. Then brainstorm the points you might cover in each section.

4 What style should the memo be written in?
   (As it says in the Style guide, memos are short, official notes that will be read by people within a company. Memos are usually less formal than business letters. The language is simple and clear and the tone is normally neutral.)

5 What phrases might be appropriate for your memo?
   (See the Style guide, particularly the phrases for making recommendations on page 16.)

6 Now go ahead and write the memo.

7 When you have finished, check your writing for: logical structure, clarity of ideas, accuracy of language, appropriateness of style.

- Style guide, Memos, page 16
- Style guide, General rules, page 3
- Skills Book, Writing 3, Memos, page 46
- Teacher's Book, page 149
- Teacher's Book, Writing preparation framework, page 188
- Teacher's Book, Writing feedback framework, page 189

> **Memo: Suggested answer (80 words)**
> To: Directors of Sunshine Foods
> From: (student's name)
> Date: (today's date)
> Subject: Best organic producer
> I think that Annie's Kitchen offers the best business opportunity for Sunshine Foods because it produces both yoghurt and ice cream. The company produces a good product. It also has 80 employees and could develop into a bigger business. The company has a distribution problem, but Sunshine Foods could help with this. The company is in financial difficulties, so we could negotiate a good deal.

Unit 6: Future

UNIT OBJECTIVES	
Reading:	An elevator to space
Language:	Modals of possibility
Vocabulary:	Financing ventures
	Collocations
Career skills:	Making predictions
Culture at work:	Past or future?
Dilemma & Decision:	Risky ventures (memo)

Some companies are confident enough to encourage employees to develop entrepreneurial activities within the company; this is also called corporate venturing or intrapreneurship. 3M, for example, allows staff to spend time working on their own projects. Those that show the most potential may end up being adopted by the company. However, many large organisations can be resistant to new ideas and reluctant to fund new ventures. This means that those with innovative ideas may be forced to go it alone and find funding for their project. The private space industry is an area that can have problems finding financial backers. One of the main reasons is that most space-related projects cannot offer a quick return to investors. However, it might be possible to raise money by finding other companies who are interested in working on a joint venture, where two or more companies could work together on a project. Some space-related ventures include: commercial zero gravity flights in adapted high altitude planes, which are already being offered at $3,000 per person; and space tourism – some predict that public flights into space will be available in the near future. Space enthusiasts with available funds include Nevada millionaire Robert Biglow, who is offering a $50-million prize for the first private orbital space vehicle. Other space-related companies remain firmly terrestrial and only venture as far as cyberspace; for example, one entrepreneur sells acres of the moon, and a number of internet companies charge to name a 'star' after a loved one.

Keynotes

Point to the picture and ask: *Where is this?* (space). Ask Ss to suggest some business ventures connected with space (for example, one internet company sells acres of the moon). Read through the keynotes with your class. Check that they understand the terms in bold. Ask Ss: *Do you think that new technology will open up new business opportunities? Can you think of any examples?* Draw Ss' attention to the glossary for this unit at the back of the book.

Coursebook, Glossary, Unit 6, page 149

Preview

Books closed. Draw a rocket and planet on the board and ask Ss to brainstorm words connected with space. Open books and ask Ss to look at the photos and say what they show (an astronaut, a satellite, a rocket launch). Ask Ss to work in pairs / small groups to discuss the questions. You may wish to tell Ss about some of the private space industry ventures mentioned above.

Reading 1

Check that Ss understand *elevator*. Ask: *Is this word British English or American English?* (American). Elicit the British English word (*lift*). Check that Ss understand the meaning of any difficult words (*cable, permanently, platform, equator, capsule*). Ask Ss to read the text and answer the questions.

> 1 One platform will be on the sea, near the equator; the other in space at the same height as most satellites.
> 2 a very strong cable
> 3 They can travel inside a capsule that moves up and down the cable.

Speaking

In pairs / small groups Ss discuss the questions. Ask pairs/groups to join together to compare ideas. Ask Ss if they would like to use the elevator themselves.

Reading 2

Ss are going to read a longer article about the space elevator. Ask Ss to read through the questions and check understanding. Draw Ss' attention to the glossary box and remind them of the glossary for Unit 6 at the back of the book. Ss read through the article and answer the questions. When Ss have finished, check answers around the class. Ask Ss to say the numbers in exercise 2. Get Ss to point out and say all the other figures in the article. Ask Ss if this reading changed their opinion of the space elevator.

INTELLIGENT BUSINESS (PRE-INTERMEDIATE) TEACHER'S BOOK: COURSEBOOK

> **1**
> 1 cost of launching and insurance; impossible to repair a satellite if something goes wrong with it
> 2 private
> 3 raising money for the construction; finding a material strong enough for the cable
> 4 set up joint ventures with other technology businesses
> 5 They will charge to deliver kilos of stuff into space: the elevator can carry a lot of material and Laine expects that there will be a big demand for the service.
>
> **2**
> 1 the year when LiftPort expects to complete the space elevator
> 2 the cost of launching a satellite into space
> 3 the start-up cost for the construction of the elevator
> 4 the cost of delivering one kilo of material into space using rocket launch
> 5 the amount of material that the elevator could carry in one day

Speaking

Ask Ss to discuss the questions in groups. Do Ss think that the space elevator would be a good investment? Why? / Why not?

Vocabulary 1

Run through the words/phrases 1–6 and check pronunciation. Ask Ss to match the words with the meanings a–f. Do the first one together to demonstrate. As Ss finish, they use the words to complete the text. Circulate, helping where necessary. Check answers around the class. Ask check questions about the text, e.g. *Why don't private investors like investing in space? How long do people have to wait for a return on investment?*

> **1**
> 1 c 2 e 3 a 4 f 5 b 6 d
>
> **2**
> 1 capital
> 2 start-up cost
> 3 payback period
> 4 return on investment
> 5 potential
> 6 a tight budget

> **Optional activity**
> This is a quick activity to practice the vocabulary from Vocabulary 1. Ask Ss to work in pairs. One S reads one of the definitions a–f from exercise 1. Their partner, books closed, says the word being described.

Vocabulary 2 **1**

Remind Ss of the term *collocation* and ask them what it means (words that go together, see Unit 5). Ask Ss to cross out the noun that does not go with each verb set. Do the first one together to demonstrate.

> 1 budget   2 a satellite   3 a rocket
> 4 a cost   5 an investment

Vocabulary 2 **2**

Ask Ss to work with a partner and match each of the definitions to a verb/noun collocation from exercise 1.

> 1 raise capital
> 2 take a risk
> 3 launch a new product
> 4 set up a joint venture
> 5 make an investment

> **Optional activity**
> Ss work in pairs / small groups and choose three more verb/noun collocations. Ss write a definition for each collocation on a piece of paper (but they do not write down the collocation). Pairs/groups exchange lists and try to find the collocations.

Listening 1 **1**

Before reading, close books and ask Ss what they know about venture capitalists. What sort of companies do they invest in? Some Ss may think that venture capitalists are connected only with new companies (start-ups, see Unit 5). However, they also invest in existing companies which want to develop products or expand. Open books and point to the large picture. Ask Ss where it could have been taken (a laboratory). Ask Ss to discuss questions 1–3 with a partner.

Listening 1 **2**

Play the recording. Ss listen and compare their answers with Christoph Wiesenthal's.

> 1 b   2 b   3 a

Listening 1 **3**

Ss listen again and decide if the statements are true or false. Ask Ss to correct the false statements.

> 1 T   2 F   3 F

UNIT 6

Speaking

Ask Ss to discuss the questions in pairs / small groups. Encourage Ss to give reasons for their answers. If Ss are not responding, ask them to note a list of the advantages and disadvantages of being a venture capitalist and compare ideas with a partner.

Language check

Before asking Ss to read the information about modals of possibility, write on the board:

a) *He might not complete the project on time.*
b) *He won't complete the project on time.*

Ask Ss which is more certain (b). Point out that modal verbs do not change form in the third person. You may also wish to highlight the form (*will/may/might* + infinitive without *to*). Point to *won't* and ask Ss to say the long form (*will not*). Get Ss to say what the positive version of both sentences is (*He might complete it on time / He will complete it on time*). Now ask Ss to read the information about modals of possibility and complete the rules (circle the correct alternative in the first two and fill the gaps in the remainder).

Point out that when talking about future predictions, we often use *think + will* (e.g. *I think people will work longer hours in the future / I don't think people will work longer hours in the future*).

1 will	2 will
3 may; might; could	4 he will
5 will not	

Coursebook, Grammar reference, Modals of possibility, page 158

Practice 1

Ask Ss to use the sentences to take turns making predictions to their partner. (Depending on your class, Ss can write the sentences first.) Point out that all the statements are about 2020.

1 In 2020, most people will work from home.
2 Most meetings may/might/could take place via video.
3 That means there will be much less traffic on the road.
4 Electric cars may/might/could be common.
5 People may/might/could have more free time.
6 You will carry your medical details on a chip under your skin.
7 There may not / might not be enough oil to meet world demand.

Practice 2

Now ask Ss to complete the text using *will*, *may*, *might* or *could*. Ask Ss questions about the completed article, e.g. *Do you think Ted Foster's company will be a success? How much is the price of a ticket? Who do you think would buy one?*

1 will
2 will
3 won't
4 may/might/could
5 will
6 may/might/could
7 won't / may/might/could not
8 won't

Workbook, page 26

Speaking

Ask Ss to look again at the predictions in Practice exercise 1. Ask them to change the sentences as necessary so that they make statements that they agree with. Ask Ss to work in pairs / small groups and discuss the questions. Encourage Ss to make more predictions about what they think life will be like in 2020.

Optional activity

To introduce Career skills you could give each S an A4 sheet of paper and ask them to tear it into three strips. On the first strip of paper ask them to write *Unlikely*, on the second strip *Probably* and on the third strip *Definitely*. Check Ss understand the meaning of each word. Read the sentences below (or personalise sentences for your class). Ask Ss to hold up the piece of paper that describes how likely they think it is that the event will happen.
In ten years, one of the people in this room will be a millionaire.
Taxes will continue to rise.
I won't give you any homework at the end of the lesson.
Interest rates will fall next month.
In 20 years, cars will run on an alternative fuel to petrol.
Mobile phones will get smaller.

Career skills

Ask Ss to read the information and look through the phrases. Have they heard any of these used in conversation? Go through the phrases with Ss and check they understand the meaning. Get Ss to work in pairs and decide which phrases describe something that is certain, probable, possible or impossible. Do the first one with the whole class to

47

INTELLIGENT BUSINESS (PRE-INTERMEDIATE) TEACHER'S BOOK: COURSEBOOK

demonstrate. You may wish to point out that we often stress key words such as:

*It's **possible** that ...*
*I'm **sure** it will ...*
*It will **probably** ...*
*This will **definitely** ...*

Word stress can also change meaning:

*I **don't** think it **will** cost more.*
(I'm confident that it won't cost more.)
*I don't **think** it will cost more.*
(I'm not confident that it won't cost more.)

It's possible that ...	? ?
I don't think it will ...	✗ ?
I expect it will ...	✓ ?
I'm sure it will ...	✓
I think it's unlikely ...	✗ ?
It will probably ...	✓ ?
This will definitely ...	✓
It may / It might / It could ...	? ?

Listening 2 **1**

Books closed. Ask Ss to work in pairs / small groups and talk about jobs that they dislike doing around the house. Note ideas on the board. Open books and draw Ss' attention to the picture. Ask: *What do you think it is?* Read the information about the Intelligent Garbage Can. Do Ss think it is an interesting product? Ask Ss if *garbage* is British English or American English (American English). What is the British English word? (*rubbish*) Tell Ss that they are going to hear four people make predictions about whether the Intelligent Garbage Can will be a success or not. Ask Ss to listen and complete only column A (Prediction) of the table. Pause briefly after each speaker to allow Ss to make notes.

Listening 2 **2**

Ask Ss to look again at the phrases for Making predictions. Ss listen again and note the phrases that each speaker uses. Ask Ss to work with a partner and say if they think that the product will be a success or not. Ask Ss to give reasons why / why not.

	A Prediction	B Phrase
John	It will sell only in the luxury market.	It will probably ...
Jemima	It's possible the price will come down and by 2020 it will be in every home.	(It) may ... (It) could ...
Jim	It will solve all our garbage problems and be a big success.	This will definitely ...
Jo	It won't solve garbage problems; it won't sell in big numbers ...	I don't think it will ...

Speaking

Check that Ss understand the four products. Ask Ss to work in pairs / small groups and give their opinions and make predictions about each product. Get pairs/groups to report back. Ask the class to vote on which product they think would be most successful and least successful. Encourage Ss to give reasons for their opinions.

Culture at work

Ask Ss to read the information individually and then discuss the information about the past or future in pairs or small groups. Ask Ss to give examples from their own experience, i.e. say which attitude is more usual in a culture / cultures that they know well. Can they think of any examples of companies that focus on past history/success or on future developments? You may find it helpful to look at the Culture at work box from page 30 of the Skills Book; this is reproduced below. You may also find it useful to refer to the relevant section on Culture at work in the teacher's notes supporting the Skills Book.

Future focus	Past focus
You talk about what the company is doing today.	The history of a company is very important.
Past performance is less important than future goals.	You refer to the past in order to give a context to present performance.
You emphasise future plans and developments.	Future plans build on past traditions.

Skills Book, Culture at work, page 30

Teacher's Book, page 136

UNIT 6

Dilemma

Tell Ss that they are going to be venture capitalists. Read the brief with the class and clarify any unfamiliar vocabulary. Ask Ss to summarise the information in order to check comprehension. Remind Ss of the interview with venture capitalist Christoph Wiesenthal. Ask if Ss can remember any comments that he made about investing in technology. If Ss can't remember, you might want to play the recording again, or ask Ss to turn to the audioscript on page 167.

Task 1: Divide Ss into three groups. Ask Group A to turn to page 138 and read the information about Celf Cure. Group B turns to page 142 and reads the information about Space Travel Inc. Group C turns to page 145 and reads the information about Fingertip. Each group should discuss their venture and make notes. Tell Ss that they will have to use their notes to prepare a presentation in Task 2.

Task 2: Ss work with their group to prepare a short presentation, using their notes from Task 1. Go through the Useful phrases box and ask which phrases Ss could use to explain how the technology works, how the company wants to develop it and its future market potential.

Task 3: Two possibilities for how groups make their presentations are:

a) Nominate a spokesperson who presents the idea to the rest of the class.

b) Divide the presentation into three parts (how the technology works / how the company wants to develop it / future market potential). A different person presents each part.

Task 4: Divide the class into groups of three or six. Each group should comprise equal numbers of members from Group A, B or C. Groups discuss which idea is the best investment. Have a feedback session where each group says which idea they chose and why.

Decision

Ss are going to listen again to venture capitalist Christoph Wiesenthal. This time he talks about which project he thinks has the most potential. Ask Ss which venture they think Christoph will choose. Play the recording and ask the class to identify which idea he chose (Celf Cure). What do they think of his decision? Play the recording again and ask Ss to identify the positive and negative things he identified in each project. (Space Travel Inc. – positive: there are people who would love to be space tourists; negative: cost, small market, risky venture, not much return on investment. Fingertip – positive: great idea; negative: very small market – luxury hotels and corporations, new start-up so greater risk. Celf Cure – positive: technique can be used to treat several common diseases, big demand, less risk because it is an existing company; negative: no negative comments.)

Write it up

Tell Ss that they are going to write a memo to colleagues in their venture capital firm, Copernica, to say which venture they want to invest in. Ss should give reasons why they think the project will be a success. You may wish to ask Ss to prepare the writing in class, complete it for homework and then compare with a partner in the next lesson before handing it in to be marked. Give each S a photocopy of the Writing preparation framework from page 188. Then use the Writing focus (Writing focus: Memos) below to link the use of the framework and the Style guide as Ss plan their writing. It may be helpful to use the Writing feedback framework on page 189 when marking Ss' writing.

Writing focus: Memos

1 First, decide who you are.
   (In this case, Ss are venture capitalists working for Copernica.)

2 Every time you start to write, you need to ask yourself two questions:
   a What is the purpose of this piece of writing?
   b Who am I writing to?
   (Here Ss identify the project that they want to invest in and give reasons why. The memo will be read by colleagues at the venture capital company.)

3 Look at the section on Memos on page 16 of the Style guide. Notice the suggested structure for a memo:
   To/From/Subject/Date
   No opening greeting necessary
   Main message
   Recommendations
   Name or initials of the writer (optional)
   Is this structure appropriate for this memo? What are you going to put on the subject line? Plan the sections you are going to divide the memo into. Then brainstorm the points you might cover in each section.

4 What style should the memo be written in?
   (As it says in the Style guide, memos are short, official notes that will be read by people within a company. Memos are usually less formal than business letters. The language is simple and clear and the tone is normally neutral.)

5 What phrases might be appropriate for your memo?
   (See the Style guide, particularly the phrases for making recommendations on page 16. See also the Useful phrases from Task 2 on page 56 of the Coursebook and the phrases for making predictions on page 55 of the Coursebook.)

6 Now go ahead and write the memo.

7 When you have finished, check your writing for: logical structure, clarity of ideas, accuracy of language, appropriateness of style.

INTELLIGENT BUSINESS (PRE-INTERMEDIATE) TEACHER'S BOOK: COURSEBOOK

- Style guide, Memos, page 16
- Style guide, General rules, page 3
- Skills Book, Writing 3, Memos, page 46
- Teacher's Book, page 149
- Teacher's Book, Writing preparation framework, page 188
- Teacher's Book, Writing feedback framework, page 189

> **Memo: Suggested answer (64 words)**
> To: All staff
> From: (student's name)
> Subject: Celf Cure
> Date: (today's date)
> I recommend that we invest in the Celf Cure venture. The techniques can be used on a variety of diseases, so there will always be a big demand for this treatment. Celf Cure is an existing company that has already made a success with other medical products, so there is less risk.

Review 2

On the next two pages of the Coursebook you will find Review 2, which reviews language, vocabulary and functional language from Units 4, 5 and 6. It can be used in a number of ways that can be adapted to suit your class, for example:

- Ss can do selected exercises for homework.
- Use in class and guide Ss to particular exercises according to their individual needs. Alternatively, if your class has similar needs, focus on exercises where they can have more practice together (Ss can work individually or in pairs).
- Use as a short progress test and review any necessary points before moving on to Unit 7.

- Coursebook Review: Answers, page 102

Unit 7: Location

UNIT OBJECTIVES	
Reading:	Arabia's field of dreams
Language:	Future plans and intentions
Vocabulary:	Collocations
	Multi-part verbs
Career skills:	Making an appointment
Culture at work:	To plan or not to plan?
Dilemma & Decision:	A new location (memo)

This unit focuses on location. On marketing courses, students are taught the four Ps: price, product, promotion and place. It is often the last of these which is given the least attention. Yet a company's location can be vital for the success of a company. Premises need to be suitable for both clients and employees, and this is the case for a small start-up as much as for a multi-national company. Whether it is in the centre of town, in a rural location or on a retail park or industrial park, a company needs to take into account the convenience of the location, its cost and the suitability for its function. Facilities such as transport links, proximity to key suppliers or related businesses, and the availability of a workforce all have to be researched to avoid costly mistakes.

Keynotes

Point to the picture and ask: *Where can you see this building?* (Dubai). Ask Ss if they know the name of the building (the Burj Al Arab hotel, the world's only seven-star hotel). Ask Ss to name some things that are important when considering the location of a business (e.g. good transport links, access to markets, good telecommunications, etc.).

Ask Ss to read through the keynotes. Check that they understand the terms in bold. Ask Ss if any of their ideas about location were mentioned. Draw Ss' attention to the glossary for this unit at the back of the book.

Coursebook, Glossary, Unit 7, page 150

Preview

Look at the business activities 1–5 and ask Ss which ones they have in their town or city. Check Ss understand all the words. Ask Ss to work in pairs / small groups and discuss which location a–e is best for each of the business activities. You might like to ask Ss to say other business activities which are often found at each location. Go through the answers, pointing out that 'a' is a possible answer for 1 and 'c' is a possible answer for 2 – but they aren't the *best* places.

| 1 c | 2 d | 3 e | 4 a | 5 b |

Vocabulary 1

Books closed. Before doing the exercise, write *Tourist resort* and *Business centre* on the board. Ask Ss to work in pairs and brainstorm facilities that a region would need in order to develop in each of these areas. After two or three minutes, have a brief feedback session and write Ss' ideas under the appropriate heading.

Open books and go through the words in the box. Make sure that Ss understand the headings, particularly *Infrastructure*. Then Ss work in pairs to put the words in the correct group. As Ss finish, ask them to add one or two more words to each list, possibly from the facilities they brainstormed earlier. Compare ideas around the class and note the new words on the board to check spelling and pronunciation. Ask Ss: *What facilities does your region have? What facilities does it need?*

Accommodation: apartment blocks, villas, hotel
Infrastructure: airport, road links, port
Attractions: theme park, beaches, shopping

Reading 1

Tell Ss that they are going to read an article about Dubai. Ask Ss what they know about Dubai and note ideas on the board. Then ask Ss what information they would like to know about Dubai. Get Ss to work in pairs and write three questions that they would like the article to answer. Draw Ss' attention to the map and ask them to locate Dubai on it. Then look at the picture and ask Ss what they think it is. Ask Ss to read through the article quickly and answer the questions. Point out the glossary and remind Ss that there is a glossary at the back of the book. Check answers around the class. Ask Ss: *Did the article answer any of your questions about Dubai? Did any of the information surprise you?*

c

Reading 2

Ask Ss to read the article again slowly and answer the questions. You might also wish to revise numbers by asking more questions about the text (e.g. *How many villas sold out in a week? How many hotels does Dubai have? How many hotel rooms?* etc.).

51

> 1 houses/villas
> 2 ten years
> 3 beaches, hotels, theme park, tax-free shopping, sporting events, desert safaris, dhow cruises
> 4 1.5 million; 20 per cent are from Dubai
> 5 multi-nationals, IT and computing companies, media and TV, banks and financial companies

Reading 3

Ask Ss what they can remember about each of the four attractions. Check that Ss understand *under construction*. Ss answer the questions. Ask Ss which of the attractions they would most/least like to visit.

> C: Media City
> U: Dubailand, Burj Dubai
> P: Knowledge Village

Speaking

In pairs / small groups Ss discuss the question. Encourage Ss to give reasons.

Optional activity
Photocopiable resource 7.1 (page 110)

Give each S a copy of the Talk outline. Ask Ss to work individually to prepare a short talk about a town or area that they think could be developed as a tourist resort and a business centre. Ss can talk about their own town/area or a place that they know. If Ss are having problems thinking of an area, they can use the information about Dubai on page 61 of the Coursebook. Refer Ss to the vocabulary for facilities in Vocabulary 1, page 60.
In section 1 Ss insert their name and the name of the place that they are going to talk about. In section 2 Ss note where the place is and any other useful information they want to include (check that Ss understand *population* and *climate*). In section 3 Ss look at three facilities for tourism and business that exist in their chosen place at the moment (Ss should consider accommodation, infrastructure and attractions). In section 4 Ss point out two facilities that the town does not have at present. In section 5 Ss recommend two or three improvements that would help the area develop as a tourist resort and business centre. Encourage Ss to think of different points to those used in section 4. Finally, in section 6 Ss thank the audience.
When Ss are ready, ask them to work in small groups and take turns to give their talk.

Vocabulary 2 1

Remind Ss of the term *collocation*. Ask them to read the definitions 1–6. Check that Ss understand the meaning. Then Ss decide which words from A and B can go together to make a phrase. Ss then read the definitions again and match the definitions with their phrases.

> 1 service sector
> 2 regional office
> 3 capital market
> 4 investment bank
> 5 shopping mall
> 6 multi-national company

Vocabulary 2 2

Ask Ss to use the collocations in exercise 1 to complete the sentences. Check answers around the class.

> 1 multi-national company
> 2 service sector
> 3 investment bank
> 4 regional office
> 5 shopping mall
> 6 capital market

Vocabulary 3

Multi-part verbs are also known as *multi-word verbs* and *phrasal verbs*. Ss can sometimes feel intimidated by this type of verb, so it will be worth spending some time introducing Ss to some of their features. Ask Ss for examples of any multi-part verbs that they know. As an example, you could write on the board (accompany with drawings if possible):

1 He looked up at the window.
2 He looked up a word in the dictionary.

Ask Ss which sentence uses a multi-part verb (2). Check that Ss understand that a multi-part verb does not simply mean that a word is added to the existing verb, but that the meaning of the verb changes (in sentence 1, *up* is simply a preposition to show where he is looking; in sentence 2 the addition of *up* changes the meaning of the verb). Ask Ss to work in pairs and choose the correct word/phrase in italics to complete the sentences. Depending on your class, you may wish to ask Ss to identify which verbs can be separated from their particles. *Run out, sell out, grow up* are multi-part verbs that cannot be separated from their particle (you cannot say *I run it out*). *Set up* and *build up* can be separated from their particles. It is possible to say: *I'm planning to set it up in July* (but **not** *I'm planning to set up it in July*) and *It took 20 years to build it up* (but **not** *It took 20 years to build up it*).

1 set	2 set up	3 run out
4 run	5 sold	6 sold out
7 growing	8 growing up	9 build up
10 build		

Speaking

With books closed, ask Ss to think about what factors a company should consider if they are thinking of setting up a regional office abroad. Open books and compare the factors Ss thought of with the list in Listening.

Listening

Tell Ss that they are going to hear Declan Murphy talk about setting up a regional office in a foreign company. Play the recording once and ask Ss to check if he mentions any of their ideas from the speaking exercise. Play it again and ask Ss to tick the topics that he mentions.

economy, inflation, currency, prospects for growth, infrastructure, cost of renting office space, taxation, attitudes to foreign business

Vocabulary 4

Here Ss look at collocations of adjectives and nouns to make phrases, which have to be positive, e.g. *low inflation* not *high inflation*. In pairs / small groups, ask Ss to match the words in the box with a topic from the list. Point out that it is possible to use some words in the box more than once. It is not possible to use *high* or *weak*.

strong economy (*good/stable* are also possible)
low inflation / unemployment
stable currency (*strong* is also possible)
good prospects for growth / infrastructure / access to regional markets (*easy accesss* is also possible)
low cost of renting office space / labour costs / taxation
positive attitudes to foreign business (*good* is also possible)

Language check

Ss look at the use of *will/won't*, *going to* and the present continuous to talk about future plans and intentions. Ss will already be familiar with the form of the present continuous and *will/won't*, but will need some practice of the form of *going to* + infinitive as well as the negative and question forms. Spend some time underlining the function of the present continuous for the future. *Going to* and the present continuous are often interchangeable; however, use the guidelines in the Language check to highlight the difference between an intention (you plan to go to Paris but you haven't booked the tickets yet) and a firm arrangement (you have made all the travel arrangements and booked the hotel, etc.).

Ask Ss to read the examples and complete the rules. Check answers around the class.

1 *will / won't*
2 *(be) going to* + infinitive
3 the present continuous

Coursebook, Grammar reference: Future forms, page 159

Practice 1

Do the first sentence together to demonstrate the exercise. Refer Ss to the Language check rules.

1 are ('re) going to set up
2 am ('m) travelling
3 am ('m) going to look at
4 are you going to travel / will you travel
5 is meeting
6 am ('m) going to collect
7 will ('ll) present

Practice 2

Ask Ss to say what the dialogue is about (A is planning a meeting, B is unable to go). Reassure Ss that more than one answer is possible in some cases. Do the first one together to demonstrate the exercise. When checking answers, ask Ss to identify where more than one answer was possible and elicit the alternative. Ask Ss to practice the dialogue with a partner.

1 We are (We're) discussing / are going to discuss
2 I am (I'm) leaving
3 I am (I'm) attending / I am (I'm) going to attend
4 are you coming back
5 I am (I'm) staying / I am (I'm) going to stay
6 I will (I'll)

Workbook, page 30

Speaking

Find out if any Ss have visited or are planning to visit Singapore. Ask Ss to read through the plan. Ask check questions, e.g. *What's happening at 13:30 on Tuesday?* Draw Ss' attention to the sample questions and response. Get Ss to spend five minutes noting some questions about the plan. Then ask Ss to work with a partner and discuss the plan, and decide who will do what. Get pairs to report back briefly on who is doing what in the plan.

Writing

Tell Ss that they are going to write an email to the colleagues who are visiting. The reason for writing is to explain who is going to pick the colleagues up when they arrive in Singapore next Monday. Briefly run through appropriate openings to the email.

Style guide, page 6

Optional activity

You could ask Ss to tell their partner what their real plans are for next week. What things have they made firm arrangements about? What things do they intend to do?

Career skills

Draw Ss' attention to the picture and ask: *What is she doing?* Find out what sort of appointments Ss make on the phone. Ask Ss to work with a partner and discuss what tips they would give to someone who is going to make an appointment on the telephone in English (e.g. *speak clearly, repeat important information such as dates and times*, etc.). Remind Ss of the phrases for offers and requests and saying no politely from Unit 3. On the board write:

A I want to arrange an appointment with you next Tuesday.
B No. I'm busy Tuesday.

Ask Ss to suggest phrases to make the dialogue more polite (e.g. *I'd like to arrange an appointment with you next Tuesday. / Sorry, I'm busy Tuesday.*) Then ask Ss to read the information in the box. Ss can work with a partner and read the suggestions and responses as a phone conversation. Read the suggestions again and encourage Ss to think of alternative expressions to those in the response column.

Focus Ss on the dialogue and ask them to suggest which sentence would go next in the conversation. Ask Ss to work in pairs to put the rest of the dialogue in the correct order and then read it with their partner. You may wish to remind Ss to use rising intonation for the end of the questions.

1. Can we meet next week to talk about the trip to Panama?
2. Good idea. What about Thursday morning?
3. I'm afraid I can't make Thursday.
4. Can we meet on Friday then?
5. Well – I'm busy on Friday morning, but I'm free in the afternoon.
6. Friday afternoon is good for me. Let's say 3 o'clock?
7. Yes, that's fine. See you on Friday afternoon at 3.

Speaking

Before Ss do this exercise you may wish to spend a short time revising days, dates and times. Ask Ss what day, time and date it is now. Ask them to say the day, date and time of your next English lesson. There is more practice of days, dates and times in the Workbook, Unit 7. Tell Ss that they are going to plan a trip. Ask Ss to work with a partner and decide where they are going on their trip and their departure and arrival days and times (tell them that they could decide to go to more than one place). They should note this information in the diary at the bottom of page 65. Then, individually, Ss think of two appointments and note these in the diary. Ss should then role-play a telephone conversation to arrange a new appointment with each other. Before they begin their role-play, you may wish to ask Ss to suggest phrases that they could use to start and end the telephone call. It would also make the situation more realistic if Ss can sit back-to-back during the call.

Culture at work

Ask Ss to discuss the questions in groups. Encourage them to give examples from their own experience where possible (e.g. trips or projects that they have planned in the past or are planning in the future). You may find it helpful to look at the Culture at work box from page 37 of the Skills Book; this is reproduced below. You may also find it useful to refer to the relevant section on Culture at work in the teacher's notes supporting the Skills Book.

Flexible	Fixed
You are spontaneous and can make arrangements at short notice.	You want to plan schedules carefully and fix arrangements well in advance.
You do not consider it a problem to cancel or change appointments.	You like to keep appointments. You do not like to cancel or change arrangements.
If you make an arrangement to meet at a certain time, it does not matter if you are a little late.	If you make an arrangement to meet at a certain time, it is important to be punctual.

Skills Book, Culture at work, page 37

Teacher's Book, page 142

Dilemma

Ask Ss to read the brief and clarify any unfamiliar vocabulary. Then ask Ss to summarise the information in order to check comprehension. Draw Ss' attention to the map and ask them to locate Luton, Swindon and Exeter. Check that Ss understand the difference between a motorway and a

UNIT 7

main road. Ask Ss to identify some motorways, main roads and railways on the map (see the key on the map) and ask what other transport facility the map shows (airports).

Task 1: Read through the list with the class and check they understand the meaning of the first three points. Ask Ss to work individually and tick the factors that they think are most important for the Whiterose Hotel Division. Encourage Ss to add other factors to the list.

Task 2: Divide the class into three groups, A, B and C. Groups read information about one of the three towns on their respective pages at the back of the book. As they read and discuss the information, they will identify what factors in the list in Task 1 their town can provide. They should then write a list of advantages and disadvantages for moving there. Ask Ss to keep clear notes from their discussion because they will be presenting their ideas to the other groups.

Task 3: Each group takes it in turn to present the information about their town. Encourage groups to divide up their presentation so that as many people in the group as possible get the chance to present information.

Task 4: The whole class then has a meeting to decide which town would be the best location for the new offices of the Hotel Division. Encourage Ss to give reasons for their ideas.

Decision

Ask Ss to listen to Charles Jerome, who has a commercial property agency that gives relocation advice to businesses, as he explains the decision that Whiterose took (Luton). Ask Ss if they agree with the decision. Why? / Why not? Play the recording again and ask Ss to name the three key elements in deciding where to locate a new office that Charles Jerome mentions (infrastructure, living environment, business environment). What disadvantages did he identify in Exeter and Swindon? What advantages did he say Luton had?

Write it up

Tell Ss that they are going to write a memo to the staff of the Hotel Division. They will say what town they think will be the best location and give reasons why. You may wish to ask Ss to prepare the writing in class, complete it for homework and then compare with a partner in the next lesson before handing it in to be marked. Give each S a photocopy of the Writing preparation framework from page 188. Then use the Writing focus (Writing focus: Memos) opposite to link the use of the framework and the Style guide as Ss plan their writing. It may be helpful to use the Writing feedback framework on page 189 when marking Ss' writing. If the exercise is done for homework, encourage Ss to look up the town that they chose on the internet and find out what facilities it has.

Writing focus: Memos

1 First, decide who you are.
(In this case, Ss are part of a team working for the Whiterose Hotel Division.)

2 Every time you start to write, you need to ask yourself two questions:
a What is the purpose of this piece of writing?
b Who am I writing to?
(Here Ss identify the town that they think the Hotel Division should move to and give reasons why. The memo will be read by all the staff of the Hotel Division.)

3 Look at the section on Memos on page 16 of the Style guide. Notice the suggested structure for a memo:
To/From/Subject/Date
No opening greeting necessary
Main message
Recommendations
Name or initials of the writer (optional)
Is this structure appropriate for this memo? What are you going to put on the subject line? Plan the sections you are going to divide the memo into. Then brainstorm the points you might cover in each section.

4 What style should the memo be written in?
(As it says in the Style guide, memos are short, official notes that will be read by people within a company. Memos are usually less formal than business letters. The language is simple and clear and the tone is normally neutral.)

5 What phrases might be appropriate for your memo?
(See the Style guide.)

6 Now go ahead and write the memo.

7 When you have finished, check your writing for: logical structure, clarity of ideas, accuracy of language, appropriateness of style.

- Style guide, Memos, page 16
- Style guide, General rules, page 3
- Skills Book, Writing 3, Memos, page 46
- Teacher's Book, page 149
- Teacher's Book, Writing preparation framework, page 188
- Teacher's Book, Writing feedback framework, page 189

INTELLIGENT BUSINESS (PRE-INTERMEDIATE) TEACHER'S BOOK: COURSEBOOK

Memo: Suggested answer (100 words)
To: The staff of the Hotel Division
From: (student's name)
Subject: Location of new offices
Date: (today's date)
The Whiterose Head Office can no longer provide enough space for all our employees. We are planning to relocate the staff of the Hotel Division to new offices in Luton. We believe this will be an excellent location because it is close to London, so most staff will not need to move house. Luton also has good communications with the rest of Britain and internationally. This means that if you have to travel on business, you can fly from your local airport.

Unit 8: Job-seeking

UNIT OBJECTIVES	
Reading:	The online job market
Language:	The imperative
Vocabulary:	Activities
	The application process
	Finding a job
Career skills:	Explaining what to do
Culture at work:	Fixed procedures or flexibility?
Dilemma & Decision:	For love or money? (informal letter)

This unit looks at job-seeking and focuses on the practicalities of looking and applying for a job as well as the application process and preparing a Curriculum Vitae (CV). The job-search process usually begins with a general analysis of the work market for the sector that a person is hoping to enter. This is then followed by more detailed research, identifying the exact job(s) that will be applied for. An applicant generally applies for a job either by completing an application form or by submitting a covering letter and a CV. Depending on the organisation, this can be sent by post or electronically. It is a good idea to keep the covering letter brief (one page), but it should outline why the applicant is interested in the job/company and what contribution they can make to the organisation. The relevant department in the company (often the Human Resources Department) will then go through the selection procedure, look at all applications and draw up a short list of candidates to be interviewed for the position. It is at the interview stage that the applicant can make their case about why they are the best candidate for the job. It is important to ask questions about the company during the interview (for example about training and professional development that the company/role can offer). As well as showing that the candidate is keen, the information will also be useful later in helping the applicant to make up his/her mind about accepting the position if it was offered. It is a useful exercise to have a career plan with one-year and five-year targets to note how you see your career developing. Information can include ambitions and career goals as well as identifying what new skills you plan/need to acquire to achieve those objectives. It should also include non-work related objectives, too, in order to maintain a healthy work–life balance.

Keynotes

Before opening books, write *Job-seeking* on the board. Ask Ss to work with a partner and write down as many words as they can think of connected with looking for a job. Open books, and ask Ss to read through the keynotes. Check that they understand the terms in bold. Ask Ss if any of their words were mentioned. Draw Ss' attention to the glossary for this unit at the back of the book.

Coursebook, Glossary, Unit 8, page 150

Preview

Ask Ss to work in pairs and discuss the question. Put pairs together to form groups of four to compare lists. Ask Ss how easy/difficult it is to find jobs in the area that they are interested in working in. If your Ss are in work or have worked in the past, ask which ways they used to find their last job. Ask Ss which methods for finding a job they think are most effective. Why?

Vocabulary 1

Ask Ss if they think it is important to get experience in the work area that they want to enter. Encourage Ss to suggest ways to gain experience. Get Ss to match the words/phrases 1–3 with the definitions a–c. Ss can use dictionaries if necessary. In the US, *graduate trainee schemes* are also called *internships*. An apprenticeship is more connected to technical jobs, and the pay is often low to begin with and rises as the apprentice gains more experience. Ask Ss if they would consider doing any of the schemes. Which ones wouldn't they like to do? Why?

| 1 c | 2 a | 3 b |

Speaking

Ask Ss to discuss the question in pairs / small groups. Ask Ss if they intend to try any of the ways suggested in Vocabulary 1. Which do they think will be most/least effective? Why?

Listening 1

Ask Ss to look at the photographs and guess what job the two men have. How do they think they got started in their careers? Ask Ss to listen and answer the questions. Elicit the names of the companies that Michael and Sanjay work for (Volkswagen and Meridian).

INTELLIGENT BUSINESS (PRE-INTERMEDIATE) TEACHER'S BOOK: COURSEBOOK

> 1 He thought it would be a good company to work for.
> 2 A family friend told him about the organisation.

Listening 1 **2**

Ss listen to Michael again and answer the questions. Ask Ss to work in pairs and think of an advantage and disadvantage to the way that Michael started his career (e.g. advantage: it allowed Michael to get to know the company properly; disadvantage: it took a long time – three years' apprenticeship plus college course).

> 1 designer (works in the design department and makes models for the exterior design of new cars)
> 2 600
> 3 design and modelling

Listening 1 **3**

Look at the questions with Ss and ask them to suggest answers. Play the listening again while Ss note their answers.

> 1 management
> 2 during the summer holidays
> 3 research consultant

Reading **1**

Ask Ss what they know about Monster.com. Even if they don't know anything about the company, the name Monster.com should alert Ss to the fact that it is an internet company. Focus Ss' attention on the title of the article and ask: *What sort of company do you think Monster.com is?* Read through the questions together and clarify any unfamiliar vocabulary. Draw Ss' attention to the glossary and remind them of the glossary at the back of the book. Ask Ss to read the article and answer the questions.

> 1 **name:** the firm's single biggest success factor
> 2 **image:** youthful fun
> 3 **contribution:** speeds up hiring and increases the accuracy of job-searching
> 4 **headhunting firms:** have lost business to Monster.com

Reading **2**

Ask Ss to work in pairs and answer the questions. Have a feedback session with the whole class.

> 1 yes
> 2 get free job-search service, can get advice on career management, can contact each other to ask questions
> 3 get quick responses, search large numbers of resumés with accuracy
> 4 newspapers, headhunting firms
> 5 You should know exactly what you want; check that your resumé is clear about what you want.

Speaking

Still in pairs, Ss discuss the question. Encourage Ss to give reasons for their answers. Ask Ss if they know any other online job-search sites. Are these sites popular in their country?

Vocabulary 2

Go through the activities and check understanding. Look back at the glossary in the reading text and draw attention to the fact that *resumé* is American English (though this word is often used in the UK) and that *CV* (or curriculum vitae) is British English. Ask Ss to decide who does each activity: an employer or a job-seeker.

> **Employer:** post a job ad, hire, scan resumés, fill jobs, recruit staff
> **Job-seeker:** search job ads, supply resumés, use a career management service, join a firm

Vocabulary 3

With books closed, ask Ss to work in pairs / small groups and brainstorm the stages in applying for a job, starting from when the job is advertised. Compare ideas around the class. Then ask Ss to open their books and complete the diagram, using the words in the box. Get Ss to look through the application process and compare it with the way that this is done in their country. Encourage Ss to point out similarities/differences.

> 1 advertisement   2 apply
> 3 candidates   4 invites
> 5 attend   6 offers
> 7 accepts

Vocabulary 4

Ask Ss to complete the text about Esther Garcia using the words and phrases in the box. Get Ss to compare answers with a partner.

58

UNIT 8

1 job ads	2 applications
3 resumé	4 interview
5 recruit	6 offered
7 selected	8 accept

Optional activity
You could ask Ss to work individually or in pairs and prepare five questions about Esther Garcia. Then work with another S/pair to ask and answer their questions.

Reading 2 **1**

Ask Ss to read through the job ad from the Monster.com site. Get Ss to summarise what the job is and what it involves. Then ask Ss to decide if the job would be suitable for people described in 1–6. Encourage Ss to give reasons for their choices.

1 No	2 No	3 No	4 Yes	5 Yes	6 Yes

Reading 2 **2**

Now ask Ss to look through the job ad again and find words/phrases with the same meaning as 1–6.

1 ideal candidates
2 at least
3 proficiency
4 excellent communication skills
5 compensation
6 benefits package

Speaking

First, ask Ss to work individually and note things that they think would be interesting / not interesting about this job, with reasons. Then get Ss to compare ideas in pairs / small groups. Ask Ss if they would consider applying for a job like this. Do they know anyone who would be good at this job?

Language check

The imperative is not normally a difficult concept for Ss to grasp. Make sure that Ss realise that it is often used in orders. It is effective for information that has to be communicated quickly (*Don't touch that!*) but can sound impolite in more general conversation (*Close the door!*). However, adding *please* at the end would make this polite. The examples include imperatives that are used for advice (*Check that your resumé is clear / If you aren't sure, ask for help*) and 'softer' imperatives that can be used as suggestions (*Let's take a break*). Focus Ss' attention on the signs and ask

where you might see signs like these. Point out the written signs and then ask Ss to suggest what the picture signs might mean (Do not enter; Do not smoke). Ask Ss to read the examples of the imperative 1–5. Ask Ss to identify how the imperative is formed (the infinitive without *to*). Then ask Ss to match the examples with the uses a–e.

1 d	2 a	3 b	4 e	5 c

Coursebook, Grammar reference: The imperative, page 159

Practice **1**

Ask Ss to complete the exercise and compare answers with a partner. Do the first one together to demonstrate the exercise. Ask Ss to take turns saying the sentences with their partner.

1 Please (Let's)	2 Don't	3 Let's	4 Don't
5 Please	6 Let's	7 Please	

Practice **2**

Now ask Ss to complete the instructions. Ask Ss where they might hear someone say these things (for example: 1, 3, 4 – at work; 2 – at school/college; 5 – at a hotel; 6 – at work or at school/college).

1 phone	2 don't understand
3 tell	4 don't enter
5 ask	6 are ('re)

Workbook, page 33

Speaking

Start by drawing Ss' attention to the example. Ask Ss to suggest a 'don't' for finding the right university or college. Ask Ss to work in pairs and choose one of the three situations. Ss write a list of six 'dos and don'ts' to help someone in that situation. Pairs take it in turns to present their list to the rest of the group. Encourage Ss to say if they agree/disagree with the advice and give reasons why. If you noticed any problems using the imperative when Ss were reporting their lists, you might wish to spend a little time going over it again where necessary.

Career skills

Find out if Ss have ever had to explain to another person how to do something. Get examples around the class. Ask Ss to read the information and the phrases, and to identify which ones they would use to give important instructions and which they would use for suggestions.

59

INTELLIGENT BUSINESS (PRE-INTERMEDIATE) TEACHER'S BOOK: COURSEBOOK

Important instructions: 1, 2, 3, 4
Suggestions: 5, 6

Listening 2 ■1

Ask Ss if they have ever prepared a CV. What information did they include? Ask Ss to note down three pieces of advice they would give someone preparing a CV for a UK job. Tell Ss that they are going to hear Barry Hampton, a careers adviser, explain how to prepare a CV for a UK job. Ask Ss what a careers adviser does. Have they ever visited one? As they listen, Ss tick the information that is correct and change any incorrect information. Check if Barry used any of the advice which Ss noted.

1 Don't write more than two pages.
2 Start with your personal details and qualifications.
3 ✓
4 Write something about special interests or hobbies.
5 ✓

Listening 2 ■2

Focus Ss back on to the phrases in the Career skills box. Play the recording again while Ss tick the phrases they hear. You may wish to spend a short time modelling pronunciation and intonation.

It may be better to …
Make sure that …
It's essential (that) …
It's a good idea to …
Don't forget to …
Remember to …

Optional activity
Photocopiable resource 8.1 (page 111)

Ss can make notes for information to include in a CV. Photocopy the sheet on page 111. This will help Ss to organise their ideas, using their own experience. Point out that this is *not* a framework to send to employers; it is a useful way for Ss to check that they have included important information. Ask Ss to prepare at home as a writing exercise and compare with a partner before handing it in to be checked. You could then show Ss a copy of your CV or a fictional CV and ask them to use it to practise writing their own CV, using the notes that they made.

Speaking ■1

Ask Ss to prepare the advice individually, referring to the corrected list in the listening exercise and phrases from the Career skills box. Then ask Ss to work in pairs and take turns giving advice.

Speaking ■2

Ask Ss to work in pairs, with each S in a pair choosing a different topic to make notes on. They should use phrases from the Career skills box and imperatives. Ss then take turns explaining what to do to their partner. They could then repeat the activity, explaining a different topic.

Culture at work

Ask Ss to discuss the questions in groups. Encourage them to give examples from their own experience where possible (e.g. trips or projects that they have planned in the past or are planning in the future). You may find it helpful to look at the Culture at work box from page 41 of the Skills Book; this is reproduced below. You may also find it useful to refer to the relevant section on Culture at work in the teacher's notes supporting the Skills Book.

More fixed	Less fixed
Procedures should be fixed and clear.	Procedures are important, but they should be flexible.
People need to know what is expected of them.	People like to show initiative and adapt to new situations.
It is uncomfortable when you do not know exactly what to expect in a situation.	It is boring when you know what to expect every day.

Skills Book, Culture at work, page 41
Teacher's Book, page 145

Dilemma

To introduce the subject, ask Ss what they would do if they were offered two good jobs each offering the same salary. What factors would help them decide which job to choose? Get Ss to read the brief and ask them to summarise the information in order to check comprehension.

Task 1: Divide the class into three groups, A, B and C. Groups A and B are each going to read about one of the companies that are offering Kate a job. They will learn about the company and discover more information about the job that Kate is being offered. Group C is going to read about Kate's personality and preferences. Ask groups to turn to the relevant page at the back of the book for their information.

UNIT 8

Task 2: Divide the class into groups of three. Each group should have at least one person from Groups A, B and C. First ask Ss to exchange information about what they learnt about the companies and Kate's personality. Then Ss discuss the advantages and disadvantages of each job offer. They use this information to match the advantages of each job with Kate, taking into account what they now know about her personality and ambitions. Groups should consider topics 1–4 as they decide which job will suit Kate better. Ask Ss to compare ideas with the rest of the class.

Decision

Tell Ss that they will listen to Barbara Kingsland, a careers adviser, give advice to Kate and then they will hear Kate say what decision she made and what happened next. Pause the recording after Barbara Kingsland and ask Ss if they agree with her advice. Ask Ss to predict which job Kate chose (Wide World Tours) and if she was happy with her decision (yes). Play the rest of the recording for Ss to check. Ask Ss if they would have made the same decision as Kate. Why? / Why not?

Write it up

Tell Ss that they are going to write an informal letter to Kate. Ss will tell Kate the decision that they made in Task 2 and their reasons why. You may wish to ask Ss to prepare the writing in class, complete it for homework and then compare with a partner in the next lesson before handing it in to be marked. Give each S a photocopy of the Writing preparation framework from page 188. Then use the Writing focus (Writing focus: Letters) below to link the use of the framework and the Style guide as Ss plan their writing. It may be helpful to use the Writing feedback framework on page 189 when marking Ss' writing.

Writing focus: Letters

1 First, be clear about the perspective you are writing from.
   (In this case, Ss are themselves.)

2 Every time you start to write, you need to ask yourself two questions:
   a What is the purpose of this piece of writing?
   b Who am I writing to?
   (Here Ss are giving informal advice. The letter will be read by Kate Gray, the recipient of the advice.)

3 Look at the section on Letters on page 10 of the Style guide. Notice the suggested structure and layout of the letter. Is this appropriate for the letter in this situation?
   (The guidance about layout in the Style guide is general and appropriate for all formal or semi-formal letters. It is also important to decide what should go in the body of the text and plan the paragraphs needed. A possible structure for the body of the letter is as follows:
   Opening: reason for writing
   Body: advice and reasons why
   Friendly closing comment
   Standard closure.)

4 What style should the letter be written in?
   (As it says in the Style guide, business letters are usually quite formal in style. This is an informal letter, so a friendly opening [Dear Kate] and informal phrases/vocabulary are acceptable.)

5 What phrases might be appropriate for your letter?
   (See the Style guide and also the Useful phrases box on Coursebook page 74.)

6 Now go ahead and plan the letter. Then write the letter.

7 When you have finished, check your writing for: logical structure, clear ideas, accurate language, appropriate style.

- Style guide, Letters, page 10
- Style guide, General rules, page 3
- Skills Book, Writing 4, Letters, page 60
- Teacher's Book, page 161
- Teacher's Book, Writing preparation framework, page 188
- Teacher's Book, Writing feedback framework, page 189

Informal letter: Suggested answer (87 words)

Dear Kate,
I'm writing to give you some advice about which job to take.
It may be better to take the job with Wide World Tours because it is a bigger company. You are ambitious and it is important to work for a company that can help you to develop your career. It is a good idea to think about your long term career and what the company and job can offer you in the future.
Good luck and best wishes for the future.
Kind regards,
LD

INTELLIGENT BUSINESS (PRE-INTERMEDIATE) TEACHER'S BOOK: COURSEBOOK

Unit 9: Selling

UNIT OBJECTIVES

Reading: Marketing to students
Language: Modals of obligation
Vocabulary: Word building
Career skills: Making suggestions
Culture at work: Showing reactions
Dilemma & Decision: Guerrilla marketing (email)

Marketing attempts to identify and anticipate the needs of potential customers. This may be achieved through carrying out market research to find out what customers want. Sales, on the other hand, focuses on persuading the customer that the product or service that will meet this need can be provided. The marketing mix refers to:
- Developing the right product
- Establishing a price
- Getting the product to where consumers can buy it
- Promoting the product so that potential customers know about it.

This is also known as the four Ps: product, price, place and promotion. Traditional ways to promote a product or service include 'above the line' advertising (e.g. TV, radio, press) and 'below the line' (e.g. direct mail). However, for targeting groups which might not respond to traditional techniques, less traditional methods have been developed. Guerrilla marketing (see Dilemma & Decision) is a term coined by the business marketing expert Jay Conrad Levinson. It describes how conventional goals of traditional marketing (i.e. profit) can be achieved through unconventional methods. Guerrilla marketing tends to use unconventional (and often less expensive) ways to promote a product, such as using easy to remember telephone numbers, running unusual competitions or promotions or advertising in unusual spaces where customers would not normally expect to see a product promoted. The aim with these unconventional methods is to use imagination to capture attention, while using minimum resources. An example of guerrilla marketing techniques can be seen in the photograph at the start of the unit. Rather than using traditional marketing techniques that students might be resistant to, Red Bull (a company that makes energy drinks) recruits students to drive to campus events and hand out free samples from a fridge installed in the car Red Bull provides them with (see Reading, page 77).

Keynotes

Before opening books, ask the class to think of ways to advertise a product (e.g. TV, radio, press, direct mail, billboards, etc.). Ask the class to open their books and draw Ss' attention to the picture. Ask: *What company are they promoting?* (Red Bull). Check whether Ss know what Red Bull is (an energy drink). Do Ss think this is an interesting way to promote a product? What target group might like this sort of promotion? Would it interest Ss in the product? Why? / Why not? Check that Ss understand the terms in bold. Ask questions such as: *Can you think of any companies that sell direct to the consumer? What was the last flyer or catalogue that you received? What were they selling?* If appropriate for your class, ask: *How does your company promote its goods or services?* Ask Ss to read the keynotes and check they understand the terms in bold. Draw Ss' attention to the glossary for this unit at the back of the book.

Coursebook, Glossary, Unit 9, page 151

Preview

Get Ss to close their books and brainstorm different methods of selling. If your Ss do not respond, write some of the words from 1–6 on the board with letters or words missing (e.g. A _ v _ r _ i _ i _ g or Personal s_____). Ask Ss to guess the letters/words needed to complete the word or phrase. Open books and ask Ss to look at the picture and say what is happening (a yacht race). Draw Ss' attention to the logo on the side of the yacht and ask them to identify what company it is promoting (Audi). Get Ss to quickly look through the methods of selling 1–6 and say which is being used in the picture (sponsorship). Ask the whole class to look at the notes and suggest different advertising media. Then ask Ss to work in pairs and discuss how to complete the other notes. Point out that Ss should write any notes on a separate sheet of paper or in a notebook, as they will complete the form in the Coursebook for Listening 1.

Listening 1

Compare ideas from the Preview discussion. Then play the recording while Ss complete the notes. Choose three or four methods of selling and ask Ss to think of examples.

UNIT 9

1 radio, the press (newspapers and magazines), cinema, the internet
2 sales representatives
3 discounts, competitions, free gifts
4 news (information about the company in the press or on TV)
5 TV and internet shopping, telephone selling
6 event; person

Reading 1

Focus Ss on the title of the article and the picture and ask: *Why do you think students are an important market? What methods of selling do you think students like/dislike?* Check Ss understand the questions. Draw attention to the glossary and remind Ss of the glossary for Unit 9 at the back of the book. Spend time going over any other vocabulary that your class may have problems with (e.g. *marketers, trends analyst, ethical, debt, university campuses, extremely, field staff*). Ask Ss to read the article and answer the questions. Then get Ss to compare answers with a partner.

1 £13 billion
2 Students are hard to reach and they are cynical.
3 It runs career fairs and offers discounts on its products.
4 Teams of students who have a Red Bull car and fridge – they sell drinks on campus at sporting events and at times when students need an energy boost.
5 You need to have an approach that doesn't look like a sales pitch.
6 By having insiders on the campus, a database of students who act as field staff.

Reading 2

First, write companies 1–4 on the board and then ask Ss to read through the article again and identify which product/service each company sells. Working individually, ask Ss to match each company with the promotion methods a–e, pointing out that one company uses two methods. Then ask Ss to read the article again to check.

1 d   2 a, e   3 b   4 c

Speaking 1

Write the word *Students* on the board. Ask Ss to:
a) suggest adjectives that describe modern students
b) identify topics that students are concerned about.

Encourage Ss to use their own experience as much as possible to make suggestions. Ask a S to read out the quote, making sure that Ss understand *ethical* (in paragraph 2 of the article – related to the principles of what is right and wrong). In pairs / small groups ask Ss to answer the questions. If there are a number of nationalities in your class, mix the groups as much as possible.

Speaking 2

Ask Ss to change partners/groups and discuss the questions. Exchange ideas around the class. Ask Ss if there are any companies that they choose to buy from for ethical reasons.

Vocabulary 1

Check Ss' understanding of the words in the box. If Ss are unsure of any words, ask them to scan the article and try to guess the meaning of the word from context or remind them of any of these words you dealt with during the reading exercise. Ask Ss to complete the sentences and compare answers with a partner. You may wish to ask Ss if university students in their country usually finish their degree in debt and how long it usually takes to pay the debt off. You could teach Ss the phrases *in the red* (someone with a negative balance in their bank account) and *in the black* (someone with a positive balance in their bank account).

1 worth
2 estimate
3 high-earning, spending power
4 debt
5 pay off
6 discount
7 method
8 boost

Vocabulary 2

Word families are a useful way for Ss to build their vocabulary. You may wish to remind Ss of some of the ways that you discussed noting vocabulary in Unit 2. Ask Ss to suggest ideas to complete the first noun and person. Ask Ss to complete the table and compare answers around the class. You may wish to spend some time checking pronunciation, syllable stress and spelling.

1 sponsorship   2 sponsor
3 consumer   4 consume
5 marketer   6 market
7 organisation 8 organiser
9 analyst   10 analyse
11 agency

INTELLIGENT BUSINESS (PRE-INTERMEDIATE) TEACHER'S BOOK: COURSEBOOK

Vocabulary 2 **2**

Ask Ss to work in pairs and change the word in italics using one of the words from the table in exercise 1. After checking answers, ask Ss if they would buy the espresso machine. Why? / Why not?

1 marketing	2 consumption
3 analysis	4 agency
5 consume	6 consumers
7 sponsor	8 sponsorship

Optional activity
Photocopiable resource 9.1 (page 112)

Ask Ss to work in pairs / small groups. Photocopy resource 9.1 Give half the groups information about company A and half information about company B (the instructions are the same on both A/B sheets). Go over the information and check understanding. Tell pairs/groups that they are going to prepare a short presentation to give to the marketing team. Give each pair/group ten minutes to prepare and then ask them to present their ideas to another pair/group. Encourage them to divide their presentation in such a way as to allow each S to take part and to present a similar amount. You could set a time limit of one or two minutes for each presentation.

Listening 2 **1**

Ask Ss to think of new products that have been launched recently. What did the companies do to attract consumer/media attention? In pairs / small groups, ask Ss to answer the question. Ask Ss to compare ideas around the class.

Listening 2 **2**

Check that Ss understand what a wireless modem is (a modem that does not need to connect to telephone lines – and therefore requires no wires). Ask Ss to read through the questions and predict what Michio Yano will say. The Ss listen and choose the best option to complete the sentences. You could ask Ss to work with a partner and take turns to describe how TNP launched the wireless modem; their partner should listen and correct any information that is incorrect.

1 b	2 b	3 b	4 a	5 c

Speaking

Ask Ss to work in pairs / small groups and discuss the questions. Ask Ss how they react when companies try to contact them by email. Does it make them want to buy the product? Why? / Why not?

Language check

In Unit 6, Ss looked at modals of possibility (*will*, *may*, *might*, *could*). In this unit, Ss focus on modals of obligation. On the board write:

	1) need to	
Companies	2) must	research their target
	3) should	market.

Ask Ss to put the modals 1–3 in the correct order of strength (1 being the 'strongest'). Discuss suggestions with the class (1 *must* 2 *need to* 3 *should*). Ask Ss what the negative forms of these modals would be (*mustn't / must not*, *don't need to*, *shouldn't / should not*). Note that in this unit the focus is on *don't need to* rather than *needn't*, which means the same. This is purely to avoid overloading Ss at this level. However, if Ss have also heard *needn't*, reassure them that both forms are possible and equally correct.

Must and *have to* can be used in similar ways and are often interchangeable. The main difference is that *must* is generally used in situations where we are giving a personal opinion (e.g. *We must tell the team the good news*) while *have to* usually expresses a fact, rule or law that has been imposed by someone other than ourselves (e.g. *We have to arrange visas for any staff attending the international sales conference*).

Make sure that Ss understand the difference between *don't have to* and *mustn't*. Write on the board:

a) You don't have to invite Charles to the launch party.
b) You mustn't invite Charles to the launch party.

Ask Ss: *Which sentence says that it is important **not** to do something?* (b) *Which sentence says that it is **not necessary** to do something?* (a). Tell Ss that *don't need to* is also used in this way to mean that something is not necessary. Ask Ss to work in pairs and complete the table using the modal in bold in the example sentences. Focus Ss on the advice at the bottom of the page to help decide when to use *must* or *have to*.

1, 2 have to / must
3 should
4 need to
5 mustn't
6 shouldn't
7, 8 don't have to / don't need to

Coursebook, Grammar reference: Modals of obligation, page 158

Practice **1**

Draw Ss' attention to the picture and ask Ss what features they think a good camera should have. Explain that the eight sentences are rules in a competition by *Camera Eye* magazine. Do the first one together with the class. Ask Ss to complete the remaining rules individually. Circulate and help where necessary. If you find that Ss are having problems

64

with particular areas, go over the relevant area of modals again to clarify. Check answers together and choose two or three sentences to ask Ss why they made their choice. Point out that alternatives are possible.

1 mustn't
2 have to (must)
3 don't need to / don't have to
4 need to (have to / must)
5 mustn't
6 don't need to / don't have to
7 have to (must)
8 have to (must)

Practice 2

Ask Ss to close books. Tell Ss that they are going to read a sales trainer's advice to shop assistants. Ask the class to brainstorm advice that they would give to a sales assistant to help them do their job better. Open books and focus Ss on the example. Ask Ss to complete the sentences with a partner. Check answers around the class.

1 You **must** know as much as possible about the products.
2 You **shouldn't** be afraid to start a conversation with the customer.
3 You **shouldn't** start with a sales pitch straightaway.
4 You **should** ask a few questions to find out your customer's needs.
5 You **should/must** make the customer feel comfortable and important.
6 You **should** suggest different products that the customer could be interested in.
7 You **must** stress the benefits of the product, not the features.
8 You **mustn't** spend too long with one customer when others are waiting.

Workbook, page 39

Optional activity
Ss could work individually to note a list of 'dos and don'ts' for driving. Then ask Ss to tell their partner their ideas using modal verbs.

Speaking

Ask Ss to close their books again and write the word *Sales representative* on the board. Ask Ss to suggest characteristics a good sales representative should have and characteristics that would make a bad sales representative (e.g. a good sales representative should be enthusiastic, doesn't have to be fashionable, must have good communication skills, etc.). Open books and ask Ss to read the information. Are any of the characteristics that they suggested on the list? Ask Ss to work with a partner and discuss which qualities in the list are essential, which are quite important and which are not necessary.

Optional activity
You could ask Ss to work in small groups and draw up a similar list of qualities for another job of their choice. Groups then exchange lists and discuss the qualities using modals.

Career skills

Ask Ss if they have ever worked in a team. Did they find it easy or difficult to suggest ideas? Then ask Ss to think of other work situations where they may need to make suggestions. Ask Ss to look at the information and phrases 1–5. Make sure that Ss understand that after *How about / What about* the verb will take *-ing* (e.g. *How about **having** a celebration at the end of term?*). The other phrases 2–5 take the infinitive form (e.g. *Why not **have** a celebration party at the end of term?*). Then focus Ss on the responses and ask them to identify which phrases mean *yes* and which mean *no*.

Responses meaning *yes*:
That's a good idea.
I like that!
Brilliant!

Responses meaning *no*:
I'm not sure about that.
That could be difficult.

Optional activity
You may wish to ask Ss to work in pairs / small groups and discuss other ways to celebrate the end of term or to think of ways that they could improve their English outside English classes. Encourage Ss to use the phrases and responses in the Career skills box. Keep the activity brief and compare ideas around the class.

Listening 3

Introduce the activity by asking Ss to focus on the people watching the chef in the photo and ask: *What are they doing?* Have any of the class attended a cookery course? Where did they go? What was it like? Ask Ss to read the instructions and get the class to summarise to check understanding. Read through the suggestions together. Focus Ss' attention on the ✓/✗ column. Play the recording while Ss note whether the suggestions met with a positive or negative response.

Ss listen again and note the phrases (from the Career skills box) that are used for making and responding to suggestions.

1	✓	1	a
2	✓	2	d
3	–	4	–
4	✓	5	b
5	✓	1	e

Speaking

Check that Ss understand what *a chain of hairdressing salons* is (a number of hairdressing salons in different locations, run by the same company). Then give Ss time to work individually to think of suggestions to promote the salons to young people. Ask Ss to work in small groups and ask each group to think of a name for their chain. Ss discuss their ideas for promoting the salons. Ask each group to present some of their ideas to the class.

Culture at work

Ask Ss to read the information individually and discuss in pairs or small groups. You may find it helpful to look at the Culture at work box from page 43 of the Skills Book; this is reproduced below. You may also find it useful to refer to the relevant section on Culture at work in the teacher's notes supporting the Skills Book.

Visible response	Neutral response
If the person is happy, angry or surprised, it often shows in their expression.	If the person is happy, angry or surprised, their expression may remain neutral.
People use hands to emphasise what they are saying.	People keep hands and body still when speaking.
People do not feel comfortable with silence and will usually respond to a suggestion quickly to avoid breaks in the conversation.	People feel comfortable with silence and like to take time to consider the suggestion before responding.

Skills Book, Culture at work, page 43

Teacher's Book, page 147

Dilemma

As a lead-in, ask Ss to look at the Virgin logo and suggest some sectors that the business is involved in (transport, travel, insurance, music, telecommunications, cosmetics, space tourism, wine, etc.; see www.Virgin.com for more information about the company's activities). Can they name the founder of the company? (Richard Branson) Ask Ss to read the brief and summarise the information in order to check comprehension.

Task 1: Divide Ss into three groups. Ask Group A to turn to page 139, Group B to turn to page 143 and Group C to turn to page 145. Each group reads about their group's option individually, and then talks about the three discussion points on their role card with their group. Highlight the Useful phrases box and also remind Ss about the phrases for making and responding to suggestions in the Career skills box on page 81.

Task 2: Ss now work in new groups of three. Each group should contain one person from Groups A, B and C from Task 1. Each person takes it in turns to explain their option and present the ideas from their discussion in Task 1.

Task 3: In the same groups, Ss discuss the three options. Ss exchange ideas about why each option would / would not work. Then groups decide on which option would be most effective. Remind Ss that, if they wish, they can combine two options. Ask each group to present their ideas to the class.

Decision

Tell Ss that they are going to hear Nikki Lambert from Virgin Mobile talk about the method that the company used to identify student marketers. Ask Ss to predict which option or combination of options Virgin Mobile chose and then listen to check (standard recruitment methods and competitions). Ask Ss if they think that Virgin Mobile chose good options for identifying student marketers. Get Ss to listen again and describe the three stages of the competition that Nikki describes (personality test; promotional ideas; persuade other students to vote for them).

Write it up

Ss write an email to Virgin Mobile to say which option they think would be most effective. The email should include an explanation of why they chose that decision and suggestions as to how it could work. You may wish to ask Ss to prepare the writing in class, complete it for homework and then compare with a partner in the next lesson before handing it in to be marked. Give each S a photocopy of the Writing preparation framework from page 188. Then use the Writing focus (Writing focus: Emails) on the following page to link the use of the framework and the Style guide as Ss plan their writing. It may be helpful to use the Writing feedback framework on page 189 when marking Ss' writing.

UNIT 9

Writing focus: Emails

1 First, decide who you are.
  (In this case, you are a marketing consultant.)

2 Every time you start to write, you need to ask yourself two questions:
  a What is the purpose of this piece of writing?
  b Who am I writing to?
  (Here Ss are writing to Virgin Mobile to recommend the best option for recruiting student marketers and giving reasons why.)

3 Look at the section on Emails on page 6 of the Style guide. Notice the suggested structure of an email:
  From/To/Cc/Date/Subject
  Greeting
  Message
  Closing phrase
  Name
  Start with the most important information. Put less important information in the second paragraph.
  Is this structure appropriate for this email? Plan the paragraphs you are going to divide the email into. Then brainstorm the points you might cover in each paragraph.

4 What style should the email be written in?
  (As it says in the Style guide, it is a good idea to keep emails short and use short sentences and simple language. This is a business email, so the style should be formal.)

5 What words and phrases might be appropriate in your email?
  (See the Style guide and also the Useful phrases on Coursebook page 82 and the phrases for making suggestions in the Career skills box on page 81.)

6 Now go ahead and write the email.

7 When you have finished, check your writing for: logical structure, clarity of ideas, accuracy of language, appropriateness of style.

- Style guide, page 6
- Style guide, General rules, page 3
- Skills Book, Writing 2, Emails, page 32
- Teacher's Book, page 138
- Teacher's Book, Writing preparation framework, page 188
- Teacher's Book, Writing feedback framework, page 189

Email: Suggested answer (177 words)
From: (student's name), Marketing consultant
To: Virgin Mobile Directors
Date: (today's date)
Subject: Student marketers
Dear Sir or Madam
I think that the most effective strategy would be to combine two options and recruit people at student fairs and also have a competition.
Student fairs attract students from a wide range of colleges and universities. Virgin Mobile could have a stand at the student fair advertising the competition. The competition could then be advertised at each campus.
The competition would be in two stages. In the first stage, students would complete an entry form and suggest a way to promote Virgin Mobile on their campus. In the second stage, the ten best suggestions would win a prize and Virgin would pay for each student to run their promotion (each student would have the same amount of money to finance their promotion). The student who runs the most successful promotion would be offered the job as student marketer and have their college fees paid for a year.
I hope these suggestions are useful for you.
Yours faithfully
GL

Review 3

On the next two pages of the Coursebook you will find Review 3, which reviews language, vocabulary and functional language from Units 7, 8 and 9. It can be used in a number of ways that can be adapted to suit your class, for example:

- Ss can do selected exercises for homework.
- Use in class and guide Ss to particular exercises according to their individual needs. Alternatively, if your class has similar needs, focus on exercises where they can have more practice together (Ss can work individually or in pairs).
- Use as a short progress test and review any necessary points before moving on to Unit 10.

- Coursebook Review: Answers, page 103

INTELLIGENT BUSINESS (PRE-INTERMEDIATE) TEACHER'S BOOK: COURSEBOOK

Unit 10: Price

UNIT OBJECTIVES

Reading:	Make it cheaper and cheaper
Language:	Present perfect
Vocabulary:	Synonyms
	Verbs that take an object
Career skills:	Describing a graph
Culture at work:	How much explanation?
Dilemma & Decision:	Stock market challenge

Visual aids can help to enliven a presentation. A well thought-out diagram can clarify something that would take several hundred words to explain. However, an over reliance on visual aids for presentations can lead to the presenter simply reading the information to the audience, rather than using it to illustrate key points. A common problem with visual aids is when they are too complex or detailed. This can distract the audience's attention from important information. Another common problem is when visual aids are left up too long, which means that the audience will focus their attention on what they see, and may not notice that the speaker has moved on to another point. Technology provides speakers with new tools to illustrate presentations, such as Powerpoint and interactive whiteboards, although the more traditional overhead transparencies (OHTs) or slides and flipcharts can be equally effective. The most important factor is that the speaker should use methods that they feel comfortable with and which they are able to practise prior to giving their talk.

Keynotes

Ask Ss to look at the picture and say where it was taken (a supermarket). Ask Ss: *Do most people shop at supermarkets in your country?* Ask Ss to name the biggest or most popular supermarkets in their country. Get Ss to read the keynotes and check they understand the terms in bold. Draw Ss' attention to the glossary for this unit at the back of the book. Ask Ss if prices in supermarkets have gone up or down in the last year.

Coursebook, Glossary, Unit 10, page 151

Preview 1

Ask the class to brainstorm ideas for products that are increasing in price at the moment. If Ss do not respond, then make suggestions (houses, cars, petrol, health insurance) and ask Ss to say if these are increasing in price at the moment. Get Ss to suggest things that are getting cheaper at the moment.

Preview 2

Draw Ss' attention to the graph. Ask Ss what four spending trends it shows. Check Ss understand *increased, decreased, rose* and *fell*.

Ask Ss to complete the sentences and then compare their answers with partner.

1 food
2 communications
3 leisure
4 household equipment

Speaking

Write *Price* on the board and get Ss to brainstorm words connected with it. You may wish to remind Ss of some of the vocabulary from Unit 4 (*value for money, high/low quality* and the difference between *inexpensive* and *cheap*). Check that Ss understand the questions. Ask Ss to answer for themselves and then work in pairs / small groups and answer the questions. Ask: *What helps you decide if something is good value for money?*

Reading 1

Draw Ss' attention to the picture and ask: *What section of the supermarket is this?* (fruit and vegetable or greengrocery). Focus Ss on the sign and ask Ss what *special offer* means (reduced price for a limited period). Get Ss to say the price and ask: *How much were the melons originally?* (*save 30p* means that the melons were originally £1.09). Go over any vocabulary that your class may have problems with (e.g. *benefited, plentiful, scale*).

Focus Ss on the title of the article and ask Ss to say what is being made *cheaper and cheaper* (food). Encourage Ss to suggest pros and cons for making food cheaper and then ask them to scan the article quickly to see if their ideas are mentioned. Check Ss understand the questions. Draw attention to the glossary and remind Ss of the glossary for Unit 10 at the back of the book. Ask Ss to read the article and match the headings with paragraphs a–d. Then compare answers around the class.

68

1 b   2 d   3 a   4 c

Reading 2

Now Ss read the article again more carefully and decide if the statements are true or false. Ask Ss if the article has changed their ideas about their list of pros and cons for cheaper food.

1 T   2 T   3 T   4 F   5 T   6 T   7 F

Speaking

Ask Ss to work in pairs / small groups and answer the questions. Encourage Ss to give examples of chain stores and smaller shops in their country. When Ss say which type of store they prefer to shop in, encourage them to give reasons why. If Ss enquire about British/American English you could point out that British English often uses the word *shop* and American English *store*. However, in recent years, *store* has also become widely used in British English, particularly when talking about larger supermarkets and chains.

Vocabulary 1

Point out that the words 1–6 are taken from the text. You may wish to ask Ss to find the words in the article first, so that they can see them in context. Ask Ss to match the words with the meanings and compare their answers with a partner before checking with the whole class.

1 d   2 a   3 f   4 b   5 c   6 e

Vocabulary 2

Check that Ss know what a synonym is (a word with the same meaning). Ask Ss if *cut* means the same as *increase* or *decrease* (decrease). Do the same for *put up* (increase). Ask Ss to complete the table and compare answers around the class. Spend some time checking pronunciation. Encourage Ss to note down new vocabulary with synonyms and related words to help build their vocabulary.

increase: put up, raise, rise, rocket
decrease: cut, drop, fall, lower, reduce, push down

Vocabulary 3

Verbs can generally be divided into those that take an object (i.e. a noun or a pronoun), which are called transitive verbs, and those that don't take an object, known as intransitive verbs. Ss often confuse pairs of verbs such as *tell* (*I told John*) and *speak* (*I spoke to John*). We cannot say ~~*I spoke John*~~ because it is not possible to put an object after the verb *speak*. Equally, we cannot say *I told* without adding an object (e.g. *I told him*). Some verbs can be used both with and without an object (such as *drop* and *decrease* from Vocabulary 2). There is no simple rule for deciding whether a verb takes or does not take an object. Instead, it is helpful, when introducing new verbs, to make Ss aware whether each verb takes an object or not and encourage them to note the information in their vocabulary notebooks. It is also useful if Ss have access to a good dictionary, which will note whether a verb is transitive or intransitive. Look at the examples together and ask Ss to work in pairs and identify which other verbs in the table in Vocabulary 2 take an object. Point out that two of the verbs can be used with or without an object.

cut, drop (both with and without object), lower, put up, raise, reduce, push down, increase (both with and without object), decrease (both with and without object)

Vocabulary 4

Ask Ss to complete the text by choosing the correct verbs in italics. Do the first one together to demonstrate the exercise. If appropriate for your class, encourage Ss to give reasons for their choice and to identify whether the verb they chose takes an object or not.

1 rose   2 pushed up
3 increased   4 go up
5 cut   6 reduce
7 increasing

Speaking

Ask Ss to work in pairs / small groups and discuss the three ideas for improving profitability. Which idea do they think is best?

Listening 1

Tell the class that they are going to hear a radio programme about business. A marketing expert, Callum Taylor, will look at each of the ideas from the speaking exercise and say how much a company can expect to increase profitability using each strategy. Focus Ss on the *Profit increase (%)* column in the table and ask them to complete it as they listen to part one. Ask Ss if they agree with Callum's ideas.

1 2.3%   2 3.3%   3 11%

Listening 1 [2]

Ask Ss to look at sentences 1–5 and predict any words that they think could be used to fill the gaps. Then play part two of the recording and ask Ss to complete the sentences. Ask Ss to compare answers with a partner and then play the recording a final time to check.

> 1 produce; profit margin
> 2 customers; spend
> 3 competition
> 4 target customers; product; service; selling
> 5 think of a price

Language check [1]

Ask Ss to look at the example sentences and identify the verbs that are in the past simple (*rose, was*). Check if Ss can identify the other tense used in bold (present perfect). To focus on the use of the present perfect, write on the board this amended sentence from the article on page 87:

Spending on food has fallen for many years, and continues to drop.

Ask: *When did spending start to fall, in the past or the present?* (past) *Is spending still falling now?* (yes). The key point is that the event started in the past and continues to the present. Then write:

In the last month, prices have increased by 12%.

Ask Ss if the prices increased a long time ago or if it is a recent event (a recent event). Draw Ss' attention to the rules on page 89. Rules 1–3 focus on the form of the present perfect, while rules 4 and 5 look at the use of the past simple and present perfect. Ask Ss to complete the rules by choosing the correct word/phrase in italics in each sentence 1–5. Get Ss to compare answers with a partner before checking answers around the class. Point out that the past participle of regular verbs is, like the past simple, formed by adding -*ed* (e.g. *rocketed*). With regular verbs ending in *e*, simply add *d* (e.g. *reduced, increased*). Irregular verbs need to be learnt individually.

> 1 has or have   4 past simple
> 2 has or have   5 present perfect
> 3 hasn't or haven't

Language check [2]

This exercise compares time expressions that refer to a finished event in the past and those that refer to time up to now. Ask Ss to say which phrases they think refer to finished time in the past (*last year, six months ago, in 1999*) and ask which tense they think should be used with these time expressions (the past simple). Focus Ss on the information that these expressions contain (a reference to past time, *ago*, a date in the past). Now ask Ss to identify which expressions we usually use with the present perfect. Point out that none of these expressions refers to a finished time in the past; instead they all refer to the past leading up to the present (time up to now). Depending on your class, you may also wish to point out that while *ago* always refers to a finished time in the past, there are also specific words that are often used with the present perfect, e.g.:

*He has been the CEO **since** 2002.*
*He has worked at ICI **for** two years.*

Since refers to *when* the event started, and indicates that it continues to the present day. *For* refers to *how long* the event has been taking place.

> Time expressions used with the present perfect: *in the last three months, recently, in recent years*

Coursebook, Grammar reference: Present perfect, page 160

> **Optional activity**
> **Photocopiable resource 10.1 (page 113)**
> You may wish to do a sorting activity to review the infinitive, past simple and past participle form of some common irregular verbs. To start the activity, check Ss understand the terms and then point out that although each form is generally different (e.g. *take, took, taken*), many verbs are the same in the past simple and past participle (e.g. *have, had, had*) and some are the same in all three forms (e.g. *put, put, put*). Ask Ss to work in pairs. Photocopy and cut up one set of cards for each pair. Keep one photocopiable sheet intact to check answers with the class. Get Ss to place the infinitive, past simple and past participle cards face up on the table. The remaining cards should be shuffled and put on the table face down. Ss take turns to pick up a card and decide if it goes in the infinitive, past simple or past participle column (point out that some verbs may go in more than one column). In a later lesson, the cards could be used for revision; hold up a card (e.g. *written*) and elicit whether it is the infinitive, past simple or past participle (past participle) and elicit the infinitive (*write*) and past simple (*wrote*) forms.

Practice [1]

Take time over these exercises and reassure Ss that you will go over any points that they are not sure of. This is an introduction to the present perfect, so Ss do not need to grasp all the information in one go. First, ask Ss to identify the sentences that are correct. Then ask them to change the incorrect sentences. Check answers around the class. Ask: *What words helped you to decide which sentences were wrong?*

UNIT 10

1 ~~we have seen~~ we saw
2 ~~fell~~ has fallen
3 correct
4 ~~we didn't raise~~ we haven't raised
5 correct
6 ~~We have reviewed~~ We reviewed

Practice 2

Read out the verbs in the box and ask Ss to say if they mean *increase* or *decrease*. Draw Ss' attention to the chart and ask Ss what it gives information on (house prices). Choose one or two countries from the chart and ask Ss if prices have risen or fallen. Ask Ss to identify the country where prices have risen the most and fallen the most. Focus Ss on the example. Ask Ss to read the text about world trends in house prices and then complete it using the present perfect forms of the verbs in the box. Point out that each verb can be used only once.

2 have risen
3 have doubled
4 have dropped / fallen
5 have been
6 have dropped / fallen

Workbook, page 42

Speaking

Choose one of the topics and have a general discussion around the class about whether prices have increased, decreased or stayed the same in recent months. Ask Ss to work with a partner and discuss the prices of the other items on the list in their own country.

Career skills

Ask Ss if they have attended any presentations recently that used visuals to illustrate information. You could ask Ss to suggest different ways of presenting information (graphs, tables of figures, bar charts, etc.). Ask Ss to read the information and match the phrases with the graphs. Then ask Ss to look at the graphs and complete the phrases with the missing numbers or dates. Tell Ss that they will listen to descriptions of the five graphs to check their answers.

Listening 2 1

Play the recording for Ss to check answers. Check answers around the class. Focus Ss on the title of each graph. Ask Ss to suggest what some of the missing words might be.

1 105 – Graph A
2 2003 – Graph D
3 3.5 – Graph E
4 150 – Graph C
5 30 – Graph B

Listening 2 2

Play the recording again for Ss to complete the titles.

Graph A: share price
Graph B: the price; oil
Graph C: renting; apartment
Graph D: London; Paris
Graph E: Rate; inflation

Speaking 1

Ask Ss to work in pairs and take turns to describe the graphs. As a variation, one S could describe one of the graphs without saying the title, while their partner guesses which graph they are describing.

Speaking 2

Give Ss time to read the information and study their graph. Encourage Ss to use phrases from the Career skills box and any other useful phrases from the lesson. Ask Ss to describe their graph to their partner. As each S describes their graph, you could ask their partner to try to draw the graph that is being described. Ss can then check each other's graphs and compare them with the ones in the back of the book.

Optional activity
Ss could make a similar graph for themselves, showing earnings or expenditure.

Culture at work

Ask Ss to think about the last presentation that they went to. Did the speaker give a lot of information or a little? Ask Ss to read the information individually and discuss in pairs or small groups. Encourage Ss to give examples from their own experience. You may find it helpful to look at the Culture at work box from page 50 of the Skills Book; this is reproduced on the following page. You may also find it useful to refer to the relevant section on Culture at work in the teacher's notes supporting the Skills Book.

A little	A lot
You like to communicate fast. You don't need a lot of words to say what you mean.	You like to be clear. You use a lot of words to say what you mean.
You use graphs and visuals to illustrate what you say.	When you use graphs and visuals you prefer to explain in detail what the information means.
The audience knows what you are talking about. You don't need to spend too much time on details.	You give background information to help the audience understand.

Skills Book, Culture at work, page 50

Teacher's Book, page 152

Dilemma

As a lead-in, ask Ss if they have made any investments recently. If they were making investments, how would they decide what companies to invest in? Tell Ss that they are members of an investment group. Point to the pictures and ask Ss what sort of company they think the group invested in (airline). Ask Ss to read the brief and the text *Guide to making money on the stock exchange*. Ask Ss if they agree with the guide. Why? / Why not? Ask Ss to summarise the brief to check comprehension.

Task 1: Ask Ss to work in small groups. Make sure that Ss read through and understand what they have to do prior to listening. Listen to the news bulletins for March, June and September. Go over the Useful phrases box. Elicit any other suitable phrases that Ss know or language from the lesson which would help in discussion. Play each month's bulletin individually, check what the share price is and give groups time to note information and discuss what to do. Ss then use the table to note the value of their group's investments and decisions at the end of each quarter (March, June, September). Circulate and help where necessary.

Task 2: Play the final news bulletin for December for Ss to fill in the information for the fourth quarter. Give groups time to calculate how much money they have in shares and cash. Ask each group to tell the class about the decisions that they took and how much money they made.

> **Optional activity**
> To add an extra dimension to the activity, you could tell Ss to calculate the interest on their cash fund at a rate of one per cent per three months.

Decision

Still working in their original groups, ask Ss to turn to page 146 and look at the graph. Encourage groups to compare the information in the graph with the decisions that they took and to discuss how much money their group could have made. Ask Ss what decisions they would have changed, and why.

Unit 11: Insurance

UNIT OBJECTIVES	
Reading:	Fighting fraud
Language:	Passives
Vocabulary:	Problems
	Insurance
	Insurance fraud
Career skills:	Expressing arguments
Culture at work:	To interrupt or not?
Dilemma & Decision:	A fair decision? (letter)

This unit looks at insurance. Insurance can be arranged by contacting a company directly or by going through a broker. A broker will look at a range of insurers and recommend the one that they think offers the appropriate type of cover.
Compulsory insurance is insurance that the law stipulates a person most hold. The most common form of compulsory insurance is for vehicles where a minimum amount of cover is required to drive on a public road. For businesses there are a number of different insurances that need to be considered. In the UK, compulsory insurances for businesses include: **Motor** insurance for all business vehicles. **Employer liability** insurance, which enables a business to meet the cost of compensation for employees who suffer illness, injury or disease through their employment. It is the law under the Employers' Liability Compulsory Insurance Act 1969 that employers have this insurance and are covered for a minimum of £5 million.
Those who give professional advice through their work often take out **Professional indemnity**, which covers legal costs and damages arising if clients sue over recommendations they were given in a professional capacity. Certain professional bodies (e.g. The Association of Chartered Certified Accountants) make this insurance a requirement for membership.
Voluntary insurances cover other types of liability, such as **Public liability** insurance, which protects members of the public who suffer injury or damage to property by a business.
Product liability covers businesses from claims from people who do not work for the company, who have suffered from products manufactured, supplied or repaired by a business. Directors and executive officers of a company are liable for over 200 areas of statutory liability under the 1985 and 1989 Companies Acts for actions or decisions on behalf of a company, so many take out **Director's and Officers liability** insurance.
Companies are protected if a debtor goes bankrupt owing them money through **Credit** insurance.
Small and medium-sized businesses may consider taking out **Business interruption** insurance, for example if files were lost or destroyed it would provide cover for the time it would take to get the business up and running again.
Business premises are covered by **Buildings** insurance and **Contents** insurance. Products that are transported by a company's vehicles or couriers can be insured for loss or damage by **Goods in transit** insurance.
With so many different forms of business insurance, premiums can be high. Businesses can choose to pay a higher excess (the amount they can afford to pay out initially before making a claim) in order to lower premiums.

Keynotes

Draw Ss' attention to the cartoon. Ask: *What sort of company is this?* (an insurance company). Point to the man in the hat and his children and ask: *What have they been doing?* (fishing) *What are they trying to show with their hands?* (the size of the fish that got away). The joke plays on the idea that fishermen always exaggerate the size of the fish that they catch, particularly ones that get away. In the cartoon, the fisherman is trying to make an insurance claim for the fish that got away, his demonstration of the size of the fish contrasting with the size demonstrated by his children. Ask Ss to read the keynotes and check they understand the terms in bold. You could also ask Ss to brainstorm any other words that they know connected with insurance. Draw Ss' attention to the glossary for this unit at the back of the book.

Coursebook, Glossary, Unit 11, page 152

Preview

You can do this as a whole-class discussion or ask Ss to compare ideas in pairs before sharing ideas with the class. Encourage Ss to use dictionaries to look up words to describe the types of insurance that they have and types of insurance that are compulsory.

Reading 1

Introduce the subject by asking Ss to name any insurance companies that they know. Where do these companies advertise? Ask Ss to read the extract from the insurance company website. Draw Ss' attention to the glossary box and

73

INTELLIGENT BUSINESS (PRE-INTERMEDIATE) TEACHER'S BOOK: COURSEBOOK

remind them of the glossary for Unit 11 at the back of the book. Then ask Ss to match the headings with paragraphs 1–4. Check answers around the class and ask Ss if they mentioned any of these types of insurance in their Preview discussion.

| 1 Commercial | 2 Life |
| 3 Auto | 4 Home |

Speaking

Ask Ss to work in pairs / small groups and discuss the question (some examples of unusual insurance include pet insurance and dangerous sports insurance for activities such as cliff diving and heliskiing).

Vocabulary 1

Tell Ss that they are going to read extracts from insurance claims. Ask Ss to read through the extracts and summarise what has happened in each. Then go over the words in the box and check Ss' understanding. Ask Ss to complete the claims with the words in the box. Get Ss to compare their answers with a partner before checking with the class.

1 injured	2 damaged
3 stolen	4 lost
5 destroyed	

Listening 1 1

Tell Ss that they are going to listen to Irene Foster from the insurance company, Green Shield, explain how an insurance company is structured. It is not necessary to explain vocabulary terms such as *underwriter* at this stage as they will become clear in the exercise that Ss are about to do. Point out that each person 1–3 matches with two job activities a–f. Play part one of the recording for Ss to complete the exercise. Check answers around the class and ask Ss to summarise what an underwriter does. Ask Ss if they would like to do any of the three jobs mentioned.

| 1 d, a | 2 b, e | 3 f, c |

Listening 1 2

Ask Ss to listen to part two and answer the questions. Check answers around the class.

1 three; a four-year period
2 A customer who made several claims for theft lived in an area of high crime, but then moved to a new address.
3 higher; cover

Vocabulary 2

Read the words 1–6 with the class to practise pronunciation. Check if Ss know the meaning of any of the words. Then ask Ss to match the words with the meanings a–f.

| 1 e | 2 f | 3 a | 4 b | 5 d | 6 c |

Vocabulary 3

Check that Ss understand the terms *fraud* (deceiving someone in order to obtain money) and *fraudulent* (the adjective from *fraud*). Read through the sentences with the class to check understanding. In pairs / small groups, ask Ss to decide which of the actions 1–6 could be described as fraud. Ask Ss: *Is fraud considered a serious crime in your country? What happens to someone if they commit fraud?* To extend the activity, you could ask Ss to work in their groups and think of other examples of fraudulent behaviour.

2, 3, 5

Reading 2 1

Ss are going to read a longer article about fighting insurance fraud. Before reading, ask Ss to look at questions 1 and 2 and guess the answer (Ss do not need to write this, they can call out suggestions and you note them on the board). Draw Ss' attention to the glossary box, check comprehension and remind them of the glossary for Unit 11 at the back of the book. Then Ss read through the text quickly and answer the questions. Ask Ss if they were surprised at how much insurance fraud costs. Which Ss guessed the figure closest to the $80 billion mentioned in the article? Do Ss think that the voice analysers are a good idea?

1 $80 billion a year
2 Layered Voice Analyzer (LVA) and Voice Risk Analyzer (VRA)
3 more than £3 million

Reading 2 2

Now Ss have to read the text carefully to decide where sentences A–E fit best. Ask Ss to insert the letter for the correct sentence in the text. Do the first one together to demonstrate the exercise. Read the article with the class, pausing to ask Ss to insert the correct sentence in the gaps.

| 1 E | 2 A | 3 D | 4 B | 5 C |

UNIT 11

Vocabulary 4

This exercise requires Ss to decide which of three possible words is best to complete each sentence. Some of the words have similar meanings, so Ss need to consider carefully which word to choose. Ss can use a dictionary if they need to check meaning. Ask Ss to complete the exercise and compare answers with a partner. When checking answers with the class, you could ask Ss to explain the difference between some pairs of words (e.g. *What is the difference between 'screen' and 'detect'?*).

| 1 a | 2 c | 3 c | 4 b | 5 b | 6 c |

Speaking

Go through the six scenarios and check Ss' comprehension. Ask Ss to work individually and put the six actions in order from most to least serious. Then get Ss to work in pairs / small groups and compare answers. Encourage Ss to give reasons where possible. You could ask Ss to consider whether they think it is worse to be dishonest with someone that you know or a company. Ask Ss to give reasons. For fun you could ask Ss if the amount makes a difference (e.g. in question 4, would it make a difference if it was €500 rather than €100? Or if it was €5?).

Language check

Point out to the class that the passive is often used in formal written English, for example reports or when describing processes. This unit focuses on the present simple, present continuous and past simple forms of the passive.

Write on the board:

The VRA program screens voices.

Ask Ss: *Is this an active or passive sentence?* (active). If Ss are not sure, you could explain that this active sentence describes what the VRA program does (i.e. the action it performs). Then write the following on the board and elicit how to make the active sentence passive:

Voices a_____ screen_____ b_____ the VRA program.

(Voices **are** screen**ed by** the VRA program.)

Draw Ss' attention to the second sentence and point out that this passive sentence focuses on what happens to the voices (not the action the program performs). Spend some time focusing on the form of the passive. Ask Ss to look at the examples on page 98 of the Coursebook and choose the best alternative in italics to complete the rules. Go over the rules with the class to check understanding. Ask Ss to identify the tense in each sentence (the first three sentences are present simple, the fourth present continuous, the fifth present perfect, the sixth past simple). You may wish to focus on some of the example sentences to demonstrate that it is not always necessary to name the agent (e.g. *My car has been stolen!*) but when the agent is named we use *by* (e.g *Three houses were destroyed by the storm*).

| 1 to be | 2 active |
| 3 passive | 4 by |

Coursebook, Grammar reference: Passive verbs, page 160

Practice 1

Make sure that Ss are aware that the sentences are all about Howard Baines's company. First, ask Ss to identify any sentences where the agent could be omitted (2, 3, 6, 7). Ask Ss to identify the tense of each sentence. Do the first sentence together to demonstrate the exercise. Give Ss plenty of time to complete the sentences. Circulate and note any problem areas. Then go over the sentences together on the board.

1 The company was set up by Howard Baines in 1978.
2 To begin with, it was divided into three departments.
3 Since then, it has been restructured into five departments.
4 Each department is headed by a manager.
5 Four thousand people are now employed by the company.
6 A new head office is being built for 2,000 staff.
7 The new building will be completed next month.

Practice 2

Before reading the text, ask Ss if they think a person's job makes their car insurance higher or lower. If Ss think that jobs are relevant to the cost of car insurance, ask them for examples of jobs that they think might pay the highest and lowest rates for car insurance. Ask Ss to complete the text by putting the verb in brackets into the correct passive form. If your class needs more support with the passive, you could ask Ss to identify which sentences they think will use the present simple and which will use the past simple. Do the first one together to demonstrate the exercise. After checking answers around the class, you could ask Ss if they agree or disagree with the ideas in the text. You could also ask Ss to summarise key information in the text.

1 are charged	2 was quoted
3 was offered	4 are attracted
5 are seen	6 are paid
7 are believed	

Workbook, page 46

75

INTELLIGENT BUSINESS (PRE-INTERMEDIATE) TEACHER'S BOOK: COURSEBOOK

Career skills

Tell Ss about a difficult decision that you have made in the past or one that you are making at the moment. Ask Ss to suggest ways to help make a decision. Have they had to make any difficult decisions recently? Ask Ss to read the information and phrases in the box. Focus on the phrases for responding on the right and ask Ss to identify which phrases you can use to agree (*That's right*) and which you can use to disagree (*Yes, but ...* and *I understand your point, but ...*). Which phrase would you use to give an alternative point of view? (*On the other hand ...*) The phrases for disagreeing may seem confusing to Ss because they appear at first to agree. You may wish to point out that in British English *I disagree* can sometimes seem too direct, and that people often use indirect phrases to soften the language.

Listening 2

Ss heard Irene from Green Shield in Listening 1. In this listening, Ss hear Irene and two other underwriters from Green Shield discuss a special case. Ask Ss to read the information and listen to see how many people think that the man should be offered insurance. Then Ss listen again and tick the phrases that they hear in the Career skills box. All the phrases are used in the recording, so as an alternative you could ask Ss to use the boxes to number the phrases in the order that they hear them. Ask Ss to summarise the arguments for and against that the three underwriters use. You may wish to ask Ss to turn to the audioscript on page 172 of the Coursebook. Drill stress (or, alternatively, play the recording again while Ss mark word stress on the audioscript). Then ask Ss to work in groups of three and role-play the conversation.

1 One person is for – Jane.

Optional activity
Photocopiable resource 11.1 (page 114)

This is an activity which consolidates the vocabulary from Vocabulary 1 and 2. Divide the class into two groups, A and B. Give each S in Group A a photocopy of information A. Give each S in Group B a photocopy of information B. In their groups, Ss complete the letter using the missing words in the box (*quote*; *premium*; *terms*; *claim*). Then ask Ss to use the prompts to write questions (*How much is the premium each year/month? What are the terms of the policy? What can I claim for?*). Next ask Ss to work in A/B pairs and take turns to ask their partner the questions about their insurance company. Ss use the information in their letter to answer. Finally, ask Ss to use the information to decide which company they would choose to insure with.

Speaking

Ask Ss to summarise again the case of the man in Listening 2. Ask Ss to work individually and note arguments for and against Green Shield insuring his house. Get Ss to look at their list and decide if they think the company should insure him. Then ask Ss to work in pairs and put forward arguments for and against the idea. Next ask Ss to prepare arguments for and against the second idea. After Ss have discussed with a partner, open the discussion up to the whole class. Encourage Ss to respond to the ideas.

Culture at work

Ask Ss to discuss the questions in groups. Encourage them to give examples from their own experience where possible (e.g. meetings that they have attended in the past). You may find it helpful to look at the Culture at work box from page 54 of the Skills Book; this is reproduced below. You may also find it useful to refer to the relevant section on Culture at work in the teacher's notes supporting the Skills Book.

Silence not OK	Silence OK
People may respond immediately after a person stops talking.	It is respectful to leave a short silence before responding, to show that you are considering what has been said.
People may speak at the same time.	Allow the other person to finish what they have to say before speaking.
It is usual to politely interrupt in meetings or conversations.	It is not polite to interrupt in meetings or conversations.
People may use expressive body language to respond or interrupt or to underline their opinion.	It is more usual to have a neutral tone of voice and body language.

Skills Book, Culture at work, page 54

Teacher's Book, page 156

Dilemma

To introduce the subject, ask Ss if they have ever had problems with an insurance company. What did they do? Ask Ss to read the first paragraph of the brief. Pause and check that Ss understand what the role of an ombudsman is. Ask Ss if they have ombudsmen in their country. Then ask Ss to read the rest of the brief. Ask Ss to summarise the information to check comprehension.

Task 1: Divide the class into two groups. Group A reads about the insurance company's decision (on page 139) and group B about Jane Buxton's point of view (on page 143). Ask Ss to look at the Useful phrases box and also the Career skills box on page 99. Tell Ss that they will be putting forward their arguments for and against in the next task, so they need to make a note of any phrases that will help them.

Task 2: Ask Ss to work in groups of four – two Ss who read about the insurance company's decision, and two Ss who read about Jane Buxton's point of view. Remind Ss that they are working for the Financial Ombudsman Service, so they should look at the arguments for and against objectively and come to a solution. Ask groups to tell the rest of the class about the decision that they came to and explain why.

Decision

Tell Ss that they are going to listen to Carl Herring, a member of the Financial Ombudsman Service. Ask Ss what decision they think the ombudsman will make. Play the recording to check and then play it again and elicit some of the reasons that Carl gave for the decision (Jane wasn't told to change the locks; changing the locks is very expensive, and it would be unreasonable to expect someone with an old car to pay so much).

Write it up

Tell Ss that they are going to write a formal letter to the insurance company. They should tell the company the decision that they made in their group and explain their arguments. If Ss wish to change their decision, after having heard Carl Herring, they can do so. Give each S a photocopy of the Writing preparation framework from page 188. Then use the Writing focus (Writing focus: Letters) below to link the use of the framework and the Style guide as Ss plan their writing. It may be helpful to use the Writing feedback framework on page 189 when marking Ss' writing.

Writing focus: Letters

1 First, be clear about the perspective you are writing from.
(In this case, Ss are members of the Financial Ombudsman Service.)

2 Every time you start to write, you need to ask yourself two questions:
a What is the purpose of this piece of writing?
b Who am I writing to?
(Here Ss are writing an official letter informing an insurance company of the decision that the Financial Ombudsman Service has come to. The letter will be read by the insurance company.)

3 Look at the section on Letters on page 10 of the Style guide. Notice the suggested structure and layout of the letter. Is this appropriate for the letter in this situation?
(The guidance about layout in the Style guide is general and appropriate for all formal or semi-formal letters. It is also important to decide what should go in the body of the text and plan the paragraphs needed. A possible structure for the body of the letter is as follows:
Opening: reason for writing
Body 1: presenting your decision
Body 2: explaining arguments
Standard closure.)

4 What style should the letter be written in?
(As it says in the Style guide, business letters are usually quite formal in style. Informal phrases/vocabulary and contractions would not be acceptable. We do not have a contact name, so the letter should begin 'Dear Sir or Madam' and end 'Yours faithfully'.)

5 What phrases might be appropriate for your letter?
(See the Style guide, in particular the phrases in Referring to subject and Explain the purpose of the letter.)

6 Now go ahead and plan the letter. Then write the letter.

7 When you have finished, check your writing for: logical structure, clear ideas, accurate language, appropriate style.

- Style guide, Letters, page 10
- Style guide, General rules, page 3
- Skills Book, Writing 4, Letters, page 60
- Teacher's Book, page 161
- Teacher's Book, Writing preparation framework, page 188
- Teacher's Book, Writing feedback framework, page 189

Formal letter: Suggested answer (126 words)

Dear Sir or Madam,
Regarding the question of Jane Buxton's insurance claim, I am writing to inform you that the Financial Ombudsman Service has come to the decision that your company's refusal to settle the claim was unfair.
It is our opinion that Ms Buxton took reasonable steps to prevent the theft. She changed the locks on her house, but she was not advised to change the locks on her car. If your insurance company thought that this was important, then you should have contacted Ms Buxton and discussed the matter with her. In the circumstances, it is unreasonable to expect that Ms Buxton would know that it was her responsibility to do so. We recommend that your company settles the claim without delay.
Yours faithfully,

INTELLIGENT BUSINESS (PRE-INTERMEDIATE) TEACHER'S BOOK: COURSEBOOK

Unit 12: Service

UNIT OBJECTIVES

Reading:	Getting better service
Language:	Conditional 1
Vocabulary:	Feedback on service
	Dealing with complaints
	Synonyms
	Collocations
Career skills:	Dealing with problems
Culture at work:	Showing emotion
Dilemma & Decision:	Service not included (short report)

This unit begins by looking at customer service. Meeting customer requirements is essential if a company is to grow. This means that a company needs to keep up-to-date with its customers' changing needs. One of the reasons that this is necessary is because it takes more time, money and effort to find new customers than it does to retain existing customers. Good customer service has to be consistent, so it is important to review processes and procedures regularly (for example, how customers are billed and how complaints are dealt with). More and more companies use focus groups, questionnaires and customer feedback to try to anticipate what customers want. The service sector accounts for over 70% of the GDP of most developed countries, so it is worth getting it right. However, there is always the possibility that things can go wrong and it is how a company deals with complaints that is often key to customer satisfaction.

Keynotes

Introduce the topic by drawing Ss' attention to the photo. Ask: *What do you think these people are doing?* (Vocabulary note: British English = *queueing*; American English = *waiting in line*). Ask: *Why is the man looking at his watch? Do they look like satisfied customers? Why? / Why not? Have you waited in a queue recently? Did you have to wait a long time? How did you feel?* Ask Ss to read the keynotes and check that they understand the terms in bold. Draw their attention to the glossary for this unit at the back of the book. You might wish to ask Ss if they have had any experiences of good customer service. Have they had any experiences of poor service?

Coursebook, Glossary, Unit 12, page 152

Preview

Tell Ss about a time when you have had to complain about something. You may wish to highlight the different parts of speech: *complain* (verb) and *complaint* (noun). Focus on the situations 1–7 and check Ss understand the meaning. Ask Ss which situation is illustrated by the cartoon (1). Ask Ss to work in pairs or small groups to discuss in which situations they would complain. You could go through the situations that Ss identified and ask Ss to suggest what phrases they would use to complain. Have a brief feedback session and then brainstorm more situations where Ss would complain.

Vocabulary 1

Check that Ss understand the words in the box, particularly words which may be used in a way that they are not familiar with (e.g. *poor = bad*). Get Ss to say which words are positive (*friendly, pleased, excellent, useful*) and which are negative (all the remaining words). Focus Ss' attention on the small faces beside each speech bubble and ask them to identify which represent positive and negative comments. These are important as grammatically some words can go with more than one speech bubble (e.g. *pleased* could go with 3: *Very pleased to receive the receipt ...* and with 4: *We were very pleased with the service at the hotel*; however, the face indicates that 4 is a negative comment and so *pleased* would not fit in context there). You may wish to go over any vocabulary that is unfamiliar to your class (*resort, receipt, confirmation, quoted, pointed out*). Ask Ss to work with a partner and complete the comments using words in the box.

1 excellent	2 friendly	3 pleased
4 dissatisfied	5 dirty	6 rude
7 wrong	8 mistake	9 apology
10 useful	11 poor	

Optional activity
Ask Ss to work in pairs and tell their partner about good or bad service that they received on holiday or on a business trip.

Reading 1

Get Ss to read the article quickly and choose the sentence that describes its main point. Ask Ss to tell you what information helped them to choose their answer.

b

78

UNIT 12

Reading 2

Ask Ss to read again more carefully and answer the questions. Draw Ss' attention to the words in the glossary and remind them of the glossary for Unit 12 at the back of the book. Get Ss to check their answers with a partner. Ask Ss to summarise the Australian, British and American attitudes to complaining.

| 1 F | 2 T | 3 F | 4 F | 5 T | 6 F |

Speaking

Ask Ss to work in pairs / small groups and answer the questions. Encourage Ss to give examples. You could then open it up for a whole-class discussion.

Vocabulary 2

Ask Ss to look at the article again and say what company trains their employees in the LEARN routine (the Marriott Group). Ask Ss to close their books and write the five steps of the routine on the board:

Listen
Empathise
Apologise
React
Notify

Check Ss understand the meaning of each word and practise pronunciation with the class. Ss open their books and match the steps in the LEARN routine with the explanations. Ask Ss to suggest phrases that customer service staff could use at each stage of the routine to deal with a complaint (e.g. *Could you tell me what the problem is? That must have been frustrating, I'm really sorry ... , I'll deal with the problem immediately, I'll talk to the manager about this*). Ask Ss if they think that the routine would be effective. Close books and clear the board and ask Ss to help you remember the five stages of the LEARN routine.

| 1 c | 2 a | 3 e | 4 d | 5 b |

Vocabulary 3

Check that Ss remember what a synonym is (synonyms were introduced in Unit 10). Ask Ss to read the sentences. All the words in italics appear in the text. If your Ss need help to do the exercise, encourage them to find the words in italics in the article first, to guess meaning from context. Ask Ss to complete the exercise and check answers around the class.

| 1 c | 2 a | 3 c | 4 b |

Vocabulary 4 1

Do the first one together to demonstrate the exercise. When Ss finish, you could ask them to brainstorm other nouns connected with customer service that can be used with each verb 1–5.

1 a customer	2 a service
3 a need	4 a complaint
5 a complaint	

Vocabulary 4 2

Now Ss choose which verbs in italics complete the text. Ask Ss if they have ever complained to a company. How did the company handle their complaint?

1 satisfy	2 makes
3 deal with	4 satisfy
5 offers	6 make

Listening 1

Ask Ss to work in pairs and match the situations 1–5 with the actions a–e. Play the recording for Ss to check their answers.

Ss listen again in more detail and answer the questions. Ask Ss to compare their answers with their partner. Ask Ss if they think that this is good advice to customer service staff. Would Ss like to work in customer services? Why? / Why not? What do they think the pros and cons of the job would be?

1/2
1 c   2 e   3 a   4 b   5 d

3
1 I didn't make the mistake. This isn't my responsibility.
2 stay calm; deal with the complaint even if it isn't your fault; follow a fixed routine to solve the problem
3 *will* (not *might* or *can't*)

Language check

Before asking Ss to read the information on conditional 1, write a conditional sentence on the board, e.g.:

If you explain the problem, I'll try to help.

Point to the contraction and ask Ss to say the long form (*I will*). Point out the comma separating the clauses in the sentence. You may also wish to inform Ss that the *if* clause can come at the beginning or end of a sentence (e.g *I'll try to help if you explain the problem*). Note that when the *if* clause is placed at the end of the sentence, a comma is not used. We use conditional 1 to say what we think the future consequence of an action will be (e.g. action: you explain the

79

INTELLIGENT BUSINESS (PRE-INTERMEDIATE) TEACHER'S BOOK: COURSEBOOK

problem, consequence: *I'll try to help*). It is generally used to talk about realistic situations and likely outcomes. Ss look at conditional 2 (which is used for hypothetical situations) in Unit 14. Ask Ss to read the examples and complete the rules using *present* or *future*. Draw Ss' attention to the information about using *can/could* instead of *will*.

| 1 present | 2 future | 3 future |

Coursebook, Grammar reference: Conditional 1, page 160

Practice 1

To introduce the topic, ask Ss to suggest different ways to pay for goods or services (e.g. cash, credit card, cheque, etc.). Focus Ss on the example and ask Ss to work in pairs to write conditional 1 sentences. After checking answers, you could ask Ss to rewrite some of the sentences, putting the *if* clause at the end of the sentence (e.g. *You will receive a discount if you pay within 10 days*).

1 If you pay by credit card, we will add a charge of 2 per cent to your bill.
2 If we don't receive payment by the due date, we will charge interest at 2.5 per cent a month.
3 If you request delivery within 24 hours, there will be an additional charge of €20.
4 If you decide not to keep the product, we will refund your money in full.

Practice 2

Ask Ss to read through the extracts from a company brochure and complete the information using the present simple or future form of the verbs. Get Ss to compare answers in pairs before checking answers around the class. Ask questions such as: *What will the company give you if you are dissatisfied with the service? What is the telephone number of the sales department? What date do you need to place an order by to qualify for a discount?*

1 find	2 will refund	3 are
4 will send	5 will deduct	6 order
7 cancel	8 will be	9 require
10 will be		

Workbook, page 51

Speaking 1

Ask Ss to prepare ideas individually and then work in pairs and discuss with their partner.

Speaking 2

Depending on how confident your class is, you may wish to brainstorm some situations with your class before asking them to discuss their possible actions with a partner, e.g.:

Book a night in an economy or an expensive hotel.
Wash my car in a carwash or do it myself.
Do my English homework as soon as I arrive home or do it later.
Cook dinner this evening or order a take-away.

Career skills

To introduce the topic, get Ss to close their books and ask them what they do when they have a problem. Write on the board:

Choose the best solution.
Note options.
Consider the result of each option.

Ask Ss in what order they would do these three problem-solving stages (Note … Consider … Choose). Now ask Ss to open their books and read the information and phrases in the box. Ask Ss to work in pairs and match the problem-solving steps with the phrases a–e. Ask Ss to repeat some of the ideas that they talked about in the speaking exercise. Rewrite the ideas on the board using some of the phrases a–e, e.g.:

If you go out with friends this evening, it will mean that you won't have time to do your English homework.
It's best if I buy a new mobile phone.
There are two possibilities: you could either look for a job abroad or you could work in your own country.

| Step 1 d |
| Step 2 e |
| Step 3 a |
| Step 4 c |
| Step 5 b |

Listening 2

Tell the class that they will hear a phone conversation between Magda Zawadski and Shane. Magda phones Shane about a problem with the delivery of some machine components. Read through the questions together and then play the recording. Check answers around the class.

80

UNIT 12

1 The supplier sent too many components and charged the wrong amount on the invoice, so Magda's company has paid too much.
2 option 1: send a credit note; option 2: request the accounts department to refund the money paid
3 She chooses option 2: refund the money. She may not order again for two to three months.
4 arrange the refund; ask the distributor to collect the extra units

Optional activity
Point out that one of the phrases that Magda and Shane use in the conversation is exactly the same as one of the phrases a–e. Play the recording again and ask Ss to say which phrase is exactly the same and which are different. You could also ask Ss what steps in the LEARN routine Shane uses in the conversation (Listen, Apologise, React).
Same:
I'll arrange (that for you).
Different:
It's better if you (refund the money).
We've got a problem …
We've got two options …
I can either (send you a credit note), or I can (request …)
If you (are ordering from us again), it'll be (easier to send …)
If I (arrange a refund,) you'll have to (wait …)

Speaking 1

Ask your class to turn to the audioscript on page 173 and role-play the conversation. If it is appropriate for your class, you could ask Ss to summarise the problem and the options. Then ask Ss to turn back to page 107 and role-play the conversation using phrases from the Career skills box or other phrases that they know. Reassure Ss that the role-play does not need to be word perfect, it is more important that they have the confidence to try new phrases and relax in the role-play.

Speaking 2

Ask Ss to work with a new partner. Give Ss time to read the information on their role cards (Student A on page 107, Student B on page 146) and prepare any phrases that they need. To make the telephone role-play more realistic, ask Ss to sit back-to-back with their partner, so that they cannot see their face. Then Ss prepare and role-play the second telephone conversation. After the conversations, ask Ss to say what options they had in each situation, and which option they chose. Encourage Ss to give reasons why.

Culture at work

Ask Ss to read the information about showing emotions. Make sure that they understand the questions. Ask Ss to discuss the questions and encourage them to give examples if they have encountered different types of behaviour from the ones described. You may find it helpful to look at the Culture at work box from page 59 of the Skills Book; this is reproduced below. You may also find it useful to refer to the relevant section on Culture at work in the teacher's notes supporting the Skills Book.

Calm	Expressive
If you show strong emotion when making a complaint, the other person will think you are aggressive.	If you show strong emotion, the other person will know that you take the matter seriously.
If you get angry, you 'lose face' and the other person will not respect you.	Showing anger can get results; it can take the other person by surprise.
It is not professional to show strong emotion in a business context.	If you do not show emotion, people will think you don't care.

Skills Book, Culture at work, page 59
Teacher's Book, page 160

Optional activity
Photocopiable resource 12.1 (page 115)
These are short role-play activities where Ss make and deal with complaints. Ask Ss to work with a partner. Photocopy and cut up enough cards to give one set to each pair. Ss place the cards face down on the table. Ss take turns to turn over a card. The S who turns over the card decides if they would deal with the situation face-to-face or on the phone. The information in brackets indicates the solution that they want for the problem. The S who has turned over the card then makes the complaint. They should begin by explaining what the problem is (they can decide whether to be calm/polite or angry/impolite). Their partner should react to the complaint (they can decide if they are going to try to deal with the complaint efficiently or if they are going to react in a negative way). Spend a short time after the activity asking pairs about some of their conversations: *Did you decide to deal with the complaint face-to-face or on the phone? Why? Did you get the result you wanted? How did your partner deal with the complaint?* You could ask Ss to choose one of the situations and deal with it by letter, being either:
a) the person writing the letter of complaint
b) the supplier responding to the complaint.

Dilemma

Ask Ss if they can name any companies that sell furniture (in their own country or internationally). Ask Ss to read the Dilemma brief and summarise the problem and possible causes. Ask: *What did the company do to find out more about the problem?* Get Ss to read through the complaints again and say which ones they think are most serious. Ask Ss to identify what the senior managers need to do and what their options are.

Task 1: Divide the class into three groups. Each group looks at more information about one of the options and possible results of the option on the relevant page at the back of the book. Circulate around the groups, checking understanding. Ss will need to explain their information and options, so give them time to prepare phrases if they wish to. Draw Ss' attention to the Useful phrases box and remind them of the language in the Career skills box on page 107.

Task 2: Now Ss work in groups of three. Each group should have one S from Group A, B or C from Task 1. Each S should present their information to their group and then discuss the possible options. The group should decide on the option that they think is best. Ask groups to present their choice to the class and explain the reasons why they chose that option.

Decision

Tell Ss that they will now hear Mandy Dunwoody, the Human Resources Director at House & Home, talk about how the company solved the problem of poor customer service. Ask Ss to listen and identify the two options that the company decided on (improve staff training and increase pay). Play the recording again and ask Ss what steps the company took to improve staff training and to increase pay levels (increased training for new staff; weekly training sessions; 3 per cent pay increase for all staff; 5 per cent for those staying for more than one year; bonuses). Ask: *What was the result of their decision?* (customers came back).

Write it up

Ask Ss to write a short report to the Directors of House & Home. Focus Ss on the structure that the report will take:

- brief summary of the problem
- possible options (make sure that Ss understand *bullet points*)
- best solution

You may wish to ask Ss to prepare the writing in class, complete it for homework and then compare with a partner in the next lesson before handing it in to be marked. Give each S a photocopy of the Writing preparation framework from page 188. Then use the Writing focus (Writing focus: Reports) opposite to link the use of the framework and the Style guide as Ss plan their writing. You may wish to set a word limit, e.g. no longer than the suggested answer below. It may be helpful to use the Writing feedback framework on page 189 when marking Ss' writing.

Writing focus: Reports

1 First, decide who you are.
(*In this case, Ss are senior managers at House & Home.*)

2 Every time you start to write, you need to ask yourself two questions:
   a What is the purpose of this piece of writing?
   b Who am I writing to?
(*Here Ss are writing to the Directors of House & Home. The purpose is to summarise the problem, identify options and recommend a solution.*)

3 Look at the section on Reports on page 18 of the Style guide. Notice the suggested structure of a report:
Title
Introduction
Key points
Conclusion/Summary
Is this structure appropriate for this report? Plan the points you want to include in your conclusion.
(*In this case, Ss are asked to focus on a brief summary of the problem, possible options (bullet points) and the best solution. The Style guide also notes that it is a good idea to make notes before preparing the report.*)

4 What style should the report be written in?
(*As it says in the Style guide, reports for senior managers usually use a formal style, i.e. correct grammar and spelling, use of full sentences and no contractions. It is also a good idea to avoid informal vocabulary or phrases. The language of the report must be clear.*)

5 What phrases might be appropriate in your report?
(*See the Style guide, in particular the sections for Giving the objectives, Give facts, Give reasons and Give the conclusion or Make a recommendation. See also the Useful phrases from Coursebook page 108.*)

6 Now go ahead and write the report.

7 When you have finished, check your writing for: easy-to-follow structure, clear ideas, accurate language, appropriate style.

- Style guide, Reports, page 18
- Style guide, General rules, page 3
- Skills Book, Writing 5, Short reports, page 74
- Teacher's Book, page 172
- Teacher's Book, Writing preparation framework, page 188
- Teacher's Book, Writing feedback framework, page 189

Report: Suggested answer (141 words)
Summary of the problem
This report looks at why sales are falling at House & Home and presents possible solutions. The main reason for loss of sales was poor customer service. We asked for customer feedback and found a number of common complaints about customer service.

Possible options
To improve the situation we could either:
- recruit more staff
- improve staff training
- offer higher pay to sales staff.

Best solution
We think that the best solution is to improve staff training. If we introduce weekly training sessions, we will help staff develop their customer service skills and increase their product information. We also recommend that all new staff should have intensive training in the importance of good customer service for the company. This will help staff to realise that if they give poor customer service, the whole company suffers.

Review 4

On the next two pages of the Coursebook, you will find Review 4, which reviews language, vocabulary and functional language from Units 10, 11 and 12. It can be used in a number of ways that can be adapted to suit your class, for example:

- Ss can do selected exercises for homework.
- Use in class and guide Ss to particular exercises according to their individual needs. Alternatively, if your class has similar needs, focus on exercises where they can have more practice together (Ss can work individually or in pairs).
- Use as a short progress test and review any necessary points before moving on to Unit 13.

Coursebook Review: Answers, page 103

INTELLIGENT BUSINESS (PRE-INTERMEDIATE) TEACHER'S BOOK: COURSEBOOK

Unit 13: Productivity

UNIT OBJECTIVES	
Reading:	Revolution in the car industry
Language:	Adjectives and adverbs
Vocabulary:	Design to delivery
	Just-in-time production
	Word building
	Efficient stock control
Career skills:	Managing time
Culture at work:	Managing time
Dilemma & Decision:	Bonus or bust? (memo)

Two of the most wide-reaching innovations in car assembly were:
- The Ford Motor Company's use of assembly line techniques to make cars in 1913, which allowed cars to be mass produced for the first time.
- The implementation by Japanese companies in the 1980s of just-in-time production (see Coursebook page 114). This sped up delivery of auto parts to the factory floor and reduced warehousing costs. It soon developed into worldwide industry practice.

Car manufacturers are faced with a number of challenges in the twenty-first century, which has been termed the 'second automobile century'. The traditional buying habits of consumers are changing. In the past, a potential customer would go to a car dealer and choose the car that most closely fitted their needs. Now the internet is playing a bigger role. It has been estimated that seven out of ten potential consumers now go online to compare prices and options before buying. Manufacturers rely on forecasts made by their sales departments when deciding how many cars of a particular model to produce. However, this 'built to forecast' production is not always reliable and can result in over-production – more cars being produced than can be sold. One solution that manufactureres are exploring is to 'build to order' (BTO). Groups have studied the possibility of the 'three-day-car', which would be built when a customer's order is actually placed and include features that they have chosen at the time of ordering. Another possibility for the near future is that manufacturers would transform themselves into 'Vehicle Brand Owners' (VBOs). This would mean that the production and assembly of cars would be outsourced to suppliers. Instead of focusing on building the cars, manufacturers would concentrate on vehicle design and brand development.

Keynotes

Introduce the topic by drawing Ss' attention to the picture. Ask: *What is this?* If Ss say that it is a car park ask: *What is strange about this car park?* (All the cars are the same model.) Ask Ss where this car park might be (at a car manufacturing plant). Ask Ss to read the keynotes. Check that they understand the terms in bold. Draw their attention to the glossary for this unit at the back of the book.

Coursebook, Glossary, Unit 13, page 153

Preview

Write the following headings on the board:

Increase productivity   Decrease productivity

Ask Ss to read through the list and decide which factors should go under which heading. Can Ss think of any other factors that would result in an increase or decrease in productivity?

Increase productivity: up-to-date technology, effective quality control, robots, efficient suppliers, good workers
Decrease productivity: delays in delivery of components, products that fail quality tests, out-of-date technology, shortage of staff

Listening 1 1

The listening contains a lot of information, so play it more than once if Ss need to listen again to answer the questions. If you do play it again, pause so that Ss can focus on the relevant information. Ask Ss to listen to Paul Gardner and tick the factors that he talks about. Then ask Ss to identify two factors that have helped to improve productivity and two that have been problems.

Paul Gardner talks about: up-to-date technology, products that fail quality tests, shortage of staff, good workers
Factors that improved productivity: up-to-date technology, good workers
Problems: poor quality products, shortage of staff

Listening 1 2

Play the recording again while Ss answer the questions. Again, you could pause at relevant points to allow Ss to focus on the information.

84

UNIT 13

1 When you increase productivity, you reduce costs and increase profit.
2 experience
3 It can produce a poor quality product which they can't sell.
4 managing people
5 People may not want to work overtime, or may be sick.
6 good teamwork

Speaking

Ask Ss to suggest ideas about how a car is produced. Then ask Ss to brainstorm problems that the car industry might have with productivity. Ask Ss to consider whether the factors that Paul Gardner talks about could help productivity in the car industry. Draw Ss' attention to the list in the preview exercise again. Do they think that any of these would cause problems or increase problems with productivity in the car industry?

Reading 1

Ask Ss: *How long does it take most manufacturers to put a car together?* Ask Ss to scan the article quickly and find the answer (18–20 hours). Is this quicker or slower than Ss predicted? Read through the statements 1–8 together and check that Ss understand. Go over the words in the glossary with the class and remind them of the glossary for Unit 13 at the back of the book. Get Ss to read the article and decide in pairs if the statements are true or false.

1 F   2 T   3 F   4 T   5 T   6 F   7 T   8 F

Reading 2

Now ask Ss to look through the list and see if they can remember which factors are mentioned in the text. If appropriate for your class, you could write the following prompts on the board and ask Ss to summarise what the article says about them:

Competition
Range of models
Delivery

1, 3, 4, 5

Speaking

Introduce the discussion by asking Ss to brainstorm features that new cars can have (e.g. satellite navigation, air conditioning, CD-player, fridge). List suggestions on the board, so that Ss can refer to them later in their discussions. Make sure that Ss understand the meaning of *built to order* (BTO). Ask Ss to work in pairs / small groups and answer the questions. Encourage Ss to give reasons for their preferences.

Vocabulary 1

Ask Ss to match the words with their meanings. Point out that all of the words 1–8 apart from *delay* appear in the article. If Ss need help, ask them to locate the words in the article so that they can check or work out meaning from context.

1 c   2 e   3 d   4 g   5 b   6 h   7 a   8 f

Vocabulary 2

Check how much Ss can remember about just-in-time production without referring back to the article. Then ask Ss to look at the article to check. Ask Ss to work in pairs and complete the stages of just-in-time production. Can Ss think of any other goods which might use this type of production? You could ask Ss to close their books and then see if they can remember the stages of just-in-time production.

1 order   2 Supplier
3 Components   4 Assembly
5 finished goods

Vocabulary 3

Word building is a useful way for Ss to increase their vocabulary. This exercise looks at noun/person/verb word families and noun/adjective families. Remind Ss to note new vocabulary. Ask Ss to work in pairs and complete the word table. You may wish to spend some time demonstrating changing word stress.

1 producer   2 produce
3 delivery   4 supplier
5 supply   6 manufacturer
7 manufacture   8 productive
9 efficiency

Vocabulary 4

Do the first one together to demonstrate the exercise. Ask Ss to complete the text individually and then compare their answers with a partner, before checking answers with the whole class.

85

INTELLIGENT BUSINESS (PRE-INTERMEDIATE) TEACHER'S BOOK: COURSEBOOK

> 1 components / parts
> 2 supplier
> 3 delay
> 4 finished goods
> 5 demand
> 6 stocks
> 7 order
> 8 delivery

Listening 2

Draw Ss' attention to Gavin Floyd's job. What do Ss think the role of a Production Improvement Manager is? Ask Ss to read through the questions and then play the recording. Play it again for Ss to check their answers.

> 1 to improve productivity
> 2 improve productivity and create a plan of the production process from raw materials to finished goods
> 3 that time or resources are being wasted on something that isn't essential
> 4 wasted time, wasted resources and wasted energy

Language check 1

Check if Ss know the difference between an adjective and an adverb. If Ss need help, you could write on the board:

a) *They lost customers because production was slow.*
b) *They lost customers because the cars were produced slowly.*

Ask Ss to look at *slow/slowly* and decide in which sentence it describes the noun (a = adjective) and in which it describes the verb (b = adverb). Ask Ss to look at the sentences in the book and find more examples of adjectives and adverbs. Then ask Ss to decide which sentences describe how you do something and which describe how often you do it. Can Ss suggest more examples of adverbs to go into each group, i.e. how / how often?

> **Adjective:** fierce
> **Adverbs (how):** quickly, easily, electronically, hard, well
> **Adverbs (how often):** frequently, usually

Language check 2

Ask Ss to work in pairs and complete the rules. Check answers around the class. Other examples of words that function as adjectives and adverbs include *early* and *late*. *Well* is an adverb which can also function as an adjective (e.g. *He isn't well at the moment / I'm well, thanks. And you?*). It is not necessary, at this stage, to go into this with your class, but if any Ss query the use of *well*, you may wish to explain.

> 1 *-ly*
> 2 *-ily*
> 3 *-ally*
> 4 well, hard, fast

Language check 3

Now Ss look at the examples again and complete the answers to each question by choosing the usual position of the adverb. Ask Ss to read out examples that demonstrate each rule. Remind Ss that adverbs which describe *how often* go **after** the verb *to be*, e.g. *Models are frequently updated.*

> 1 at the end of the sentence
> 2 in front of the main verb

Coursebook, Grammar reference: Adjectives and adverbs, page 161

Practice 1

Draw Ss' attention to the photo and ask them to guess what type of company they are going to read about (glass producer). Tell Ss that the management of the company wanted to carry out an experiment to see if workers could work more efficiently. The staff worked a 50-hour week. What do Ss think the management asked workers to do? (work fewer hours) Ask Ss to turn the adjectives in the box into adverbs. Then ask Ss to complete the text using the adverbs. What do Ss think of the experiment? Do they agree with the Managing Director? Why? / Why not?

> 2 regularly   3 Initially
> 4 easily   5 carefully
> 6 successfully 7 smoothly
> 8 necessarily

Practice 2

Ask Ss to read the sentences and circle the position that the adverb should go in. Do the first one together to demonstrate the exercise. When checking answers around the class, recycle the rules by asking Ss why they chose a particular position for their adverb.

> 1 c   2 a   3 c   4 a   5 c   6 c

86

UNIT 13

> **Optional activity**
> **Photocopiable resource 13.1 (page 115)**
> Ask Ss to work in pairs / small groups. Tell Ss that they are going to put together a story about a successful businessman called Simon. Photocopy and cut up enough sheets to give part A or part B to each pair/group. Cut part A and part B into phrases as indicated before handing them out. You may wish to tell Ss what the first sentence is. Ask the class to see which pair/group can put their story together in the quickest time. Then put A/B pairs/groups together and ask them to exchange information about Simon. For smaller groups, you could ask Ss to complete part A. Then ask Ss to predict what Simon does in his free time, before asking Ss to complete part B. More than one answer is possible (e.g. *Simon is a successful businessman. He's good at his job. / Simon is a good businessman. He's successful at his job*). Allow Ss flexibility, but check that their version of the story makes sense and is grammatically possible.

Practice 3

Ask Ss to work in pairs to find and correct one mistake in each sentence in the checklist.

1 necessary	2 important
3 constructively	4 quickly
5 tidy	6 useful
7 regularly	8 efficient
9 certain	

Workbook, page 54

Speaking

Ask Ss to look at the checklist again and tick the things that they usually do. Then Ss work with a partner to discuss the checklist and answer the questions. Open up the discussion to the whole class to discuss ways to improve efficiency. Encourage Ss to give examples of different techniques that they have tried.

Career skills

Introduce the topic by asking Ss: *What things can make a meeting go on too long? Can you think of ways to stop this happening?* Then ask Ss to read the Career skills information and phrases. Point out that it is important to say these phrases in a neutral tone of voice, to avoid sounding aggressive.

Listening 3

Tell Ss that the three extracts they will hear are from different parts of the same meeting. Ask Ss to listen and decide which extract is from the start, which is from the middle and which is from the end. Then play the recording again and ask Ss to tick the phrases that they hear. This would be a good opportunity to practise the intonation of the phrases. You could ask Ss to turn to the audioscript on page 174 and practise reading the extracts with a partner.

> 1
> **Extract 1** Middle
> **Extract 2** End
> **Extract 3** Start
> 2
> 1 e, c, f   2 g   3 a, b

Speaking

Ask Ss to work in groups of four to six. Get Ss to read the information and summarise the aim of the meeting. Set an appropriate time limit (probably around five minutes) for the meeting. When the time limit is up, ask Ss to present their ideas to the rest of the class.

Culture at work

Ask Ss to read the information about managing time. Make sure that they understand the questions. Ask Ss to work in pairs / small groups and discuss the questions. What style is more common in their own country? What about other countries? Encourage Ss to give examples from their own experience where possible. You may find it helpful to look at the Culture at work box from page 64 of the Skills Book; this is reproduced below. You may also find it useful to refer to the relevant section on Culture at work in the teacher's notes supporting the Skills Book.

Relaxed	Structured
People may come and go at different times throughout the meeting.	The meeting has a set start time and it is not polite to be late or to leave before the end.
Topics do not have to be discussed in a particular order.	A formal agenda is circulated before the meeting. Items are discussed in the order that they appear on the agenda.
The meeting goes on as long as necessary, until everyone agrees on a decision. Agreement is more important than deadlines.	The meeting has a pre-arranged time to finish and all decisions should be agreed by that time.

INTELLIGENT BUSINESS (PRE-INTERMEDIATE) TEACHER'S BOOK: COURSEBOOK

📄 Skills Book, Culture at work, page 64

📄 Teacher's Book, page 164

Dilemma

Ask Ss to read the brief and summarise the problem to check comprehension. Brainstorm possible ideas for what the directors should do.

Task 1: Ask Ss to work individually and read the information about the background to the problem. Ask check questions, such as:

Who had a disagreement?
What was it about?
What did the directors decide?
What did Patrick do?
Who became the new Production Manager?
Was he a good person for the job? Why? / Why not?

Read the options together and check understanding. Tell Ss that they are going to prepare arguments for one of the options for a meeting. It is important that Ss work on different options, so if you have a larger class you may wish to nominate which options Ss prepare. Make sure Ss are clear about what the options mean.

Task 2: Now Ss work in groups of four to seven. Arrange the groups so that each contains Ss who have prepared arguments for different options as much as possible. Ss role-play a meeting where they represent the directors of Scrutons Ltd. Before the meeting starts, ask Ss to nominate a person to lead the meeting (if this is not appropriate for your class, you can choose a leader at random for each group). Give each group a time limit of around ten to fifteen minutes. Draw Ss' attention to the Useful phrases box and also remind Ss about the phrases for managing time on page 117. The leader should: start the discussion, make sure that everyone has a chance to give their opinion and keep to the time limit. Encourage other members of the group to take responsibility for managing time during the meeting, too. When a decision has been reached, the leader should close the meeting.

Decision

Tell the class that they are going to hear George Mann, the Managing Director of Scrutons Ltd, talking about the decision the directors took. Ask each group which option they think he will choose. After Ss have listened, ask if they agree with the decision. Why? / Why not?

Write it up

Ask Ss to write a memo to all the staff of Scrutons Ltd to explain the decision that their group took. Encourage Ss to give reasons why they think this is the best decision. You may wish to ask Ss to prepare the writing in class, complete it for homework and then compare with a partner in the next lesson before handing it in to be marked. Give each S a photocopy of the Writing preparation framework from page 188. Then use the Writing focus (Writing focus: Memos) below to link the use of the framework and the Style guide as Ss plan their writing. It may be helpful to use the Writing feedback framework on page 189 when marking Ss' writing.

Writing focus: Memos

1 First decide who you are.
 (In this case, Ss represent the directors of Scrutons Ltd.)

2 Every time you start to write, you need to ask yourself two questions:
 a What is the purpose of this piece of writing?
 b Who am I writing to?
 (Here Ss are writing to recommend which option the directors have decided and explain why. The memo will be read by all the staff at Scrutons Ltd.)

3 Look at the section on Memos on page 16 of the Style guide. Notice the suggested structure for a memo:
 To/From/Subject/Date
 No opening greeting necessary
 Main message
 Recommendations
 Name or initials of the writer (optional)
 Is this structure appropriate for this memo? What are you going to put on the subject line? Plan the sections you are going to divide the memo into. Then brainstorm the points you might cover in each section.

4 What style should the memo be written in?
 (As it says in the Style guide, memos are short official notes that will be read by people within a company. Memos are usually less formal than business letters. The language is simple and clear and the tone is normally neutral.)

5 What phrases might be appropriate for your memo?
 (See the Style guide, particularly the phrases for making recommendations on page 16.)

6 Now go ahead and write the memo.

7 When you have finished, check your writing for: logical structure, clarity of ideas, accuracy of language, appropriateness of style.

📄 Style guide, Memos, page 16

📄 Style guide, General rules, page 3

📄 Skills Book, Writing 3, Memos, page 46

📄 Teacher's Book, page 149

📄 Teacher's Book, Writing preparation framework, page 188

📄 Teacher's Book, Writing feedback framework, page 189

Memo: Suggested answer (99 words)
To: All staff
From: The directors
Subject: Productivity
Date: (today's date)
Productivity has fallen in the last two years and the directors recently met to discuss how to solve the problem.
We have decided to appoint a new Production Manager in order to help set and achieve production targets. If staff meet production targets for six months, we will consider reducing the level at which workers can earn a productivity bonus.
If staff and management work together, we will find a way to increase productivity and to introduce a productivity bonus that all staff can work hard to achieve.

INTELLIGENT BUSINESS (PRE-INTERMEDIATE) TEACHER'S BOOK: COURSEBOOK

Unit 14: Creativity

UNIT OBJECTIVES

Reading:	A different perspective
Language:	Conditional 2
Vocabulary:	Multi-part verbs
	Suffixes
Career skills:	Finding creative solutions
Culture at work:	Showing disagreement
Dilemma & Decision:	Gold rush (meeting notes)

The opening page of the unit shows Leonardo Da Vinci (1452–1519), one of the most innovative of thinkers. He is an example of *Renaissance man*, someone with the ability to excel in a number of diverse areas. The artist, whose paintings include *The Last Supper* and *La Gioconda (The Mona Lisa)*, was also an accomplished scientist and inventor. Da Vinci's illustrated notebooks, which indicate the breadth of his interests, are divided into four main areas: painting, architecture, the elements of mechanics and human anatomy. They are written in a form of shorthand that he invented; some are written backwards, from right to left across the page, and can only be deciphered using a mirror. He was also a man of contradictions: an animal-loving vegetarian who was reportedly anti-war, yet he travelled for a year with Cesare Borgia's army as a military engineer. His designs include early versions of the tank, submarine and helicopter.

The ability to think creatively is a skill that is also important in modern business. Thinking creatively allows us to break out of routine patterns of thought and behaviour and can therefore help us to find innovative solutions to problems. Part of the process of becoming a creative thinker is becoming less reliant on our traditional approaches to problem-solving, which are based on logic and using methods that we have tried in the past and feel comfortable with. Instead, it is necessary to look at the situation from a different angle, challenging our previous assumptions and questioning our current ways of thinking. While creative thinking does not always produce better solutions, it can generate ideas and helps encourage new insights. It is a helpful tool when processes need to be reviewed and also for dealing with open-ended problems that can benefit from being approached in a fresh way.

Keynotes

Draw Ss' attention to the title and picture. Find out if Ss know who the person in the picture is (Leonardo Da Vinci, see notes opposite). Ask Ss what the connection between the title and Leonardo Da Vinci is. Ask Ss to read through the keynotes and check they understand the terms in bold. Find out if Ss have been in any situations recently where they had to think creatively. Draw Ss' attention to the glossary for this unit at the back of the book.

Coursebook, Glossary, Unit 14, page 153

Preview

Ask Ss to work in small groups. Tell Ss that they are going to read about two businesses. Draw Ss' attention to the two pictures and the titles of the texts and check they understand what sort of business each one is. After groups have discussed solutions, ask them to read the information on page 146. Discuss with the whole class what they think of the solutions.

Reading 1

Before reading the article, ask Ss to close their books. Tell them that a football club is having problems. It is making huge losses and needs to find ways to make money. Ask Ss to work in pairs / small groups and discuss what they think the club can do. Encourage Ss to think of unusual ideas. Ask Ss to open their books and look at the title of the article. What do they think it means? (*perspective* = a way of thinking of / looking at something) Draw Ss' attention to the picture. What can they see? What is the alternative perspective? (white = a wine glass / hourglass; black = two faces in profile) Read the question with the class and check comprehension. Ask Ss to tick the correct answers. Ask Ss what they think of Karen Brady's way of making money for Birmingham City football club. How did her ideas compare with the ideas they discussed in their groups?

2, 4, 5

Reading 2

Ss read the article again. Draw their attention to the glossary box and remind them of the Glossary for Unit 14 at the back of the book. Read the sentences a–e together and check for understanding. Point out the gaps in the article. Ss read the text and choose the correct position for each sentence. Do the first one together to demonstrate the exercise.

UNIT 14

| 1 e | 2 a | 3 c | 4 b | 5 d |

Speaking

Ask Ss to work in pairs and discuss the questions. If your class cannot think of any innovators, ask what inventions they think have most improved people's lives. Brainstorm ideas and then ask Ss to focus on the people who invented or developed those things. Some classes may find the second question more challenging. You could work together and look at the room that you are in from the perspective of an artist (if Ss do not respond, encourage them to think about what an artist would focus on, e.g. colour, shape, composition, etc.). Then in pairs, ask Ss to think of the same place as if they are a child and then as if a martian. Exchange ideas around the class.

Vocabulary 1

Ask Ss to look at the words and phrases in italics and choose which one could replace the word(s) in bold in each sentence. Do the first one together to demonstrate the exercise.

1 unplanned
2 clear
3 because he wanted to
4 changed
5 successful

Vocabulary 2 1

Remind Ss of the multi-part verbs they studied in Unit 7 of the Coursebook. This exercise focuses on how the verb *look* can change meaning when combined with different words. Ask Ss which of the five multi-part verbs take an object (they all do). Then do the matching exercise.

| 1 c | 2 a | 3 d | 4 b | 5 e |

Vocabulary 2 2

Ss use the five different combinations with *look* to complete the text. After checking, you may wish to ask Ss to think of other multi-part verbs that use *look* (e.g. *look over*, *look through*, *look up*, *look up to*).

1 look at
2 looks like
3 looking for
4 looks after
5 looking forward to

Vocabulary 3

Check that Ss understand what a suffix is (letters that we add to the end of a word to make a new word). Refer Ss back to Unit 13, where they saw how suffixes change adjectives into adverbs. They are now going to look at how adjectives can be formed by adding a suffix to a noun. Explain that some suffixes are simply added to the end of the noun (e.g. *tradition – traditional*, *profit – profitable*), while with others the end of the noun changes (e.g. *imagination – imaginative*, *beauty – beautiful*). Ss look at the above examples in their book and then do the exercise. Encourage them to use a good dictionary, such as Longman's *Wordwise*, to complete the exercise. Check answers around the class. Focus on the nouns ending in *e* (*practice*, *care*) and ask Ss to notice what happens to the *e* in each case when the adjective is formed. Rather than go into spelling rules at this stage, it may be more helpful to make Ss aware of patterns and encourage them to notice these when recording vocabulary.

1 practical	2 successful
3 competitive	4 accidental
5 innovative	6 careful
7 reasonable	8 fashionable

Pronunciation

Draw Ss' attention to the example. Model pronunciation with the class. Ask Ss to listen and write the noun and adjective. Play the recording again and this time ask Ss to mark the stressed syllable in each of the words. Check the stress with the class. Point out that the stress is not always predictable and that Ss should note and learn the correct pronunciation, including the stress, of new vocabulary. Drill pronunciation for the nouns and adjectives and ask Ss to practise with a partner.

1 imagi<u>na</u>tion, i<u>ma</u>ginative
2 compe<u>ti</u>tion, com<u>pe</u>titive
3 <u>ac</u>cident, acci<u>den</u>tal
4 inno<u>va</u>tion, <u>in</u>novative

Listening 1 1

To introduce the topic, ask what types of business Ss think it is important to think creatively in. Can they think of ways that a company can develop creativity in its staff? Go over the questions and make sure that Ss understand them. Before listening, get Ss to discuss possible answers. Then ask Ss to listen and answer the questions.

1 every field of business
2 There's lot of competition (so companies need to be more competitive).

Listening 1 **2**

Ask Ss to look at the gapped sentences and suggest the missing part(s) of speech for each gap (e.g. 1 = adjective; noun). Tell them that more than one word is needed to fill some of the gaps and then play part two of the recording for them to do the exercise.

> 1 careful and realistic; details
> 2 making improvements
> 3 radical changes; take risks
> 4 things are changing
> 5 make suggestions
> 6 take risks (and accept the possibility of failure)

Language check

Remind Ss of conditional 1 from Unit 12 and elicit rules. Write the following sentences on the board:

a) If we buy at a lower price, we will sell at a profit.
b) If we bought at lower price, we would sell at a profit.

Ask Ss which sentence suggests that the situation is more likely (a). You may wish to introduce your class to the word *hypothetical* to talk about situations which are unreal or improbable. Go over the examples with the class and ask Ss to identify what tense the verb following *if* is in (the past simple). Ask Ss to work in pairs and complete the rules. Refer Ss to the Grammar reference on page 160. You may wish to spend some time contrasting the examples of conditional 1 and 2 there.

> 1 past simple
> 2 would; could
> 3 In the first sentence, taking a boat is a real possibility (you may be actually at the river or planning a trip to the river). In the second sentence, you are not able to take a boat or you are not planning to take a boat, so it is an unreal or hypothetical situation.
> 4 not correct: talk about the future result of a possible action

Coursebook, Grammar reference: Conditional 2, page 160

Practice **1**

Ask Ss to work in pairs and choose the correct form of the verb in italics. Point out that some of the sentences use conditional 1 and some use conditional 2. Check answers together and go over the rules again if necessary.

> | 1 I'll | 2 could | 3 weren't |
> | 4 had | 5 make | 6 Would |
> | 7 didn't | 8 failed | |

Practice **2**

Ask Ss to look at the illustration and say what some of the people are doing (talking, arguing, having phone conversations). Ask Ss to think of adjectives to describe the office (*noisy, messy, crowded*). Does it look like the sort of place where they would like to work? Why? / Why not? Draw Ss' attention to the example and the fact that it's a conditional 2 sentence. Ask Ss to read through and summarise the information about Marta, Don, Trudy and Felipe. They then write a conditional sentence based on the information for each of them. Get Ss to compare their sentence with a partner, before checking answers around the class.

> 1 If I worked flexi-time, I could meet my children from school.
> 2 If I travelled less, I could spend more time with my family.
> 3 If I worked from home, I would/could save time and costs.
> 4 If I had a more sympathetic boss, I'd feel less stressed.

Workbook, page 57

Speaking

Tell Ss about something that would make your life easier (e.g. more time, a larger workspace, a new computer). Tell Ss what you would like to change and why, using conditional 2 sentences as appropriate. You could give Ss a few minutes to think and prepare individually, before asking them to work in small groups to discuss the questions.

Career skills

This section looks at two stages for finding creative solutions: brainstorming ideas and then evaluating the ideas that have been generated. Although Ss will have used brainstorming in earlier units of the book, they may not be fully aware of all the techniques that should be used. Point out that when brainstorming, Ss should not interrupt or comment on individual ideas. Similarly, the ideas expressed should be fairly short and quick. The aim of a brainstorming session is to generate as many ideas as possible. The ideas can be as creative and unusual as possible. All suggested ideas, however far-fetched they might be, need to be noted down (either by all individuals or a group can ask someone to volunteer to do this). After the brainstorming session comes the evaluation, where each idea is looked at individually. Sometimes it helps to identify all the ideas that definitely would not work and focus on the possibilities that are left. Ask Ss if they use these techniques. What situations do they use them in? Do they find them useful? Ask Ss to study the information and phrases in the Career skills box and answer the questions. Then ask Ss to read the problem. Ask Ss to summarise for comprehension. Ask them to work in small groups and brainstorm solutions to the problem.

Each group should nominate someone to note all the ideas. Set a time limit (five minutes). Ask Ss to spend a short time evaluating the suggestions and decide on two or three that are possible solutions.

> **Brainstorming:** Would it help if … ? What else could we do? What if we … ?
> **Evaluating:** If we did that, it would be … That could be a solution. That wouldn't work / wouldn't help.
> **Defining:** What we really want is …

Listening 2 **1**

Tell Ss that they will hear three members of the finance company discussing three possible solutions to the problem. Before listening to part one, ask Ss to look at the solutions and say which they think would/wouldn't work. Why? / Why not? Play the recording and ask Ss to identify which ideas the people speaking think will work / not work. Then play it again and ask Ss what reasons the speakers give.

> Reprint all the brochures – too expensive
> Fire the person responsible – wouldn't help
> Print labels – would work but would take a long time; it would be obvious they had made a mistake

Listening 2 **2**

Tell Ss that they are going to hear someone suggesting a new idea. Ask Ss to suggest what the idea might be. Play part two of the recording and ask Ss to answer the questions. Ask Ss to think of the advantages and disadvantages of the suggestion. If they worked for the company, which of the four suggestions would they choose? Why?

> **Idea:** Ask the telephone company to change the customer enquiries number to match the one on the brochure.
> It could work if that number was available.

Speaking

Some Ss might prefer a short time to prepare ideas. However, if your class are confident enough to go straight into brainstorming, this would be most useful. Ask Ss to work in small groups. Make sure that one of the group volunteers / is nominated to note ideas or that all Ss in the group agree to do so. Give Ss five minutes for the brainstorming part of the discussion and five or ten minutes to evaluate ideas. Ask groups to decide which idea or ideas would work best. Have a feedback session with the whole class for Ss to share ideas.

Culture at work

Ask Ss to read the information and discuss it with a partner. Encourage Ss to give examples from their own experience. You may find it helpful to look at the Culture at work box from page 67 of the Skills Book; this is reproduced below. You may also find it useful to refer to the relevant section on Culture at work in the teacher's notes supporting the Skills Book.

Refuse indirectly	Refuse directly
People prefer to avoid confrontation.	People prefer to say 'No' directly.
Communication is tactful. A direct 'Yes' or 'No' might offend.	Communication is clear, direct and to the point.
People often use indirect ways of saying 'No', for example: *Yes, but …* *I'm afraid that's not possible.* *I'm not sure that we can do that.*	People often use direct ways of saying 'No', for example: *No.* *No, we won't do that.*

Skills Book, Culture at work, page 67

Teacher's Book, page 167

Dilemma

Ask the class if anyone is wearing something made of gold or hold up something that you have that is made of gold and ask Ss: *What is this made of?* Ask Ss where gold is found (focus on under/above ground rather that geographic location, i.e. under ground). How do companies get it? What is this process called? (mining) What can gold be used for? You may wish to draw Ss' attention to the word family that goes with the verb *to mine*. Ask Ss to name the place (*a mine*), the job (*a miner*) and the concept/process (*mining*). Ask Ss if they can think of any other jobs that people who work for a mining company might do (e.g. *engineers, geologists, administrative staff*). Can Ss think of any other types of mine? (e.g. *coal, iron, diamond*) Ask Ss to read the brief and summarise the information to check understanding. Check Ss are familiar with the terms used (*productive, ounces, extracted, low grade, exploration*).

Task: Ask Ss to work in small groups. Tell them that they are going to hold a meeting to evaluate the possible solutions in the brief. They should then brainstorm some other creative solutions and evaluate those, too. Ask Ss to add at least one more idea to the list in the brief. Draw Ss' attention to the Useful phrases box and remind Ss about the phrases for brainstorming and evaluating on page 125. Circulate and help where necessary.

INTELLIGENT BUSINESS (PRE-INTERMEDIATE) TEACHER'S BOOK: COURSEBOOK

Write it up

Ask Ss to work with their group to write a summary of the meeting. They should list the main solutions that they discussed (it is not necessary to list every idea from their brainstorming session, only those ideas from the brief and any other solutions that the group agreed were a good idea). Give each S a photocopy of the Writing preparation framework from page 188; then use the Writing focus (Writing focus: Meeting notes) opposite to link the use of the framework and the Style guide as Ss plan their writing. It may be a good idea to set a word limit, e.g. no longer than the suggested answer below, or to give Ss a time limit to write their summary (ten to fifteen minutes). If you do not wish your class to do this as a group exercise, ask Ss to prepare their summary of the meeting individually and then compare with other members of their group before handing it in to be marked. It may be helpful to use the Writing feedback framework on page 189 when marking Ss' writing.

Decision

Ask Ss to listen to a financial news report about Goldcorp. Did Rob McEwen choose the same solution (a competition) as their team? Why do they think he chose that solution?

Writing focus: Meeting notes

1 First, decide who you are.
 (In this case, Ss are employees of Goldcorp.)

2 Every time you start to write, you need to ask yourself two questions:
 a What is the purpose of this piece of writing?
 b Who am I writing to?
 (Here Ss are writing to give a summary of a meeting looking at possible solutions to Goldcorp's problems. The notes will be read by the other people at the meeting.)

3 Look at the section on Meeting notes on page 20 of the Style guide. Notice the suggested structure for the notes:
 Subject and date of the meeting
 A list of the people who attended
 A list of the points that you discussed
 Is this structure appropriate for these meeting notes? What are you going to put as the subject of the meeting? Plan the sections you are going to divide the notes into.

4 What style should the memo be written in?
 (As it says in the Style guide, if your notes are going only to colleagues and co-workers, you can write in an informal style, using familiar abbreviations and contractions. Full sentences are not always necessary.)

5 What phrases might be appropriate for your meeting notes?
 (See the Style guide, particularly the sections on Reporting the discussion and Reporting decisions on page 20. There would also be opportunities for Ss to use conditional 2 when noting what could or would happen.)

6 Now go ahead and write the report.

7 When you have finished, check your writing for: easy-to-follow structure, clear ideas, accurate language, appropriate style.

Style guide, Meeting notes, page 20

Teacher's Book, Writing preparation framework, page 188

Teacher's Book, Writing feedback framework, page 189

UNIT 14

Meeting notes: Suggested answer (295 words)

Meeting to discuss possible solutions, 24th October 2007

Present: RG, KPD, YS, FJ

We discussed possible solutions to Goldcorp's current problems and brainstormed some new ideas. We also outlined what could happen in each possible situation.

- **Close the mine.**

If we closed the mine, all the company's staff would be made redundant. This would not be a good option for the staff and could be expensive for the company. It would be better to consider other possible solutions first.

- **Invest in more geologists and new equipment.**

This option could result in further losses for the company if the geologists were still unable to find the gold.

- **Continue to explore with the existing team and no new investment.**

We cannot guarantee that the existing team will find any results. It is also taking too long. The costs of running the mine are high and we will make further losses if a solution is not found quickly.

- **Hold a competition to find the gold.**

The company could offer a prize for any individual or team who finds the gold. This would mean that the company would have not one team, but many working on the project, but would not have to fund the research (which would be very expensive). This could be a good solution.

- **Offer our team of geologists a bonus if they find the gold within a time limit.**

This would also be a good solution.

- **Offer our geologists the same amount of money as we would offer as prize money.**

The bonus would be reduced every week that the team fails to find gold. The chance of earning a generous bonus would motivate the team to work harder and longer and to think creatively to find the gold.

Optional activity
Photocopiable resource 14.1 (page 116)

Give each S a photocopy of the creative thinking exercises. Ask Ss to complete the first exercise individually. You may wish to demonstrate the exercise by drawing two random shapes on the board and asking Ss to suggest how to make it into a picture. Ask Ss to add lines or shapes on their page to make a picture. Then ask Ss to compare their drawings with a partner. Ask Ss to work in pairs / small groups to do exercise 2. There are no right or wrong answers to these questions; they are simply exercises for using different parts of the brain.

INTELLIGENT BUSINESS (PRE-INTERMEDIATE) TEACHER'S BOOK: COURSEBOOK

Unit 15: Motivation

UNIT OBJECTIVES

Reading: The kids are all right
Language: Present perfect and past simple
Vocabulary: Personal qualities
Management styles
Multi-part verbs
Career skills: Giving reasons
Culture at work: Formal and informal presentations
Dilemma & Decision: Hot-desking (memo)

This unit looks at factors that motivate us, including office culture and management styles. Management styles can vary from company to company and manager to manager, and can also be influenced by cultural factors. Some organisations have an authoritarian company culture. This means that the manager's role is to pass down information and implement decisions from above. Decisions are often made at the highest levels in the hierarchy, so a manager might have little true power or responsibility. This can lead to a company culture where employees avoid making decisions in case they get the blame if things go wrong. In addition, when decisions have to be made it can be time consuming, as they may need to be passed back up the management chain for approval or be decided by committee. In a participative organisation, the manager's job is to provide assistance to subordinates to allow them to do their job effectively. Subordinates may also take part in the decision-making process. Company organisation will rarely be strictly one or the other of these extremes.

It is not only the culture of a whole company which affects motivation. Employees can be motivated or demotivated according to job-satisfaction, management support, working environment and their own needs and expectations. Many workers would also want the opportunity to progress in their career and learn new skills. A positive or negative working atmosphere can also differ from department to department, and can be influenced by management style. Research suggests that there are four major management leadership styles worldwide:

- Democratic: the leader consults staff and empowers them to make decisions
- Collaborative: the leader negotiates targets and solutions with the team, becomes involved as a team player
- Autocratic: the leader controls staff, makes decisions, demands loyalty
- Paternalistic: the leader is a paternal (or maternal!) figure who looks after the group's interests.

An employee or team can be demotivated if they encounter a style of management or leadership that they have not experienced before and do not know how to adapt to. This can be a particular challenge for international managers, if they attempt to apply a style of management which is acceptable in their own culture, but which meets resistance in the culture that they are working in.

Keynotes

Ask Ss to look at the picture and say what the man is doing (he's riding a motorised scooter). Where do they think he might be going? (work) Point to the scooter and ask: *Does that look like fun? Have you had a go on one? Would you like to?* Draw Ss' attention to the title and ask: *Do people usually have fun at work? Why? / Why not?* Ask Ss to read the keynotes and check that they understand the words in bold. Refer Ss to the glossary for this unit at the back of the book. Find out if Ss agree that companies are less hierarchical now than in the past. Can they think of any examples of companies that are and are not hierarchical? Do modern employees still want to be rewarded for loyalty to the company? What things do they expect for their loyalty? What things make a good working environment? What things can make a bad working environment?

Coursebook, Glossary, Unit 15, page 154

Preview

Go through the items in the list and check Ss' understanding. Ask Ss to look at the list individually and choose three factors that motivate them to work harder. If none of the items motivates, ask Ss to think about what does motivate them. Then ask Ss to tell their partner about why they chose the three factors. Encourage Ss to look for differences and similarities.

UNIT 15

> **Optional activity**
> You might want to ask the class to brainstorm factors that can demotivate. Ask Ss to work in pairs and prioritise the five factors that are most demotivating. Choose two or three factors and ask Ss to suggest positive ways to improve the situation (e.g. if a demotivating factor is low salary, they could ask for a pay rise).

Listening 1 1

Ask Ss to think of things that a human resources manager does in his/her job (recruit staff, deal with employee training and development, find solutions to personnel problems, etc.). To preview exercise 3 before listening, you could also write *Do* and *Don't* on the board and ask Ss to brainstorm things that a manager should do and not do to motivate workers (try to encourage Ss to give short suggestions such as *do listen / don't shout*, etc.). Tell Ss that they are going to hear Dilys Breeze, a human resources manager, talking about motivating workers in her company. Which factors from the list do Ss think she will mention? Play the recording for Ss to tick the factors that she mentions.

> She mentions all the factors in the list.

Listening 1 2

Ask Ss to listen again and complete the extract. Ask Ss to take turns reading the extract to a partner. Help Ss with stress and intonation where necessary.

> 1 contribution   2 useful
> 3 listen to   4 skills
> 5 learn

Listening 1 3

Ask Ss to look at the items and tick the ones that they remember Dilys mentioning. Play the recording again for Ss to check.

> stimulate, encourage, support, listen, help

Speaking

Ask Ss to think back to the discussion that they had in Preview. Did they have similar or different ideas to Dilys Breeze? Do they agree about the things that she says about managers? Why? / Why not? Do Ss think that it is a manager's or company's duty to motivate staff, or an employee's duty to motivate himself/herself?

Reading 1

Ask Ss to look at the photo on page 129. Get Ss to think of words to describe what the office looks like (e.g. *big, crowded, open-plan*) and what sort of working environment it would be (e.g. *serious, traditional*). Do most of the people in the office look old or young? Before Ss read, ask them to work in pairs and suggest why companies are trying to attract young people. Then ask Ss to quickly read through the article and answer the question. Check ideas around the class.

> their technical skills; enthusiasm for change; they learn and relearn faster; they risk more to try new things
> (Other possible answers: they are creative and energetic)

Reading 2

Ask Ss to read the article again and answer the questions. You may wish to point out that question 1 refers to activities and working environment rather than factors such as pay. Draw Ss' attention to the glossary and remind them of the glossary for Unit 15 at the back of the book. Ask Ss to compare their answers with a partner. Encourage Ss to say what information in the text helped them to answer the questions. Ask Ss if they have ever played basketball, volleyball or pingpong (table tennis).

> 1 basketball courts, volleyball nets, Nerf guns, a games room with pingpong, bright colours inside, a monthly fun budget for each department
> 2 opportunity, responsibility, respect, challenges, rewards

Reading 3

Get Ss to go through the questions and answer them from memory and then to read the text a final time to check. You could ask Ss to put the sentences that refer to the past into the past tense.

> 1 P   2 P   3 T   4 P   5 T   6 P   7 T

Speaking

Ask Ss to discuss the questions in pairs / small groups. Encourage Ss to give reasons for their opinions. Ask Ss to think of ways that the office culture in companies in their country has changed in recent years.

INTELLIGENT BUSINESS (PRE-INTERMEDIATE) TEACHER'S BOOK: COURSEBOOK

Optional activity
Photocopiable resource 15.1 (page 116)
Ask Ss to work in pairs. Give each pair a copy of the information and a sheet of A4/A3/flipchart paper (the bigger the better). Tell Ss that they are interior designers specialising in office environments. NuBroom is a new company. It has a big budget to spend on redecorating the offices. The directors of the company want the staff to have as many things as possible to help them enjoy being at work. Ask Ss to read the information about the people and brainstorm things that they could have in the office to entertain them. The office needs to be both a creative, stimulating environment and also have areas where people can relax, rest and work quietly when they need to. Ask pairs to design the layout of the office. They can use the space in any way that they wish. Encourage Ss to think of details such as the colour of the walls, whether there would be pictures on the walls, etc. Ask pairs to join with another pair and describe the office that they created.

Vocabulary 1

Introduce the topic by asking Ss to suggest characteristics that are useful in a manager and those that are useful in an employee. Draw Ss' attention to the initial letter at the beginning of each gap and the paragraph number at the end. Encourage Ss to think about what the missing qualities might be before referring to the relevant paragraph in the text to check.

1 enthusiasm	2 courage
3 loyalty	4 talent
5 ambition	6 initiative

Vocabulary 2

Ask Ss if they can think of any management styles. If Ss do not respond, point to the illustration in the diagram and ask what it might represent (traditional hierarchy in an organisation). Ask them to describe the type of hierarchy (CEO or managing director at the top, a row of managers and then a row of employees). Go through the words in the box and check understanding. Ask Ss to work with a partner and complete the text.

Have Ss experienced any of the management styles mentioned in the text (either as a manager or as an employee)? Ask Ss to discuss which sort of company they would prefer to work for and why.

1 hierarchy	2 senior
3 subordinates	4 superiors
5 seniority	6 responsibility
7 reward	8 level

Vocabulary 3 ▇

Ss have looked at multi-part verbs in Units 7 and 14. You may wish to revise some of those verbs with the class. In this section, Ss focus on words that can combine with *take*. Go through the verbs in bold in sentences 1–6. Check which verbs Ss have seen before. Then ask Ss to work with a partner and match the examples with the meanings a–f. You could ask Ss to close books and ask one S to read out a meaning for the other Ss to say what verb it is.

| 1 b | 2 c | 3 d | 4 a | 5 f | 6 e |

Additional information about multi-part verbs

There are generally two types of multi-part verbs:
- In some cases, the second part of the verb (e.g. *on*, *of*, *up*) is a preposition and normally goes before the object (e.g. *They looked for new offices* **not** ~~*They looked new offices for*~~).
- In other cases, the second part is an adverb particle, which can go either before or after the noun. Both these sentences are possible: *They took off 10 per cent* or *They took 10 per cent off.*

For pronoun objects (e.g. *it*, *her*) the rules are different. A pronoun object must come **after** a preposition but **before** a particle:
They looked for them **not** ~~*They looked them for.*~~
They took it off **not** ~~*They took off it.*~~

Use your knowledge of your class to decide how much information your Ss require.

Vocabulary 3 ▇

Ask Ss to complete the sentences using the words in the box. Ask Ss to compare answers with a partner.

| 1 over | 2 up | 3 off |
| 4 on | 5 part | 6 place |

Language check

In Unit 10, Ss were introduced to the present perfect. You may wish to revise the form of the present perfect and ask Ss if they can remember some of the time expressions that are often used with it (e.g. *recently, in the last three months, in recent years*). In this section, Ss focus on contrasting the present perfect with the past simple. Ask Ss to look at the sentences 1–6 and match them with the rules a–e. Make sure that Ss are aware that one of the rules matches two examples. You may also want to draw Ss' attention to the way that the present perfect and past simple are used with multi-part verbs by briefly looking back to the examples in Vocabulary 3 on page 130.

1 a   2 c   3 b   4 e   5 d   6 d

Coursebook, Grammar reference: Past simple, page 159 and Present perfect, page 160

Practice 1

Ask Ss to do this in pairs. Encourage Ss to explain their choices.

1 b   2 a   3 a   4 a

Practice 2

Before starting the exercise, ask Ss to go through the text and identify the time expressions. Encourage Ss to discuss whether the time expressions are usually used with the present perfect or the past simple. Ask Ss to complete the text using the present perfect or past simple of the verb in brackets. Ask Ss: *What was the company like in the past?* (traditional). Then ask Ss to identify the things that have changed in the company since Christian began working there (flatter hierarchy, flexible working hours, bonus system).

1 has worked	2 have been
3 had	4 took over
5 has developed	6 came
7 has changed	8 received
9 have enjoyed	

Workbook, page 61

Speaking

Point out that the change does not have to be big or dramatic, but could be, for example, something that has made their life easier, a change of routine, a change in the cost of living. If Ss do not want to talk about their own life, encourage them to talk about changes in their work or country. Give Ss time to prepare, but encourage them not to read directly from notes when they speak to their partner.

Listening 2 1

Ask Ss to close their books. Tell them that they are going to hear Clark Morris, a human resources consultant, talking about employee motivation. Clark talks about the four Cs. Can Ss think of any words that would help employee motivation that begin with *c*? Then ask Ss to brainstorm things that a manager can do to help staff feel motivated. Open books. Read through the information with the class. Play the recording and ask Ss to match the factors 1–4 with the explanations a–d. Then play the recording again and ask Ss to say what managers should do to create a good climate or company culture. Ask Ss if they agree with Clark's ideas. Why? / Why not? Have Ss worked in any companies that followed any of the four Cs of motivation?

1 c   2 a   3 d   4 b

Listening 2 2

Ask Ss what they can remember about creating a good climate. Play the recording again (possibly just from 'In order to create a good climate ...' rather than the whole of it) and ask Ss to note the things Clark says that managers should do. Get Ss to check together before checking answers with the whole class.

listen to the staff; respond to their suggestions; encourage staff to have ideas and use initiative; support their team

Career skills

Point out that sometimes our reasons for doing things may not be clear to others, so we need to explain why. It helps people to understand how we arrived at our point of view or decision. Ask Ss to read the information and phrases. Then ask Ss to give reasons why you should not give them homework this week.

Listening 3 1

Read through the questions and check understanding. Then ask Ss to listen and answer. Get Ss to compare answers with a partner. Then check answers around the class.

1 Because the pay wasn't very good.
2 Because it wasn't a challenge.
3 So that she can learn something new and develop her skills.
4 The company is small. That means that the career prospects are not very good.
5 In order to improve his career prospects.

Listening 3 **2**

Play the recording again and ask Ss to tick the phrases in the Career skills box that they hear. Play it again and ask Ss to match exact phrases to the examples (or ask Ss to turn to the audioscript on page 176).

> All the phrases are used apart from *because of* (+ noun).
> 1 Because ... so ...
> 2 Because ... so ...
> 3 So that I can ...
> 4 That means that ...
> 5 In order to ... so ...

Listening 3 **3**

Ask Ss to work in pairs and complete the sentences, using the phrases from the Career skills box.

> 1 because 2 so
> 3 That means that 4 so that
> 5 Because of 6 In order to

Speaking

You could begin the exercise by telling Ss about your goals in the coming year. Encourage Ss to ask you questions and you can give reasons in response. If your class are having problems thinking of goals, draw their attention to the examples and brainstorm some more, noting suggestions on the board. Ask Ss to discuss the questions with a partner. Circulate and encourage Ss to give reasons. Make a note of any good examples of language and share them on the board to consolidate.

Culture at work

Ask Ss to read the information and discuss the questions in pairs / small groups. Encourage Ss to give examples from their own experience and also to give reasons for their preferences. You may find it helpful to look at the Culture at work box from page 71 of the Skills Book; this is reproduced opposite. You may also find it useful to refer to the relevant section on Culture at work in the teacher's notes supporting the Skills Book.

	Informal	Formal
Dress	Casual	A business suit
Language	You use everyday expressions and short sentences to explain information.	You use formal expressions with technical vocabulary.
Audience	You use humour and stories to make the audience relax.	You do not use humour or stories. You keep to factual information.

Skills Book, Culture at work, page 71

Teacher's Book, page 170

Dilemma

Check that Ss understand the term *hot-desking* and ask Ss if they have ever worked like this. What are the advantages and disadvantages of having an individual work space? What are the advantages and disadvantages of hot-desking? Encourage Ss to think of the advantages and disadvantages from the point of view of the company and employees. What sort of jobs are suitable for hot-desking? Go over any vocabulary that Ss may need help with (e.g. *B2B*, *downturn*, *rent*, *cupboard*, *unit*). Ask Ss to read the brief and the information about hot-desking and individual work spaces. Ask Ss to summarise the situation in order to check comprehension.

Task 1: Divide the class into two groups, A and B. Each group reads opinions from three members of staff on the relevant page at the back of the book. Ask Ss to discuss these opinions and decide whether to introduce hot-desking or not. All Ss should make a note of their reasons.

Task 2: Ask Ss to work in small groups. Each group should contain an equal mix of Ss from Groups A and B. Those Ss who were in Group A should present their decision and give reasons to the Ss who were in Group B. Draw Ss' attention to the Useful phrases box. As Group B Ss listen, they should ask for explanations if necessary. The Group B Ss present their decision and reasons. Group A Ss should ask for explanations where necessary.

Decision

Ask Ss to listen to Kok Tan Hiang, the CEO of a Hong Kong software design company, explaining the decision that was taken when his company moved to new offices. Ask Ss what the advantages of hot-desking were for the company (more democracy, better communication) and the staff (dynamic, creative). Who liked the new arrangements? (sales and technical teams) Who didn't like them? (lawyers) What did the company do to compromise? (made some permanent work spaces available)

UNIT 15

Write it up

Tell Ss that they are going to write a memo to the staff of Sirius to tell them the decision that was taken and explain the reasons why. You may wish to ask Ss to prepare the writing in class, complete it for homework and then compare with a partner in the next lesson before handing it in to be marked. Give each S a photocopy of the Writing preparation framework from page 188. Then use the Writing focus (Writing focus: Memos) below to link the use of the framework and the Style guide as Ss plan their writing. It may be helpful to use the Writing feedback framework on page 189 when marking Ss' writing.

Writing focus: Memos

1 First, decide who you are.
   (In this case, Ss are senior managers of Sirius.)

2 Every time you start to write, you need to ask yourself two questions:
   a What is the purpose of this piece of writing?
   b Who am I writing to?
   (Here Ss are writing to say whether staff will hot-desk or have individual work spaces.)

3 Look at the section on Memos on page 16 of the Style guide. Notice the suggested structure for a memo:
   To/From/Subject/Date
   No opening greeting necessary
   Main message
   Recommendations
   Name or initials of the writer (optional)
   Is this structure appropriate for this memo? What are you going to put on the subject line? Plan the sections you are going to divide the memo into. Then brainstorm the points you might cover in each section.

4 What style should the memo be written in?
   (As it says in the Style guide, memos are short, official notes that will be read by people within a company. Memos are usually less formal than business letters. The language is simple and clear and the tone is normally neutral.)

5 What phrases might be appropriate for your memo?
   (See the Style guide, particularly the phrases for making recommendations on page 16. See also the Useful phrases on page 133 and 134 of the Coursebook.)

6 Now go ahead and write the memo.

7 When you have finished, check your writing for: logical structure, clarity of ideas, accuracy of language, appropriateness of style.

Style guide, Memos, page 16
Style guide, General rules, page 3
Skills Book, Writing 3, Memos, page 46
Teacher's Book, page 149

Teacher's Book, Writing preparation framework, page 188
Teacher's Book, Writing feedback framework, page 189

Memo: Suggested answer (127 words)

To: All staff
From: Senior management, Sirius
Subject: Hot-desking
Date: (today's date)

As you all know, we will soon be moving to new offices. This means that we will have less space. In order to use the work space as efficiently as possible, we considered hot-desking and traditional individual work spaces.

We have decided to use hot-desking in the new offices. This is because some members of staff (for example, the sales staff) are often out of the office. Also, we hope that hot-desking will help communication and will create a relaxed atmosphere.

If any members of staff have a problem with this arrangement, we can look into alternatives. This is an exciting move for our company. We hope that you will enjoy your new working arrangements.

Optional activity
Photocopiable resource 15.2 (page 117)

Ask Ss to work in small groups. Give each group a photocopy of the board game. To move around the board, Ss should take turns flipping a coin: *heads* means move one space forwards, *tails* means move two spaces forwards. Ss should use small pieces of paper as counters. Ask Ss to take turns to move their counter and follow the instructions on the square they land on. The first person to reach the last square wins. This game can also be cut up and used as a card activity with pairs/groups taking turns to turn over a card and follow the instructions.

Review 5

On the next two pages of the Coursebook you will find Review 5, which reviews language, vocabulary and functional language from Units 13, 14 and 15. It can be used in a number of ways that can be adapted to suit your class, for example:

- Ss can do selected exercises for homework.
- Use in class and guide Ss to particular exercises according to their individual needs. Alternatively, if your class has similar needs, focus on exercises where they can have more practice together (Ss can work individually or in pairs).
- Use as a short progress test and review any necessary points.

Coursebook Review: Answers, page 104

Coursebook Review: Answers

Review 1: Answers

Language check, page 31, Present simple and continuous
1 analyses   2 is playing   3 plays
4 are working   5 are conducting   6 read
7 are buying   8 don't read

Language check, page 31, some / any / a / much / many / a lot of
1 a   2 c   3 b   4 b   5 c
6 a   7 a   8 b

Language check, page 31, Offers and requests
1 d   2 a   3 f   4 c   5 b   6 e

Language check, page 31, Consolidation
1 Could you   2 some   3 I'd like to
4 Let me   5 any   6 an
7 does that cost?   8 a lot   9 Do you have
10 costs   11 Can I   12 Do you want to
13 I'm waiting   14 could

Vocabulary check, page 32 **1**
1 founders   2 partners   3 set up
4 run   5 produce

Vocabulary check, page 32 **2**
1 c   2 a   3 a   4 b   5 c
6 a   7 a   8 c   9 a

Career skills, page 32, Explaining your job
1 d   2 b   3 a   4 c   5 e

Career skills, page 32, Checking information
1 Sorry, did you say 16 or 60?
2 Sorry, I didn't catch that.
3 So that's about half?
4 Do you mean 16 per cent of all Britons?
5 Sorry, can you repeat the last number, please?

Career skills, page 32, Being polite
1 Can I introduce; meet you
2 Would you like to; would be very nice
3 for all your help; You're welcome
4 Is it OK
5 I'm afraid

Review 2: Answers

Language check, page 57, Comparatives and superlatives
1 smaller   2 more stylish
3 more attractive   4 more comfortable
5 bigger/biggest   6 better
7 lowest   8 most expensive
9 more profitable   10 higher

Language check, page 57, The past simple
1 founded   2 took
3 didn't start   4 bought
5 developed   6 invested
7 grew   8 increased

Language check, page 57, Modals of possibility
1 could   2 won't   3 may not
4 will   5 won't

Language check, page 57, Consolidation
1 launched   2 became   3 didn't have
4 took   5 cheapest   6 sold
7 will   8 greater   9 reached
10 than   11 could   12 as
13 better   14 could   15 will

Vocabulary check, page 58
1 c   2 a   3 a   4 c   5 a
6 c   7 c   8 a   9 c   10 b
11 a   12 c   13 b

Career skills, page 58, Describing products
1 d   2 e   3 a   4 b   5 c

Career skills, page 58, Telling a story
1 To begin with,
2 Then,
3 For the next two years,
4 So what did he do?
5 After
6 And now

Career skills, page 58, Making predictions
1 I'm sure I'll
2 I think it's unlikely that I'll
3 I'll probably
4 It's possible that
5 I definitely won't

Review 3: Answers

Language check, page 83, Future plans and intentions
1 'm not coming
2 're meeting
3 'll stay
4 Are you going to come
5 'll phone
6 'll talk
7 is travelling
8 is not going to be / won't be

Language check, page 83, The imperative
1 Let's discuss …
2 If the company offers you …
3 Please don't touch …
4 Please be careful …
5 Don't use this phone …
6 … please take a message.
7 If you don't have the right qualifications …
8 Please tell me …

Language check, page 83, Modals of obligation
1 f / g / h	2 e	3 b / c
4 h	5 d	6 b / c
7 a	8 f / g / h	

Language check, page 83, Consolidation
1 you're going to start
2 is coming
3 I'm going to explain
4 have
5 must
6 please do it
7 you mustn't
8 are travelling
9 have to
10 is going to have
11 will give
12 should
13 don't have to
14 don't
15 shouldn't

Vocabulary check, page 84 1
1 a 2 b 3 b 4 c 5 a

Vocabulary check, page 84 2
1 b 2 c 3 a 4 a 5 c 6 b

Career skills, page 84, Making an appointment
1 I'd like to arrange
2 Can we meet
3 I'm afraid not
4 free
5 I can't make
6 Let's say
7 see you

Career skills, page 84, Explaining what to do
1 be better   2 important
3 a good   4 forget to
5 sure

Career skills, page 84, Making suggestions
1 How about   2 a good idea
3 we could   4 I'm not sure
5 why   6 I think we should

Review 4: Answers

Language check, page 109, The present perfect
1 hasn't been   2 has fallen
3 has stayed   4 hasn't seen
5 has risen   6 have decided
7 have introduced

Language check, page 109, Passives
1 The results of this survey are described in our latest report.
2 The new model is called the 'Robomat'.
3 A new office block is being built in the city centre.
4 The building will be completed next year.
5 A new drink has been developed by the company.
6 Salaries were raised by 4 per cent last year.
7 Only one person was offered a job.
8 The T408 is manufactured in Germany.

Language check, page 109, Conditional 1
1 will pay   2 don't have
3 don't hurry   4 won't lose
5 doesn't pay   6 will need
7 will learn   8 is

Language check, page 109, Consolidation
1 has improved   2 have found
3 read   4 are
5 are scheduled   6 have become
7 be seen   8 was
9 visit   10 has taken
11 has been reported 12 is being
13 don't   14 will be

Vocabulary check, page 110 1
1 a 2 c 3 b 4 c 5 b

Vocabulary check, page 110 2
1 a 2 a 3 c 4 a 5 c 6 b

INTELLIGENT BUSINESS (PRE-INTERMEDIATE) TEACHER'S BOOK: COURSEBOOK

Career skills, page 110, Describing a graph
1. fluctuated
2. fell to
3. remained steady
4. reached a peak of
5. dropped from 6% to 4.5%

Career skills, page 110, Expressing arguments
d e b c a

Career skills, page 110, Dealing with problems
A I've got a problem with my laptop – it isn't working.
B Right. Well there are two possibilities: we could send someone to you to look at it, or you could bring it to us.
A I can't bring it to you very easily – it's connected to other equipment at my desk.
B OK, but if we send someone to you, you may have to wait till this afternoon.
A That's OK, I can wait.
B Fine. Then I'll arrange for someone to come to you.

Review 5: Answers

Language check, page 135, Adjectives and adverbs
1 recently   2 individually
3 frequently   4 highly
5 helpful   6 high
7 productive   8 popular

Language check, page 135, Conditional 2
1 were   2 wouldn't look   3 had
4 didn't offer 5 would enjoy   6 was
7 would work   8 installed

Language check, page 135, Present perfect and past simple
1 started   2 left   3 joined
4 has been   5 has had   6 sold
7 didn't like 8 asked   9 has worked

Language check, page 135, Consolidation
1 drank
2 has become
3 have opened
4 has risen
5 recent
6 rapidly
7 close
8 has now reached
9 could
10 noisy
11 would go
12 was
13 regularly
14 would
15 was

Vocabulary check, page 136
1 b   2 a   3 b   4 c   5 b
6 a   7 a   8 b   9 c   10 b

Career skills, page 136, Managing time
1 d   2 a   3 h   4 b   5 g

Career skills, page 136, Finding creative solutions
1 What could we do
2 What if we
3 That wouldn't help
4 Would it help if
5 If we did that
6 That could be a solution

Career skills, page 136, Giving reasons
1 because   2 so that   3 in order
4 means that 5 because of

Coursebook Glossary Test: Answers

1 A   2 C   3 D   4 B   5 B
6 C   7 A   8 A   9 B   10 B
11 B   12 C   13 A   14 D   15 C
16 C   17 C   18 D   19 B   20 A
21 C   22 B   23 C   24 C   25 C
26 D   27 B   28 D   29 A   30 D
31 A   32 C   33 B   34 D   35 B
36 C   37 B   38 B   39 D   40 D
41 C   42 B   43 B   44 D   45 A

Photocopiable resource 1.1: Company activities

Company name

The name of the company is ...
The company is called ...

Main sector(s)
(e.g. technology, media)

Its main sector is ...
Its main sectors are ...
It concentrates on ...
Its core business is ...

Products/Services

It produces/manufactures ...
It provides ...

Country/Countries where the company operates

The company has factories/offices in ...
It's an international company with factories/offices in ...
The company has factories/offices in ... countries around the world.

Other
(e.g. number of employees, who runs the company, etc.)

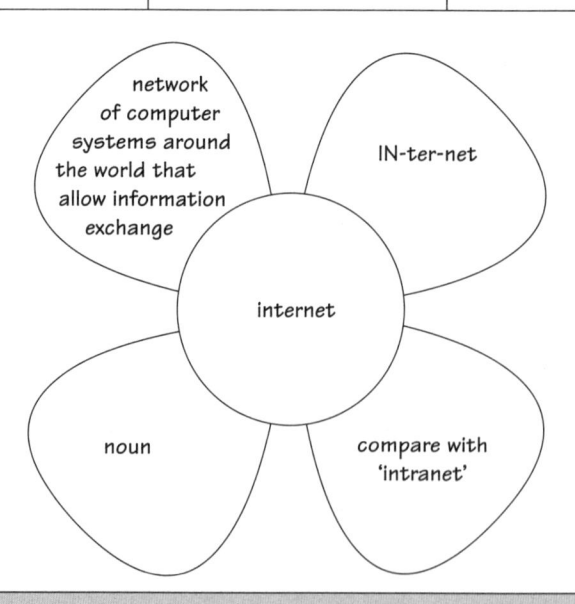

Photocopiable resource 2.1: Vocabulary

1. **Vocabulary cards**

   You can use these to note one word or a family of words. Write the main word in big letters at the top. Under this, you could write other useful information: *translation*, *pronunciation*, *word stress*, *example sentence*, *opposite*, etc. Complete the information where possible; you can add new information, *opposite*, for example, as you go through the course.

2. **Vocabulary notebook**

   Organise in categories according to subject (*presentations, telephoning expressions, hobbies, travel*, etc.). You could have a space at the front for new vocabulary and then transfer important words/phrases to the correct category at the back of the book.

3. **Word diagram/spider**

   Put the main topic in the centre and note all the words connected to it.

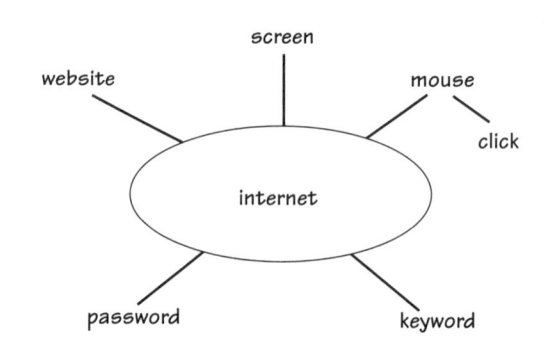

   internet — screen, website, mouse, click, password, keyword

4. **Word table**

   Organise in categories according to part of speech.

Noun	Verb	Adjective	Adverb

5. **Word flower**

   Put one vocabulary item in the circle at the centre and write different information about it in each of the four petals, e.g. its meaning, the word stress or pronunciation, what part of speech it is, and other comments.

   internet: network of computer systems around the world that allow information exchange; IN-ter-net; noun; compare with 'intranet'

Photocopiable resource 3.1: Polite phrases and responses

POLITE PHRASES	RESPONSES
Can you give me David's mobile phone number, please?	Sorry, I don't have it.
Would you like me to help you prepare your presentation?	Thanks, that's very kind of you. I could do with some help.
Do you want me to send you a copy of our new catalogue?	Thanks, but I already have one.
Is it OK to open the window?	I'd rather you didn't. It's cold in here.
Let me introduce my assistant, Laura Blake.	Hi, it's good to meet you.
Could you change the date of your business trip?	It's a bit difficult. I've already arranged meetings with clients and suppliers.
Thank you, that was a lovely meal.	You're welcome. I'm glad you enjoyed it.
Would you like another cup of coffee?	Not at the moment, thanks.
It's good to see you again!	It's great to see you, too.
Is it OK to phone a taxi to the airport?	Certainly, the phone is over here.
Would you like to join us for dinner?	I'm afraid I can't. I'm working late this evening.
I'm sorry I can't find the sales figures.	Don't worry. I have a copy in my office.

INTELLIGENT BUSINESS (PRE-INTERMEDIATE) TEACHER'S BOOK: COURSEBOOK

Photocopiable resource 4.1: Comparatives and superlatives questionnaire

Answer the questions for yourself. Then ask your partner the questions.

Question	You	Your partner
1 Is it more important for clothes to be stylish or comfortable?		
2 What is the most luxurious product that you have bought this year?		
3 What are the most famous brands you can think of for …? a) Shoes b) Cars c) Electrical goods d) Sunglasses e) Mobile phones		
4 What was the most interesting advertisement that you have seen recently? What was it selling?		
5 Who is the biggest star that you have seen in an advertisement?		
6 Put these items in order depending on which you spend most on each month (1 = spend most, 7 = spend least). Clothes and shoes Music Hobbies Books/Magazines Food/Restaurants Electrical goods Computer software		

Photocopiable resource 4.2: Product information

Product name		**Company name**	
	Company 1	Company 2	Company 3
Product image (e.g. luxury, value for money)			
Price			
Quality			
Adjectives that describe this company			

PHOTOCOPIABLE RESOURCES

Photocopiable resource 5.1: Business plan brainstorm

Business project name	
Description of product or service your company will make/provide	
Is there a demand for it?	
Who will buy it?	
How much will you charge for it?	
Do any companies already supply this product/service? (note names of competitors)	
Why is your idea better than your competitors'?	
Approximate cost of starting this business (consider how much it might cost to rent premises, buy equipment, hire staff, etc.)	
Ideas for financing the business	
Any other comments?	

PHOTOCOPIABLE © Pearson Education Limited 2006

INTELLIGENT BUSINESS (PRE-INTERMEDIATE) TEACHER'S BOOK: COURSEBOOK

Photocopiable resource 7.1: Presentation outine (Tourism and business)

Use the outline to prepare a short talk about your town or area and why it is a good area to develop as a tourist resort and business centre. If you don't want to talk about your own town, choose another place that you know, or use the information about Dubai on page 61.

---

1 Introduction
- Introduce yourself and tell the audience where you are going to talk about:
  Hello, I'm _____ . Today I'm going to talk about _____ . We'll look at the tourism and business facilities that it has at the moment and areas that could be improved in the future ...

---

2 Present information about the place
- Say where it is (what country it is in). _____
- Size (Is it a big/small town/area? What is the population?) _____
- Climate? _____

---

3 Facilities (now)
- Talk about three facilities that make it a good place for tourism and business at the moment (think about accommodation, infrastructure and attractions in the area).
  The following facilities make this a good area for tourism and business at the moment: ...

---

4 Facilities that the area doesn't have
- Talk about two facilities that it doesn't have at present.
  Unfortunately, at present the area doesn't have ...

---

5 Recommendations for the future
- Talk about two or three facilities that need to be improved in the future.
  To promote this as a tourist resort and business centre in the future, we need to improve the following areas: ...

---

6 Thank the audience
Thank you for your attention ...
Thank you for listening to my talk ...

PHOTOCOPIABLE RESOURCES

Photocopiable resource 8.1: Notes for a CV

Name	
Address	

Places of study [Note: only include secondary schools, language schools, universities, colleges, etc. where you received qualifications.]	Qualifications [Put your most recent/highest qualification first. If you have a lot of qualifications, you can make one list of academic qualifications and another of professional qualifications.]

Work experience
[Note: do include voluntary work, work placements, graduate trainee schemes or apprenticeships.]

Name of company/organisation	What you learnt from this position (e.g. new skills, how to work in a team, importance of good organisational skills, etc.)	What you contributed to the job (e.g. new ideas, energy, commitment, etc.)	What skills you demonstrated (e.g. organisational skills, keeping to deadlines, time management, initiative, etc.)

Additional information [Keep this information brief.]

Hobbies and interests:

Additional qualifications or skills:
(e.g. computer skills, training courses you attended)

Languages spoken:
(including information about level,
e.g. French: fluent, Spanish: intermediate, etc.)

References: Reference 1   Reference 2

_____   _____

_____   _____

INTELLIGENT BUSINESS (PRE-INTERMEDIATE) TEACHER'S BOOK: COURSEBOOK

Photocopiable resource 9.1: Balloon marketing

- Read the information about the company.
- Discuss the best way to market your product or service (see Preview, Promoting the product, Coursebook page 76).
- Discuss how other companies could use your product or service to market their company.
- Prepare a 1–2 minute presentation of your ideas.

A Balloon Printers

An ideal low-cost way to celebrate birthdays, weddings, etc. or to promote corporate events. The balloons are available in a range of colours and are printed to a high quality with text, slogans or company logos. They could be used in exhibitions, given to customers during promotions or printed with photographs of your product. An original and fun way to get people interested in your company. Available in packs of 20, 50 or 100.

- Read the information about the company.
- Discuss the best way to market your product or service (see Preview, Promoting the product, Coursebook page 76).
- Discuss how other companies could use your product or service to market their company.
- Prepare a 1–2 minute presentation of your ideas.

B Balloon Trips

Enjoy a once-in-a-lifetime experience travelling in a hot-air balloon over beautiful countryside. Our balloons can carry up to 20 people, so can be used for special occasions or corporate events. The trip lasts one hour and ends with a luxury picnic, including champagne or soft drinks. For special events we can print company logos or slogans on the balloons.

© Pearson Education Limited 2006   PHOTOCOPIABLE

Photocopiable resource 10.1: Card activity (infinitive, past simple, past participle)

Infinitive	Past simple	Past participle
be	was/were	been
choose	chose	chosen
come	came	come
do	did	done
fall	fell	fallen
grow	grew	grown
rise	rose	risen
see	saw	seen
take	took	taken
write	wrote	written

Photocopiable resource 11.1: Insurance quote

A Akorn

Complete the information in the letter using the words in the box.

claim	quote	terms	premium

Thank you for your letter enquiring about Akorn health insurance. We are pleased to make the following _____ :

The _____ each month is £135 for full cover.

The _____ of the policy state that you are not covered for any illnesses or injuries that you had in the past. You can go to the hospital of your choice to be treated.

You can _____ for operations, overnight stays in hospital and health check-ups. Please contact me if you would like a quote on any other insurance policy.

Now use the following prompts to prepare questions to ask your partner about their insurance company. Use the information in your letter to answer your partner's questions. Then discuss which quote you prefer.

How much / premium / each year?   What / terms / of / policy?   What / claim / for?

B Henlow Trust

Complete the information in the letter using the words in the box.

claim	quote	terms	premium

Thank you for your letter enquiring about Henlow Trust health insurance. We are pleased to make the following _____:

The _____ each year is £1,320 for full cover.

The _____ of the policy state that you are covered for any illnesses or injuries that you had in the past. You can go to any Henlow Trust hospital to be treated (there are 50 around the country).

You can _____ for operations and overnight stays hospital. Health check-ups are not included in the policy.

Please contact me if you would like a quote on any other insurance policy.

Now use the following prompts to prepare questions to ask your partner about their insurance company. Use the information in your letter to answer your partner's questions. Then discuss which quote you prefer.

How much / premium / each year?   What / terms / of / policy?   What / claim / for?

Photocopiable resource 12.1: Card activity (complaints)

You buy a new briefcase and the handle breaks the first time you use it. (refund)	Your new laptop computer stops working after a week. (replacement)	You phone a company for product information. The person on the phone is impolite. Phone the supervisor. (an apology)	You take your company car to a garage. The garage fixes it. On the way to the office, it breaks down again. Phone the garage owner. (a refund)
You book a table at a restaurant. You arrive and your table is taken by another customer. Talk to the manager. (a free meal)	You book a business class seat on a flight to Australia. When you arrive at the airport, you are told you are now in economy class. (a seat in business class and/or a free business class ticket for a future trip)	You arrive at your holiday resort. The room is dirty. It is a single room. You booked a double. Speak to the hotel manager. (a new room)	You buy a book called *How to become a millionaire*. You read it and do what it says, but you are still not a millionaire. Speak to the publishers. (£1 million)

Photocopiable resource 13.1: Simon's two lives

Part A

Simon is a | successful | businessman. He is | good | at his job and his company | is doing | well. | He runs his business | efficiently | and is | popular | with his staff. | In his work life, | Simon doesn't take | unnecessary | risks. |

Part B

In his free time, Simon enjoys | dangerous | sports. |

He | regularly | goes skydiving | and bungee jumping. |

He also likes driving | fast | cars. |

If you ask Simon for | the secret | of his success, he says: |

'I work | hard … | and I only take risks as a hobby.' |

INTELLIGENT BUSINESS (PRE-INTERMEDIATE) TEACHER'S BOOK: COURSEBOOK

Photocopiable resource 14.1: Creative thinking

1 Look at the shapes below. Spend two minutes adding lines, shapes or colour to make any picture that you want. Give the picture a title and compare with your partner.

Title: _____

2 Spend one minute discussing each of these questions in pairs or small groups.
   1 If your partner were a car, what model would they be? What sort of animal? What kind of music?
   2 What things could you make from an A4 sheet of paper?
   3 Name as many things as you can that are yellow.
   4 What connections can you make between these words?
      mountain   business   shapes
   5 Think of ways you can react if a colleague arrives at work in a bad mood.
   6 How could you get £100 cash in the next 15 minutes?
   7 What smell makes you feel relaxed?
   8 What things would make your life easier? Choose one of your partner's/group's suggestions and brainstorm ways to make it happen.

Photocopiable resource 15.1: Office design

You work for an interior design company. NuBroom, a music production company, asks you to design an office for six of its key workers. These employees often work long hours and weekends. The company wants the office to be a place where they are happy to spend time. Look at the information about the employees and then:

1 Discuss what facilities the office should have for each person to work and relax.
2 Use the paper that your trainer gives you to design the layout of the office.
3 Think about details such as colour, decoration, style of furniture, etc.

General information: All the employees need to use a desk and a computer sometimes, but most of their work is creative and they do not need to sit at a desk all day. They often work on projects together, so need to be able to have discussions.

Ali is 21. She likes rap music, going to the gym and skateboarding.	Ben is 24. He likes playing the guitar and making sculptures from junk. He can only think when he is lying down.	Fiona is 39. She likes to do yoga. She can only be creative when it is quiet and she is near water.
Jon is 44. He loves singing and basketball. He needs to eat chocolate and drink apple juice to help him think.	Mark is 28. He likes painting and gardening. He sleeps for short periods during the day.	Penny is 32. She likes space to move around and rarely sits down. She enjoys climbing and karaoke.

Photocopiable resource 15.2: Motivation game

20 What do you enjoy about your job/course? What gives you satisfaction? **You have finished – well done!**	19 What personal qualities make you a good friend? ←	18 What can you do now that you couldn't do ten years ago? ←	17 Talk about two things you hope to achieve in the next five years. ←
13 Reward talent not company loyalty. Do you agree with this statement? Why? / Why not? →	14 Talk about something you enjoyed taking part in recently. →	15 What management style do you prefer? Why? →	16 Do you think it is important to have goals? Why? / Why not? ↑
12 Would you prefer to work for a formal or informal company? Give reasons for your answer. ↑	11 Talk about one thing that you think each person you are playing with is good at. ←	10 Think of a way to reward staff who have worked hard on a project. ←	9 Name something that you learnt this year that you did not know last year. ←
5 Say three things that a good manager should do to motivate staff. →	6 Describe the sort of office that you would like to work in (think of facilities and what it should look like). →	7 What personal qualities make you a good employee or student? →	8 Is company culture important to you? Why? / Why not? ↑
4 Talk about something that you achieved this year. ↑	3 Which is more important to you – job satisfaction or earning a high salary? Give reasons. ←	2 Talk about a talent or skill that you have. ←	1 **Start**

INTELLIGENT BUSINESS (PRE-INTERMEDIATE) TEACHER'S BOOK: SKILLS BOOK

Unit 1: Let's get started

UNIT OBJECTIVES	
Skills:	Meet people for the first time
	Talk about what you do
	Open a meeting
Language:	Present simple and continuous
Culture at work:	Exchanging business cards

When introducing two people, it is helpful to say a little about what they do, e.g. *This is Jane, she's organising training courses for our Singapore branch.* The information should be brief but include enough detail to encourage conversation between the two people being introduced. This unit also looks at opening a meeting. For those Ss who need to open a meeting, the following may need to be considered:
- Welcome participants and introduce any visitors / new members
- Make sure that everyone knows the aims and objectives of the meeting.

For those who do not currently need to open meetings, introductions are also practised in a more general business context.

The following cultural factors may need to be considered when introducing people in an international context:
- Order in which people are introduced (Should the most senior person be introduced first?)
- Business cards (Can they be exchanged casually or should they be handed over with formality? Should you read the information carefully?)
- Handshake or bow? (What physical gestures are important?)
- When to use titles and first names (If you are unsure, it is better to make the introduction formal. It is a good idea to wait to be invited before using first names).

What do you think?

Introduce the topic of the lesson, meeting people, by greeting Ss as they come into class. Ask Ss to show things that they do when they meet someone for the first time (e.g. shake hands, bow, say their name). Draw Ss' attention to the picture and ask: *What is happening?* (The man at the back on the right is introducing two men.) Point to the two men who are standing and ask: *What do you think they are saying?* (The man on the right could be saying *This is [name]*. The man on the left could be saying *Pleased to meet you.*) Read through the information with Ss and clarify any words that are unfamiliar to your class (e.g. *formally/informally, business cards, coffee break, name badges*). You could give Ss different contexts for meetings by saying: *Which things would you do in a formal meeting? Which would you do in a big international meeting? Which would you do in a small meeting?* Ask Ss to discuss the questions with a partner.

Skills Book, Good business practice, Starting a meeting, page 76

What do you say? 1

Ask Ss to work in pairs and match the expressions for introducing yourself and others. Point out that two of the functions each match two phrases. Check Ss' answers and elicit more expressions to match the functions. Check that Ss are comfortable with the pronunciation of the phrases (see Language focus below).

1 I'm Robert.
2 What's your name?
3 This is …
4 Pleased to meet you. / Nice to meet you.
5 What do you do? / What's your job?
6 I'm an accountant.

Language focus: Introducing yourself and others

I'm Robert is a polite and direct way of introducing yourself. A more formal and less direct way turns the introduction into a question *Can/May I introduce myself? I'm Robert.*

When introducing others, *This is …* is neutral and is appropriate for most business situations. A more formal expression is *I'd like to introduce you to … .* A less formal expression is *Have you met … ?*

When a person has been introduced to you, *Pleased to meet you / Nice to meet you* are both semi-formal responses. They sound natural and are useful for most situations. Less formal responses include *Good to meet you / Great to meet you.* The most formal response is *How do you do?* This is used less in modern business.

If Ss are unsure how to respond, they can copy the phrase that the other person being introduced uses (including *How do you do?* although this is a question form).

UNIT 1

Listening 1

Before listening to the two conversations, ask Ss to say what words they think could complete the conversations. As they listen, Ss complete the conversations. Play the recording as many times as necessary. You may wish to point out the upward intonation at the end of the questions *What's your job?* and *What do you do, Lukas?* Get Ss to practise the conversations with a partner.

> **Conversation 1**
> 1 I'm 2 Nice 3 Pleased 4 job 5 do
> **Conversation 2**
> 1 is 2 an 3 this 4 a 5 meet

Task 1

Introduce yourself again to two or three Ss. Encourage Ss to ask you questions about what you do. Brainstorm jobs on the board or encourage Ss to look up their job title in a dictionary. Ask Ss to walk around the room, introducing themselves and asking and answering questions about what they do. If it is not suitable to move around the class, ask Ss to turn and speak to the nearest person. Keep the activity moving and encourage Ss to move on after they have made their introduction and listened to their partner's introduction. Then ask Ss to work in groups of three and take turns introducing the other two Ss in the group. Encourage them to try to include information about the person's job or company. Finally, ask Ss to move to another group of three and repeat the activity.

Analysis

Go over the Analysis questions and check understanding. Allow Ss a short time to reflect on the Analysis questions and discuss them in pairs. Ask Ss to report back and discuss their comments. Encourage Ss to give examples of phrases that they used to introduce themselves and to introduce others.

Culture at work

Draw a business card on the board and elicit what information is usually included on one. If you, or your Ss, have business cards spread them over the desk so that you can compare styles. Ask Ss to demonstrate how they normally present business cards and what they do when someone presents a business card to them. Go over the information in the Culture at work box and check understanding. Ask Ss to discuss the different ways of exchanging business cards. Encourage Ss to use their own experience to give examples. If you have a mixed class, encourage Ss of different nationalities to work with each other.

Then ask Ss to complete their own culture profile about exchanging business cards on page 82. (Ss identify and mark with a cross where they believe their culture is situated on the line ranging from formal to informal.) Ask Ss to discuss the two ways of exchanging business cards and encourage them to use examples from their own experience.

Skills Book, Culture profile, page 82

What do you say? 2

Draw Ss' attention to questions 1 and 2. Ask Ss which question would need a more detailed answer (question 2). Ask Ss to work in pairs and match the questions and responses. Then check answers around the class. Get Ss to work with a partner and practise saying the questions and responses. Also refer Ss to the Grammar reference section on page 83. Ask Ss to compare: *We manufacture sports equipment* (long-term activity) with *We are manufacturing a great new sports bag at the moment* (temporary activity).

> 1 b, c   2 d, f   3 a, e

Skills Book, Grammar reference: Present simple and continuous, page 83

Task 2

Ask Ss to work individually and prepare to answer the questions in What do you say? 2 with information about themselves. Circulate and help where necessary. Encourage Ss to use a dictionary to find vocabulary about their job/company. When Ss are confident, ask them to work in pairs and take turns asking and answering the questions. If Ss are not in work, encourage them to use details about a past job or make up information. Then tell Ss that they are waiting to go into a meeting and they meet another person, who is also attending the meeting. They are going to role-play introducing themselves and talking about their job, company and job activities. Ask Student A to read the information on page 8. Student B turns to page 97. Circulate and help Ss prepare. When Ss are ready, ask them to stand up and role-play introducing themselves and asking their partner questions.

Analysis

Allow Ss a few minutes to consider their performance in Task 2. Then ask Ss to say what questions they asked about their partner's job and company. Ask Ss to prepare information about their own job, using the same format as the role-play. You could then ask Ss to role-play the situation again, using real information.

119

INTELLIGENT BUSINESS (PRE-INTERMEDIATE) TEACHER'S BOOK: SKILLS BOOK

> **Optional activity**
> **Photocopiable resource 1.1 (page 174)**
> To extend the language to the third person, ask Ss to work in pairs. Give Student A information about Howard and Student B information about Amanda. Ask Ss to prepare questions to ask their partner to complete the information. When Ss have finished, ask them to check each other's completed information.

Listening 2

Ask Ss to read the information, then ask check questions (e.g. *Where does Natalya work? What does she do? What is the meeting about?*). Ask Ss what order they think Natalya will say the phrases in. Then Ss listen to Part 1 and check. Play the recording again and ask Ss to practise saying the introduction. Then Natalya continues the meeting by introducing two new members of the team. Ss listen to Part 2 and correct two mistakes in the notes about Karim Sahbaz and two mistakes about Noriko Yagi. Ask Ss to compare answers with a partner and then check with the whole class. Ask Ss to take turns introducing the meeting (Part 1) and introducing Karim and Noriko to the meeting (Part 2).

Part 1
d b a c

Part 2
Karim Sahbaz
Job: **PR** manager
Responsible for: **promoting** the new company logo
Noriko Yagi
Job: **Designer**
Main role: **design** the new logo

Task 3

Explain that Ss are going to prepare the opening to a meeting. First, Ss work individually and turn to their information on the relevant page at the back of the book. Remind Ss about the phrases that they heard in Listening 2. Circulate and help Ss prepare. Now Ss work in groups of three. Make sure that Ss work in groups where each person has looked at a different meeting (A, B or C). Tell Ss that they are each opening a different meeting. When each person opens his/her meeting, the other two Ss should listen and note the subject of the meeting.

Analysis

Allow Ss a little time to reflect and then ask them to discuss the questions in their groups of three. Ss should focus on how effective each opening was, and if it: welcomed participants, said what the subject of the meeting was and introduced people.

Self-assessment

Allow Ss a few minutes to think about what they have achieved from the unit and tick the boxes. Suggest what Ss can do to gain further practice.

CD-ROM

Unit 2: Make contact

UNIT OBJECTIVES	
Skills:	Get through to the right person
	Take/Leave a message
	Check information
Language:	Countable and uncountable
Culture at work:	Precise or approximate information?

This unit introduces telephoning. Making telephone calls in another language can make some Ss nervous at this level because of the lack of visual clues that usually help with context and understanding. Reassure Ss who have had little experience of speaking on the telephone in English, by setting up the role-plays carefully (giving Ss plenty of time to prepare and helping them to feel confident before they do the role-play itself). It may also be useful to consider the following when communicating on the telephone:

- Know your objective for the call: Why are you phoning? What outcome do you want? It is useful to note these before the call to help you remain focused
- Speak slowly and clearly
- Check pronunciation and spelling of names before making the call
- Give your name and company (make sure you can spell these, if necessary) and say who you want to speak to
- When you get through to the right person, explain briefly why you are calling
- Have all documents and information that you need at close hand, as well as a prepared list of any useful phrases
- When taking/leaving a message, repeat key information
- When exchanging information, check and clarify that you have understood / been understood correctly
- If someone calls you and you are unprepared, say that you are busy at the moment and will call them back.

Cultural attitudes may affect:
- How information is communicated and how questions are phrased (direct or indirect)
- Attitudes to silence
- Whether people feel comfortable/uncomfortable asking for clarification.

What do you think?

Introduce the topic of the lesson: making contact on the phone. Ask Ss what sort of business calls they make and receive in their own language and who they speak to on the phone (e.g. suppliers, clients, colleagues, etc.). What things do they do to prepare for making or receiving a call in English? Ask Ss to discuss the questions on page 10 with a partner. Encourage Ss to explain why they would choose to do certain things by phone or face-to-face.

Skills Book, Good business practice, Telephoning, Making contact, page 79

Listening 1

Explain to Ss that they are going to hear June Shen phoning James MacDonald. Play the recording the first time and ask Ss to listen. Ask: *Who does June speak to first?* (the receptionist) *Why can't she speak to James immediately?* (his line is busy). Play it again and ask Ss to tick the expressions that June and James use. It would also be a good idea to spend some time looking at the phrases that the receptionist uses and ask questions, e.g.:

What phrase does the receptionist use to ask June to wait? (One moment, please.)
What question does she ask June? (Would you like to hold?)
What does 'hold' mean? (wait)
What phrase does she use to say that James is available now? (His line's free now.)
What does she say as she connects June to James's phone? (I'll just put you through.)

1 b	2 c	3 a

Task 1

Ask Ss to work in groups of three. To introduce the task, you could ask Ss to turn to the audioscript of Listening 1 on page 105. Ask Ss to read the phone conversation together, then to switch roles and read it twice more, so that they've each played all three roles. Ss are now going to role-play a similar phone call. This is the first telephone role-play so it would be worth making sure that Ss are very clear about what they are going to do:

- Student A is the receptionist at Entel Investments; they receive a call from Student B.
- Student B uses their own name and says they want to speak to Student C (using Student C's real name).
- The line is busy, so the receptionist asks Student B to wait and then connects him/her to Student C's phone.
- Student C answers the phone.
- Student B says their name to Student C.
- Student C greets Student B.

Give each S time to prepare expressions for the call. Circulate and help. When Ss are confident, ask them to role-play the conversation. To make it more authentic, you could ask Ss to sit back-to-back in their groups. Then ask Ss to change roles and practise the conversation twice more.

Analysis

Go over the Analysis questions and check understanding. Allow Ss a short time to reflect on the questions and discuss them in pairs. Ask Ss to report back and discuss their comments. Get them to say what they found difficult about speaking in English on the phone. Ask how they overcame any problems – or how they think they could overcome problems in future conversations.

Listening 2

Before listening, you could ask Ss to say what information they include when they take a phone message in their own language (e.g. the caller's name, company, phone number, etc.). Now Ss are going to listen to James phoning June. June is not at her desk; her colleague Alex answers the phone and takes a message. Ask Ss to listen and complete the message. Check answers and get Ss to spell James MacDonald's name. You may wish to briefly revise how to say telephone numbers (see Language focus opposite). Then ask Ss to listen again and answer the questions. Finally, Ss complete the words in the phrases that Alex uses. Ask Ss to compare their answers with a partner and then play the recording again to check.

> 1
> 1 MacDonald   2 JMP   3 01632 960 0883
>
> 2
> 1 Certainly.
> 2 Can you spell … ?
> 3 Sorry, did you say … ?
> 4 Thanks for your help.
> 5 You're welcome.
>
> 3
> 1 Can I **take** a **message**?
> 2 Can I **have** your **name**?
> 3 **What**'s your **company** name?
> 4 Can I **take** your telephone number, **please**?
> 5 **I'll give** her the message.

Language focus: Telephone numbers

Can I take your telephone number, please?
Certainly – it's 01632 960 0883.

When asking for a telephone number, we can also say (in descending order of formality):

Could you tell me your telephone number?

Could/Can I have your telephone number?

What's your telephone number?

It is usually a good idea to add *please* after these phrases.

In British English, 0 is usually expressed by *oh* instead of *zero*. The double numbers in 0883, can be expressed: *oh, double eight, three.*

In American English, 0 is usually expressed by *zero* and double numbers are said individually. So, 0883 can be expressed: *zero, eight, eight, three.*

Telephone numbers are often dictated in groups for clarity, with a pause after an area code, and with numbers divided into groups of three or four, e.g:
01632 960 0883
oh, one, six, three, two (short pause) nine, six, oh (short pause) oh, double eight, three.

Task 2

Ss are going to role-play two telephone calls where they take and leave a message. Draw Ss' attention to the Useful phrases box and practise saying the phrases with the class. You may want to spend a short time focusing on intonation (rising at the end of the questions, falling at the end of the statements). It is easy to sound too direct on the phone, so friendly intonation can be important. Give Ss time to prepare. Then ask them to sit back-to-back and role-play the first phone call. Give them time to prepare again, and role-play the second phone call. Circulate and note any areas where the class might need further practice.

Analysis

Go over the Analysis questions and check understanding. Allow Ss a short time to reflect on the questions and discuss them in pairs. Ask Ss to report back and discuss their comments. Encourage Ss to give examples of phrases that they used to take and leave a message and end the call politely.

Listening 3

Note that there are quite a lot of numbers and percentages in conversation 1. Before listening, ask Ss to say the numbers in exercise 1. Check that Ss understand the vocabulary (e.g.

recruits). Tell Ss that they are going to complete phrases that are used to talk about numbers. Play the recording for Ss to complete the exercise. Make sure that Ss understand the meaning of the expressions. Ask Ss if they know any other similar phrases to talk about figures (e.g. *more than, less than, around, almost*).

The next exercise looks at phrases for checking and clarifying information. Play the recording again for Ss to put the phrases into the correct order.

Then Ss listen to conversation 2 and find the answers (on the right) to the questions. You could ask Ss to turn to the audioscript on pages 105–106 of the Skills Book and practise saying the phrases; then ask Ss to read the conversations with a partner. Encourage Ss to note any phrases that are useful for them in their vocabulary notebooks. Take the opportunity to review the countable and uncountable nouns used in the two conversations (e.g countable: *figure(s)*, *recruits*, *women*; uncountable: *information*).

1
1 over   2 About   3 Just under

2
1 Sorry, can I just check the exact figure?
2 Do you mean exactly 50 per cent?
3 Sorry, did you say Asia, Africa and America?

3
1 a, b, e   2 d, f   3 c, g

Skills Book, Grammar reference: Countable and uncountable, page 84

What do you say?

Stress is important in the English language. Incorrect stress can hamper communication as much as incorrect pronunciation. Practise saying the example phrases with the class, stressing the letters or numbers in bold. Ask Ss to work in pairs and practise sentences 1–4. Check stress with the whole class.

1 No**vem**ber   2 02**3**76
3 H**B**C   4 L-I-**Z**-A

Culture at work

Draw Ss' attention to the two ways of completing the sentence. Ask: *Which sentence gives a precise figure?* (the second) *Which gives an approximate figure?* (the first). Go over the information in the Culture at work box and check understanding. Ask Ss to discuss the different ways of talking about figures.

Then ask Ss to complete their own culture profile about precise or approximate information on page 82. (Ss identify and mark with a cross where they believe their culture is situated on the linc ranging from precise to approximate.)

Skills Book, Culture profile, page 82

> **Optional activity**
> **Photocopiable resource 2.1 (page 175)**
> To help Ss prepare for Task 3, you could give them a photocopy of the Telephone preparation worksheet. Go though the useful phrases and tips with the class and check understanding. Phrases are provided to help with the start and finish of the call. Help your class choose phrases for the main part of the call (phrases are not provided for this part, as it will depend on the individual call). In this case, Ss should prepare the questions that they will need for their telephone role-play. Although the worksheet is primarily for use in preparing to make a call, it also contains phrases that would be useful when taking a call. You may also wish to give Ss a spare copy of the sheet at the end of the lesson for them to use when preparing telephone calls in English at work.

Task 3

Explain that Ss are going to prepare and role-play two phone calls. Give Ss time to prepare. Encourage them to use language from the lesson and any other phrases that they know.

Analysis

Allow Ss a little time to reflect and then ask them to discuss the questions with their partner.

Self-assessment

Allow Ss a few minutes to think about what they have achieved from the unit and tick the boxes. Suggest what Ss can do to gain further practice.

CD-ROM

INTELLIGENT BUSINESS (PRE-INTERMEDIATE) TEACHER'S BOOK: SKILLS BOOK

Unit 3: Receive visitors

UNIT OBJECTIVES	
Skills:	Greet visitors
	Make polite offers and requests
	Make small talk
Language:	Modal verbs part 1
Culture at work:	Direct and indirect requests

In Unit 1 Ss looked at meeting people for the first time and talking about what they do. Unit 3 extends this social English with greetings, polite offers and requests, and small talk. There is a direct link between the ideas in the Culture at work section, which looks at *direct* and *indirect* cultures, and small talk. Some cultures prefer to get down to business directly and think that small talk is a waste of time. However, for many cultures small talk is an important part of establishing rapport and developing business relationships.

If your students are from a culture that does not generally practise small talk, it would be worth spending a little time looking at the process of small talk and what it entails. The most important thing to realise is that it is not necessary to be a brilliant speaker to be good at it. Small talk is all about turn-taking in conversation. Very often it starts with a general observation about the environment (e.g. *It's hot in here / That was a good presentation*, etc.). Then the conversation moves on to other more general topics, which are usually light rather than serious. The content of the conversation is less important than the process of conversation itself. Subjects are introduced and dropped casually, and participants are not expected to look at a subject too deeply or at any great length. If someone raises a conversation topic, it is the job of the other participants to comment briefly or ask a question. One person should not dominate the conversation. It is useful to ask open questions that cannot be answered with a simple *yes* or *no*. The most important factor is to relax and to listen, and respond to what the other person is saying.

What do you say? 1

To introduce the topic, ask Ss to say how they would greet someone that they are meeting for the first time (imagine that they are meeting a visitor at an airport). Then ask Ss to say phrases that they would use to greet someone they know. What questions could they ask in both situations? Ask Ss to work in pairs and put the two conversations in the correct order. Then ask Ss to practise the conversations with a partner. Ask one or two pairs to read out the conversations for the whole class to check.

Greeting someone for the first time
Good morning. I'm Marcela Janku. Welcome to Talma Finance.
Hello, Macela. Thanks for meeting me.
How was your journey?
Very good, thanks.

Greeting someone you know
Hi, Michael. Good to see you again!
It's good to see you too, Yana!
How are you?
Very well thanks, and you?
I'm fine, thanks. How is work?
Great. I'm working on a new sales project. And you?

Task 1

Step 1: To introduce the task, tell Ss to imagine that their company is hiring a famous actor or actress to star in a new advertising campaign. In pairs / small groups, Ss decide which actor or actress they would choose and why. Tell pairs/groups that they are going to meet the actor/actress at the airport. Ask them what they would say when they first meet them. What would they talk about? Tell Ss that they are going to role-play a situation where a PR manager meets a famous actor/actress at the airport. Ask Ss to read their information (Student A on page 14, Student B on page 98). Make sure that Ss realise that the name of the company is Dominion. Encourage Student B to decide on a real actor/actress they want to be.

When Ss are confident, ask them to stand and role-play the conversation. The PR manager starts by introducing themself. If there is time, Ss could change roles and role-play the conversation again.

Step 2: Ask Ss to change partners. Ss are going to role-play a meeting with someone that they know. Ask Ss to read their information (Student B on page 15, Student A on page 95). Circulate and check understanding. Less confident Ss can use the *Greeting someone you know* conversation from What do you say? 1 as a guide. Tell Ss that Chris Green is waiting for Sam Young in reception at Rondor Services. Sam Young arrives. Now ask Ss to role-play the conversation.

124

UNIT 3

Step 3: Ask Ss to work with the same partner as in Step 2. This time Ss role-play meeting for a business appointment. Ss should greet each other, and ask about current projects. Ss should use their partner's real name and information about their own current projects. If Ss are not in work, ask them to imagine projects they are working on. Encourage Ss to extend the role-play by asking other questions (about the visitor's journey, etc.).

Analysis

Give Ss a few minutes to think about their performance in the three steps of the task. Ask Ss for examples of the formal and informal greetings they used. What questions did Ss ask? How did their partner respond?

Listening

Before Ss listen to Part 1 tell them that Yasmin is meeting Tim at the airport. This is their first meeting. Can Ss predict any phrases that they will use? Ss listen to Part 1 and choose the best option to answer each question.

Then Ss listen to Part 2 and answer the questions.

Play Part 1 and Part 2 again while Ss tick the phrases for offers and requests that they hear. Point out that the phrases for accepting/refusing are longer than just *yes* or *no*. When responding to offers and requests, *yes/no* can seem too direct unless accompanied by *please* or *thank you*. Take this opportunity to review modal verbs for offers and requests (see Language focus opposite).

You could ask Ss to look at the audioscript on page 106. First, ask Ss to identify all the modal verbs and then ask them to read the conversations with a partner.

```
1
1 a    2 c    3 b
2
1 F    2 T    3 T
3
Offer     Can I help ... ? Would you like ... ?
Request   Can you ... ? Could I ... ?
Accept    Thanks, I'd like a ... That would be great.
Refuse    I'm fine, thanks. Not at the moment, thanks.
```

> ### Language focus:
> ### Modal verbs: requests and offers
>
> Requests and offers can be seen here in descending order of formality:
>
> **Offer**
> *Would you like (some help)?*
> *Could I (help)?*
> *Can I (help)?*
>
> **Request**
> *Would you (help)?*
> *Could you (help)?*
> *Can you (help)?*
>
> A modal verb (e.g. *would/could/can*) is followed by the infinitive without *to* (e.g. *help*). Modal verbs remain the same in all forms, i.e. they do not change in the third person, e.g. *Could he meet Mr Duffy at the station?* **not** *Could he meets Mr Duffy at the station?*
>
> *May I* is formal and can be used for offers and for requests / asking permission, e.g.:
>
> *May I open the door for you?* (offer)
> *May I use your pen?* (request / asking for permission)
>
> Note: It is not possible to say *May you ... ?*
>
> *Do you want ... ?* (offer) and *Is it OK to ... ?* (request) are both informal and are not modal verbs.

Culture at work

Draw Ss' attention to the two speech bubbles. Which one do they think is most direct? Which is closer to the way that they would ask for something in their culture? Ask Ss to work in pairs / small groups and read the information about direct and indirect ways of communicating. Do they agree? Can they think of any problems that could occur if a person who communicates very directly meets someone who uses indirect communication? Encourage Ss to use their own experience to give examples. If you have a mixed class, encourage Ss of different nationalities to work with each other. Then ask Ss to complete their own culture profile about exchanging business cards on page 82. (Ss identify and mark with a cross where they believe their culture is situated on the line ranging from Direct to Indirect.) You could also point out that there are differences between English-speaking countries, for example the United States and Australia are more direct and the UK is more indirect.

Task 2

This role-play consolidates phrases for introductions and greetings and also allows Ss to practise offers and requests. Tell Ss that they are going to role-play a conversation between a business consultant and a training manager. Ask Ss to work in pairs and read their information (Student A on page 16, Student B on page 98). Give Ss time to prepare. After they have role-played the conversation, ask them to change roles and practise the conversation again.

INTELLIGENT BUSINESS (PRE-INTERMEDIATE) TEACHER'S BOOK: SKILLS BOOK

Analysis

Allow Ss a moment to consider their performance in Task 2. Then ask Ss what phrases they used to make offers and requests. What phrases did they use to respond to offers and requests?

What do you think?

To introduce the topic, ask Ss to close books and work in pairs / small groups to answer the questions:

What is small talk?
Why is it important?

Ask Ss to open books and discuss the questions with the whole class. If it is more appropriate for your class to discuss the second part of the question in pairs / small groups, then do so. Some of your class might be from cultures where small talk is not an important part of business socialising. You could point out that if they are doing international business with cultures that use small talk, their business partners may find it too direct to immediately start a business discussion without any introductory conversation. Small talk is about making people feel comfortable and relaxed. It can be useful in business situations because it gives both sides a chance to get to know each other and helps build a business relationship. If your Ss are unfamiliar with the process (rather than the content) of small talk, you could use some of the information from the introduction to this unit in your discussion.

> Skills Book, Good business practice, Social English, Making small talk, page 81

What do you say? 2

Say the social questions 1–5 and ask Ss to repeat. Before starting the exercise, ask which city is in Poland (Gdansk), which is in Italy (Turin), and which country Rio is in (Rio de Janeiro is in Brazil). Then ask Ss to match the social questions with the responses. Ask Ss to work in pairs and read the questions and responses with a partner.

1 d	2 e	3 a	4 c	5 b

Task 3

Remind Ss of the conversation between the Training Manager and the business consultant in Task 2. Task 3 will extend their conversation.

Step 1: Ask Ss to work in pairs and think of conversation topics that the Training Manager and business consultant could talk about. Ss use some of their ideas to write a short dialogue, including social questions and responses such as those used in What do you say? 2. Circulate and help. As Ss finish, ask them to read their dialogues together.

Step 2: Now ask Ss to role-play the conversation between the Training Manager and business consultant. Instead of reading the dialogue, Ss use the preparation to try to have the conversation without prompts. Ask Ss to change roles and have the conversation again.

Analysis

Allow Ss a little time to think about the questions individually and then start a group discussion. Ask Ss if they changed their conversation between Steps 1 and 2. Did preparing the conversation topics make them feel more confident when they were speaking?

Self-assessment

Allow Ss a few minutes to think about what they have achieved from the unit and tick the boxes. Suggest what Ss can do to gain further practice.

> Coursebook, Unit 3 and Review 1, pages 28, 29 and 31
> CD-ROM

Optional activity
Photocopiable resource 3.1 (page 176)

Ss use a set of 15 topic cards to practise small talk. Ask Ss to work in pairs / small groups. Photocopy and cut up one set of cards for each pair/group. Give each group a set of cards, face down on the table. One S turns over a card and makes a comment about the topic. The other S(s) respond(s) with a comment or a question, e.g.:
S1 The traffic was really bad this morning.
S2 Really? Did you drive here?
The pair/group then try to keep the conversation going for no less than 30 seconds and no longer than one minute (set the time limit according to your class). When the allotted time is up, ask another S to turn over the next topic card. You could demonstrate the activity with a confident student (or the whole class). The aim of the activity is to practise turn-taking in conversation and to demonstrate the speed at which small talk topics are often introduced and dropped in conversation.

Writing 1: Messages and notes

UNIT OBJECTIVES	
Skills:	Write a telephone message
	Write a note
Language:	Present simple and continuous
	Offers and requests

Messages and notes are usually informal, so contractions are used and it is not necessary to use *Dear*. It is a good idea to keep information short and simple. Non-essential words can be omitted and abbreviations can be used. For phone messages, it is useful if the following information is included:
- The name of the caller
- Company name
- Contact numbers
- Time/Date of the call.

In case the person has any questions about the message, it helps if the person who took the message adds their name.

Style guide, Messages and notes, page 13
Teacher's book, Writing preparation framework, page 188
Teacher's book, Writing feedback framework, page 189

What do you think?

Before asking Ss to open their books, introduce the topic, writing messages and notes, by writing a short message on the board, e.g.:

Phone JD!

Tell Ss to imagine that they arrive back in their office after a five-day business trip to find this message. What would be the problem? (Who is JD?, no contact number, no indication who took the message or when it was written, etc.) Then ask Ss to open their books. Draw Ss' attention to the note and ask check questions, e.g. *Who is the note to? Who telephoned? What time did they call? What is the message?* Discuss the question in exercise 1 with the class. Then ask Ss to do exercise 2 individually. Get Ss to compare their answers with a partner before checking with the whole class.

> 2 Date and contact number(s) are not included in the message.

Language focus: Use of abbreviations

Common abbreviations are often used in messages and notes, e.g.:

asap	as soon as possible
FYI	for your information
Tel no.	telephone number
pls	please
PTO	please turn over (the page)
@	at

Task 1

Ask Ss to turn to page 95 and look at the information about Eduardo Estervez for Unit 2, Task 3, Call 2.

Ask check questions such as: *Who is the message to? Who is it from? What is the company name and contact number? What time and date will you put on the message?*

Ask Ss to write the message individually and then compare with a partner. Encourage peer correction before having a feedback session with the whole class.

> **Suggested answer**
> 10.30   4 Oct
> Sam,
> Eduardo Estervez from LNE Electronics phoned. Can he have a meeting with you on Friday at 2pm? Pls call him back. His mobile tel no. is 07700 902 738.
> Thanks
> (student's name)

What do you write? 1

In this exercise, Ss look at common punctuation. Start by drawing Ss' attention to the notes. Ask Ss to point out differences between this note and the message on page 18 (the note is longer and has more details). Elicit examples of informal elements in the note (*Kate* rather than *Dear Kate*, use of contractions, *Thanks* rather than *Regards / Yours sincerely*, etc.). Go through the punctuation words with the class and check that Ss understand the function of each of the punctuation points. Ask Ss to work in pairs and match the punctuation words with the examples in the note.

INTELLIGENT BUSINESS (PRE-INTERMEDIATE) TEACHER'S BOOK: SKILLS BOOK

1 comma	2 capital letter	3 full stop
4 question mark	5 hyphen	6 apostrophe

What do you write? 2

Ss complete the note with the correct punctuation. Point out how many of each type of punctuation Ss will need to use. When Ss finish, ask them to compare their answers with a partner. Then ask the class to dictate the note to you, including the correct punctuation.

> Robert,
> I can't come to the presentation today because I'm meeting Mr Muller at the airport. Could you take notes and give them to me on Friday?
> Thanks
> Kate

Optional activity
Ask Ss to work individually and write a short reply to the note. Write the following information on the board:

Might not go to the presentation!
Ask Kate to call as soon as possible to discuss.
Telephone number: 301 779 233.

When Ss finish, they should work in pairs and dictate their note to their partner, including correct punctuation.

Task 2

Before starting the exercise, you may wish to review offers and requests from Unit 3. Make sure that Ss are aware that they only need to write a note about one of the three subjects (you may wish to ask Ss to write a note about one of the remaining subjects for homework). Circulate and help Ss as they write. Then ask Ss to work in pairs. Ss exchange notes and write a reply accepting or declining the invitation.

Suggested answer
Noriko,
Would you like to come to a meeting about English language training courses on Thursday 12th May at 4pm?
Lydia

Suggested reply
Lydia,
I can't come to the meeting on Thursday. Could you take notes for me and give them to me on Friday in the lesson?
Noriko

Optional activity
You may wish to extend the writing task and do the activity in a more structured way. If so, consider using the Writing preparation and feedback frameworks on pages 188 and 189.

➔ Writing preparation framework, page 188
➔ Writing feedback framework, page 189

Optional activity
You may want to integrate further practice in writing notes with a review of an area of grammar – either Present simple and continuous or Offers and requests. It would be best to focus on one particular area (e.g. use of the present continuous for future fixed arrangements) and review this, referring to the relevant section in the Grammar reference on page 83 or 85. Write a note including examples of a mistake relating to the area that you wish to highlight. Photocopy the note and give a copy to each S. Ask Ss to correct the mistakes in the note and write a reply.

➔ Skills book, Grammar reference: Present simple and present continuous, page 83
➔ Skills book, Grammar reference: Offers and requests, page 85

UNIT 4

Unit 4: Be a good guest

UNIT OBJECTIVES	
Skills:	Show appreciation
	Talk about likes and dislikes
	Describe products and give opinions
Language:	Comparatives and superlatives
Culture at work:	Saying what you think

This unit complements and extends the social English introduced in Units 1 and 3. As a guest, it is useful to be able to make polite responses when being entertained by your host. Although Ss look at talking about likes and dislikes and describing products and giving opinions in the context of a social situation, the language is transferable to a wide range of business situations.

Cultural attitudes may have an impact on the following aspects of being a guest:
- Gift giving (should you bring your host/hostess a gift when you first meet?)
- Refusing food or drink (is this impolite in the culture of your host/hostess?)
- Discussing business (is it appropriate/inappropriate in a social context in the culture of your host/hostess?).

What do you think?

Draw Ss' attention to the picture and ask: *Where are these people?* (in a restaurant) *What are they doing?* (having a business lunch). Find out if your Ss have business lunches. How often? What do Ss like / not like about business lunches? Focus Ss on the title *The perfect lunch guest*. What do they think makes a good guest at a business lunch? Check that Ss understand the eight sentences. Ask Ss to underline the words or phrases in italics that are most true for their country. Ask Ss to compare their ideas with a partner and to write two or three more things that it is OK / not OK for a guest to do at a business lunch/dinner in their country. Have a feedback session around the class. Have they ever been in a situation where a lunch guest did not behave in an appropriate way? How did they react? Do your Ss agree or disagree with the advice in Good business practice on page 81? Is there any advice that they would add?

Skills Book, Good business practice, Social English, Business lunches, page 81

Listening 1 1

Before Ss listen, explain that they are going to hear part of a conversation at a business dinner. Check that Ss understand statements 1–3. Ss listen and decide if the statements are true or false.

1 F   2 T   3 F

Listening 1 2

Go over the two extracts and see if Ss can remember any of the missing words or work them out from context. Play the recording again for Ss to complete the extracts. Elicit any other phrases that Ss know for commenting on a meal or for thanking and responding to thanks. You may also like to spend some time checking that Ss are using intonation and stress to sound polite (see Language focus below). After drilling the extracts, ask Ss to practise with a partner. It would also be useful to ask Ss to turn to the audioscript on pages 106–107 and practise reading the dialogue with a partner. Check that Ss sound polite and interested.

delicious; glad; like
lovely; pleasure

Skills Book, Grammar reference: Comparatives and superlatives, page 87

Language focus: Sounding polite

Having a 'flat' intonation or not stressing the 'politeness' words in a sentence can make a statement sound indifferent even if the actual words used are polite. Make sure Ss stress words in bold when they read the extracts from Listening 1, exercise 2.

*This is **delicious**, Martha.*
*I'm **glad** you **like** it. It's a regional **speciality**.*

*Martha, **thank** you for a **lovely** meal.*
*It was my **pleasure**, Jake.*

129

INTELLIGENT BUSINESS (PRE-INTERMEDIATE) TEACHER'S BOOK: SKILLS BOOK

Language focus: Comparatives and superlatives

Ask Ss to look at the audioscript for Listening 1 on pages 106–107 and elicit the comparative forms of adjectives (*later, longer, nicer, more expensive*). Use the examples to elicit/review the rules for shorter and longer adjectives (see Grammar reference on page 87). Point out the use of *than* (*You eat dinner later ... **than** we do in England / This is much nicer **than** the staff restaurant*). Review the rules for comparatives and superlatives. Elicit the superlative form for the comparatives used in the dialogue (*latest, longest, nicest, (the) most expensive*). Also draw Ss' attention to the adjective *good* and elicit the comparative/superlative form (*better/best*). Brainstorm some more adjectives and elicit the comparative and superlative forms.

Optional activity

Ask Ss to work in groups of three. Tell Ss that they are going to talk about a restaurant that they have been to recently. Give Ss time to prepare information to give a 30-second talk about the restaurant. They should include information to answer these questions:
Where was the restaurant?
What type of food was on the menu and what did it cost?
What did the restaurant look like?
Was the restaurant smart/comfortable?
What was the service like? (slow/fast/efficient/inefficient)
What were the staff like? (polite/rude)
After listening to information about the three restaurants, Ss compare the three and decide which would be best for a business lunch, and why.

Task 1

Step 1: To introduce the topic, ask Ss to talk about meals that they have had in restaurants lately. You could brainstorm vocabulary for meat, fruit and vegetables (see CD-ROM, Unit 4). Ask Ss to write a menu with two main courses and two desserts. If Ss wish to create a longer menu with more items, e.g. starters, drinks, encourage them to do so. Circulate and help with spelling and pronunciation where necessary.

Step 2: Ss work in the same pairs and take turns being the guest and the host. Give Ss time to prepare. If your class would prefer to write notes for the conversation, allow them to. However, when they are doing the role-play, encourage Ss to refer to their notes but not read from them directly. Alternatively, they could do the role-play once using notes and then repeat it without notes. The role-play takes place at three different stages of the conversation. It would be useful if you gave Ss an indication of when they should move from stage to stage (*it is the start of the meal ... now it is during the meal ... it is the end of the meal*).

Analysis

Give Ss a few minutes to think about the questions individually and then start a group discussion. Ask Ss for examples of the phrases that they used.

Culture at work

Ss work with books closed. Ask Ss to work in pairs / small groups and talk about food that they don't like. Open the discussion to the whole class and elicit ideas of all the least favourite foods. List ideas on the board. Now ask Ss to open their books and read the information. Ask Ss to imagine that their host offers them one of the foods listed on the board that they don't like. Ask Ss to think about how they would respond. Then ask Ss to read the information about diplomatic/honest responses and say which is closer to their own response. Which is closer to the response acceptable in their country?

Ask Ss to complete their own culture profile about saying what you think on page 82. (Ss identify and mark with a cross where they believe their culture is situated on the line ranging from Diplomatic to Honest.) Ask Ss to work in pairs and discuss how they would feel if they were the host and a guest refused food or drink that they offered.

What do you say?

Ask Ss to work in pairs and put the phrases along the line ranging from Like 100% to Dislike 100%. Draw Ss' attention to the use of *really* as a qualifier to make likes and dislikes stronger. Point out word order when saying *I'm not really keen on ...* and *I don't really like ...* . Tell Ss that we generally use the question *Do you like ... ?* to discover people's likes and dislikes. Encourage the class to ask you questions about the food in exercise 2; answer using a variety of phrases for expressing likes and dislikes. Then ask Ss to practise in pairs / small groups.

a I love	b I like	
d I'm not keen on	e I don't like	f I hate

Task 2

This role-play consolidates phrases for talking about likes and dislikes. Read the information and ask check questions: *What is a buffet?* (a meal of snack foods where people serve themselves) *When are they having the buffet? What does a catering company do?* (provide all the food, drink and equipment for a function/party). Encourage Ss to look through the list of foods and check any unfamiliar vocabulary in a dictionary. Check understanding before starting the activity. Tell Ss that they should also add one other dish to the list. Next ask Ss to work in groups of four and talk about the food that they like and dislike on the list, and then agree on four dishes to order from the catering company. Have a feedback session and ask Ss to talk about the dishes that they chose. Would they be happy with this buffet if they were at a conference? Why? / Why not?

Analysis

Allow Ss a moment to consider the questions individually and then start a group discussion. Ask Ss if they can remember any of the likes and dislikes of the other members of their group. How did they agree on what four dishes to choose?

Listening 2

Explain that Ss are going to hear a conversation between Lisa and Philip who are having a business lunch. Just as they start the lunch, Lisa's mobile phone rings. Go through the questions and check understanding. Ask Ss to listen and tick the correct option to answer the questions. Check answers around the class. Ask Ss if they think the mobile phone would be useful? Why? / Why not? Then ask Ss to listen again and tick the phrases that they hear for asking questions, describing the phone and giving an opinion. Draw Ss' attention to the phrases for description (see Language focus opposite). Elicit any other phrases that Ss know and write them under the appropriate heading on the board. Ask Ss to turn to the audioscript on page 107 and read the dialogue with a partner.

> **1**
> 1 c   2 b   3 a
> **2**
> **Questions:**
> Does it have any special features?
> What's it made of?
> **Description:**
> It's designed for …
> You can use it to …
> It's made of …
> **Opinion:**
> It looks really stylish.
> Wow, that's amazing!

> **Language focus: Description**
>
> With the following phrases, *for* can be followed by a noun or by the *-ing* form of the verb, e.g.:
> *It's designed for use underwater / using underwater.*
> *It's suitable for fruit juice / making all types of fruit juice.*
> *It's designed for kitchens / opening tins.*
> *It's ideal for hot climates / keeping food cool.*
>
> Note the use of *to* (+ infinitive):
> *You can use it to keep food cool.*
> and *of* (+ noun):
> *It's made of plastic.*

Task 3

Step 1: To demonstrate the activity, choose an object in the class and elicit two questions that you could ask (e.g. *What is it made of? What can you use it for?*). Ask Ss to work in pairs and write two questions about each product. Encourage Ss to write different questions for each product.

Step 2: Now ask Ss to work individually. Check that each S chooses a different product from their partner. Ss write notes to describe one of the products in the picture and give opinions about it.

Step 3: Ss work in their original pairs and use their notes to talk about the product that they chose. Their partner should show interest by asking questions and giving their own opinions. Have a feedback session with the whole class to discuss the products and compare descriptions.

Analysis

Allow Ss a little time to think about the questions individually, then ask them to discuss with their partner.

> **Optional activity**
> **Photocopiable resource 4.1 (page 177)**
> To review and extend the language for describing products, ask Ss to work in small groups. Give each S a copy of the worksheet. Groups work together to complete the worksheet and then describe their product to another group.

Self-assessment

Allow Ss a few minutes to think about what they have achieved from the unit and tick the boxes. Suggest what Ss can do to gain further practice.

CD-ROM

INTELLIGENT BUSINESS (PRE-INTERMEDIATE) TEACHER'S BOOK: SKILLS BOOK

Unit 5: Talk about company history

UNIT OBJECTIVES	
Skills:	Introduce a talk
	Sequence events
	Present a company history
Language:	Past simple
Culture at work:	Talking about past events

This unit looks in particular at introducing a talk or presentation. This skill is further developed in Units 10 and 15. In an introduction, it is important for the speaker to:
- Introduce themself
- Give a clear overview of the subject
- Tell the audience the structure that the talk will follow
- Tell the audience whether they can ask questions during the presentation or whether there will be an opportunity to ask questions at the end of the talk.

Cultural attitudes may have an impact on the following aspects of introducing a talk or presentation:
- Formality (some cultures will start with jokes or anecdotes and others will begin more formally)
- Audience participation (some cultures will expect the audience to participate, e.g. by asking direct questions that the audience are expected to respond to; in other cultures the audience's role is less participative)
- Gestures and body language (some cultures use more expressive body language than others)
- Audience reaction (in some cultures it will be easier to judge whether the audience is enjoying the presentation than others).

What do you think?

To introduce the topic, ask Ss to think about the last presentation that they attended. What was good about it? What was not so good? Ask Ss how they prepare for making a presentation in their own language. Go through the list with the class and check understanding. Ask Ss to tick the five items that they think are most important. Then ask Ss to work in pairs and compare their ideas. If you have mixed nationalities in your class, try to get Ss to work with a partner from another country.

Skills Book, Good business practice, Presentations, Opening a presentation, page 78

What do you say? 1

Ss are going to complete a short introduction to a presentation. Ask Ss to work individually. Circulate and help where necessary. Then ask Ss to work in pairs and take turns reading their introduction to a partner. Tell Ss to take a breath before reading to help them speak slowly and clearly.

1	
1 Hello	2 (student's name)
3 Today	4 To begin with
5 Then	6 finally

Task 1

Ask Ss to use the structure in What do you say? 1 to prepare a short introduction to a talk about a current project. If this is not an appropriate subject for your Ss, brainstorm other suitable topics (e.g. a company in my country, my ideal job, learning a new language, cultural tips for someone visiting my country, etc.). Tell Ss that their introduction should last from about 30 seconds to one minute. Give Ss plenty of time to prepare and practise. When they feel confident, ask Ss to work with a partner and introduce their talk. You could then ask Ss to present their introduction to a new partner; encourage Ss to try this time to look at their 'audience' rather than reading from their notes.

Analysis

Give Ss a few minutes to think about the questions individually and then start a group discussion. Ask Ss for examples of the phrases that they used in the introduction to their talk.

Listening

Before Ss listen, explain that they are going to hear the introduction to a presentation by Bruno Cardoso about his company, The Gadget House. Tell Ss that the company sells gifts. Ask Ss for examples of gifts that they have given or received recently. Go though the list and check understanding. Then play the recording for Ss to tick the places that they hear. Play it again while Ss put the events into the correct order. Finally, Ss use the dates to write sentences about Bruno Cardoso. Ask Ss to compare answers with a partner. Then play the recording one more time for Ss check. Use exercises 2 and 3 to review the past simple (see Language focus on page 133). Ask Ss to turn to the audioscript on page 107 and work in pairs, taking turns reading the introduction to the presentation. Encourage Ss to underline words that they think should be stressed to make the presentation sound lively and interesting.

132

UNIT 5

1
warehouse   gift shop   Lisbon   Europe   Berlin
online store

2
d b f a e c

3
1 In 1985 he opened a gift shop in Lisbon.
2 In 1988 he moved to Berlin.
3 In 2005 he launched an online store.

Language focus: Past simple

Ask Ss to identify the regular verbs in exercise 2 (*moved, launched, opened, started*). Elicit how the past simple is formed with regular verbs (add *-(e)d*).

On the board write the three ways to pronounce *-ed* endings. Model how to say the endings and ask Ss to decide which ending goes with each of the verbs above:

/d/	/t/	/ɪd/
moved	launched	started
opened		

Ask Ss to go through the audioscipt on page 107 and identify all the regular (*started, opened, decided, launched*) and irregular (*grew, had, was/were, bought*) past simple verbs. Elicit how to form questions (and what the short answers are) and negatives:

Question form:
Did you open a gift shop in Portugal?
(Yes, I did. / No, I didn't.)
Negative:
Bruno didn't move to Poland.

Ask Ss to form more questions and negatives, using the verbs in the listening.

Skills Book, Grammar reference: Past simple, page 88

What do you say? 2

Ss have already briefly looked at language for sequencing events in What do you say? 1. This extends the phrases. Ask Ss to work in pairs and use the phrases to complete the sentences. You can play the recording again for Ss to check. Ask Ss to take it in turns to read the sentences. You could encourage Ss to stress the words in bold, in the answer box, as they read.

1 To **begin** with
2 **After** moving
3 For the **next**
4 **Then**
5 So **what** did I **do**?
6 **After** a while
7 **Finally**
8 And **now**

Task 2

Ss are going to prepare an introduction to a talk about Bruno Cardoso and The Gadget House company.

Step 1: Ask Ss to work individually and choose four events to include in their introduction (if Ss wish to choose more, they can do so). Encourage Ss to expand the events (adding dates and any additional information they want to) and to include the language for sequencing events from What do you say? 2. Draw Ss' attention to the opening sentence they could use, or they could prepare their own opening. Give Ss time to prepare. Ask them to read their introduction to themselves, and to underline in their presentation any words that should be stressed and where they wish to pause.

Step 2: Ask Ss to take turns presenting their introduction to their partner. Encourage Ss to speak slowly and clearly. While they are listening to their partner's introduction, Ss should note the events that are included and in what order.

Analysis

Allow Ss a moment to consider the questions individually, before discussing with their partner. Ask the class what sequencing language they used. Is there anything that they would change about their presentation if they were doing it again?

Culture at work

Ss may find it quite strange that there are different ways to talk about past events. Some cultures prefer a linear approach where the story of a company starts at the beginning (e.g. when it was started/opened/launched). It then talks about key events in the history of the company in the order that they occurred before ending at the present day. History is seen as a line moving from past to present. Other cultures would approach the story differently, by giving the listener lots of background information and moving about within the story. History is seen more as a circle with the past and present being of equal importance. Check that Ss understand the information in the box. Then ask Ss to discuss the ways of talking about past events with their partner. Ask Ss to complete their own culture profile about talking about past events on page 82. (Ss identify and mark with a cross where they believe their culture is situated on the line ranging from

133

Fixed sequence to Flexible sequence.) Ask Ss how the different ways of talking about the past might lead to different approaches when planning an introduction to a talk.

Optional activity
Photocopiable resource 5.1 (page 178)

To help Ss prepare for their presentation in Task 3, you may wish to give them a photocopy of the Talk preparation worksheet. Ss use Part 1 to prepare their talk on a company history. When Ss are listening to their group's presentations, they can use Part 2 of the sheet to note the subject of and information about their partners' talks. This will be useful when Ss analyse their performance after the talk.

Task 3

Tell Ss that they are going to prepare a talk about the history of the company that they work for, or the history of another company that they know. If Ss have access to the internet, they can research information to use in their talk. Tell Ss that they will be giving their talks in small groups (rather than to the whole class).

Step 1: Ask Ss to work individually and prepare information for their talk about the history of their own company, or any other company they would like to talk about. The talk should last about two minutes. Remind Ss as they prepare that they should:

- Greet the audience
- Introduce themselves and say what they do
- Introduce the subject of their talk
- Use language for sequencing events.

Circulate and help Ss as they prepare. Encourage Ss to self-correct where necessary. If possible in your class, try to give Ss the opportunity to read their talk aloud to themselves. Remind Ss to try to smile when they greet the audience, speak clearly, and glance up from their notes as they speak.

Step 2: Now ask Ss to work in groups of three and take it in turns to present their talk. When Ss are listening to other Ss giving their talks, they should note the subject of the talk and key events.

Analysis

Allow Ss a little time to think about the questions individually and then ask them to discuss with their group. Ask Ss to tell each other what they did well in their presentations and (if appropriate) what could be changed if they did the presentation again. If your Ss used the photocopiable resource 5.1, they could use this to structure their feedback.

Self-assessment

Allow Ss a few minutes to think about what they have achieved from the unit and tick the boxes. Suggest what Ss can do to gain further practice.

CD-ROM

Unit 6: Participate in meetings

UNIT OBJECTIVES	
Skills:	Give your opinion
	Ask for opinions
	Agree and disagree
Language:	Modals of possibility
Culture at work:	Focus on the past and future

In Unit 1, Ss looked at introductions before a meeting and opening a meeting. This unit introduces language for participating in meetings. Ss may take part in a variety of different types of meeting, from small and informal to large and formal. In addition, Ss may need to take part in international meetings, where participants come from a range of cultural backgrounds. Whatever the type of meeting, participants may need to consider the following:
- Are the aims and objectives of the meeting clear? (Why are they attending the meeting?)
- Is there anything that the participant needs to do to prepare for the meeting? (Will they be expected to comment, report, have opinions on particular topics?)

Cultural attitudes may affect the following:
- Agenda (having an agenda or having a more informal discussion with no agenda)
- How participants give opinions and agree and disagree (direct or indirect)
- Interruptions (the style of interruptions, how they are dealt with and whether they are considered acceptable)
- Style of debate (energetic or cool).

What do you think?

Introduce the topic of the unit, participating in meetings and giving and asking for opinions, by asking Ss to think about a meeting that they have recently attended. How many people attended? What was the style of the meeting (formal/informal)? What was the aim of the meeting? Ask Ss to read the information and then check understanding. Get Ss to work individually and tick the items that they think are a good idea. Then discuss the points with the whole group. Encourage Ss to give opinions. It may be worth pointing out that the final item 'Make your point in short, simple sentences' is meant to highlight that even complex ideas can be said briefly, and you are more likely to keep the attention of the other participants if you make your point easy to understand.

Listen to what people say.
Use polite phrases to agree and disagree.
Make your point in short, simple sentences.

Skills Book, Good business practice, Meetings, Participating in a meeting, page 76

Optional activity
Ask Ss to work in small groups and have a five- to ten-minute meeting to discuss the following:
1 Are most meetings a waste of time?
2 Three things that make an effective meeting are …
Each member of the group should give their opinion.
Ask Ss to tell the class their ideas.

Listening 1 1

Ask Ss to close their books and brainstorm different soft drinks that are popular in Ss' countries. Focus on one or two of the drinks and ask Ss how the drinks are marketed. Who are they aimed at? What do Ss think will influence the soft drinks market in the next ten years? Ask Ss to open their books and read the information. Play the recording while Ss note the number of each speaker next to opinions a–d.

a 4   b 3   c 1   d 2

Listening 1 2

Ss listen again to decide which speaker sounds most certain of their opinion. Encourage Ss to say what language the speaker used that helped them to come to their decision. You could point out that sounding sure/unsure is also about how we say things as well as the words that we use. If a speaker sounds confident when they are giving an opinion, it will make the listener think that they are sure about what they are saying.

Most sure: 3 (*I'm sure; definitely*)
Least sure: 4 (*It's possible that …*)

Listening 1 3

Ss listen again and complete the phrases that speakers use to introduce their ideas. Say the sentences with the class. You could ask Ss to work with a partner and take turns saying each sentence first in a confident and then in an unconfident voice, to hear the difference. This is a good point at which to

135

INTELLIGENT BUSINESS (PRE-INTERMEDIATE) TEACHER'S BOOK: SKILLS BOOK

review language for talking about possibility (see Language focus below).

| 1 think | 2 don't | 3 sure | 4 possible |

> Skills Book, Grammar reference: Modals of possibility, page 85

Language focus: Talking about possibility

In business, we often need to predict what we expect to happen in the future. We can indicate how sure we are about our predictions by the language that we choose:

Will indicates that we are certain or very sure:
*Sports drinks **will** be a big market in the future.*
(negative: *Sports drinks **won't** be a big market …*)

May/Might/Could indicate that something is possible, but that it is not certain. *Might* and *could* indicate a weaker possibility than *may*:
*The teenage market **may** grow in the next few years.*
*Health drinks **might/could** be an important area.*

Task 1

Ss are going to role-play a meeting to discuss a new anti-ageing drink that Orion (the company from Listening 1) is thinking of developing.

Step 1: Draw Ss' attention to the illustration. Ask Ss: *Would you buy a drink that would help with anti-ageing?* Can Ss think of any other foods/drinks that are being marketed at the moment as healthy or anti-ageing? Check Ss' understanding of any unfamiliar vocabulary (e.g. *eyesight*, *memory*, *healthy*, *teenagers*). Ask Ss to work individually and tick the opinions that they agree with. Encourage Ss to add at least one idea to the arguments for and arguments against list.

Step 2: Ss work in groups of four. Ss use their ideas from Step 1 to give their opinion about whether Orion should invest money in developing the product. Each S in the group should give an opinion and listen to the ideas of other members of the group. Then groups should try to agree whether or not they will recommend that Orion should develop the anti-ageing drink.

Analysis

Give Ss time to consider their performance individually and then start a group discussion. Ask for examples of language that Ss used to give their opinions. Encourage groups to say why they decided that Orion should / should not invest money in the product.

Culture at work

Ask Ss to work with their books closed. Tell Ss that you are going to dictate sentences that focus on the past and the future in different ways. Dictate the sentences from the Culture at work box, in random order. Spell any difficult words. Ask Ss to read back the sentences and check understanding. On the board, write *Future focus* and *Past focus*. Ask Ss to work in pairs and decide which things a company would do if it is future focused and which it would do if it is past focused. Get Ss to open books and read through the information. Ask them to think about which statements apply to their own culture and complete the culture profile on page 82. (Ss identify and mark with a cross where they believe their culture is situated on the line ranging from Future focus to Past focus.)

> Skills Book, Culture profile, page 82

Listening 2

Tell Ss that they are going to hear another excerpt from the meeting at Orion about the anti-ageing drink. Before listening, ask Ss what three departments they think the chairperson of the meeting will want to hear opinions from. Play the recording for Ss to check. Check verbally whether Ss think the questions should be completed with *on* or *about*. Play the recording again for Ss to check and write in the words. Encourage the class to practise saying the phrases. Point out that *What's your opinion* is often followed by *of*.

| 1 |
| R&D   Marketing   Production |
| 2 |
| 1 on   2 about   3 about   4 on |

Task 2

Ss are going to prepare for and have a meeting about what technology and equipment to purchase for a modern home office. Before doing the task, ask Ss to brainstorm what equipment and technology they expect to see in a modern home office. Encourage Ss to use dictionaries to look up any vocabulary that they need. Ask Ss if they would like to work from home. What do they think the advantages and disadvantages might be?

Step 1: Ask Ss to work individually and prepare a list of five items that they think employees need in a modern home office. They should note how much they think each item might cost. It may help Ss if they then prioritise their list in order of importance.

Step 2: Ask Ss to work in groups of four to six. Ask Ss to read through the instructions and ask check questions, e.g. *How many employees do you need to purchase equipment for?* (10) *What is the budget per person?* ($1,000). Remind Ss of the phrases that they have looked at for giving and asking for opinions. Give groups a time limit of ten minutes for their meeting.

Step 3: Give groups a few minutes to prepare, and ask each group to present their ideas to the class. If you have a large class, ask groups to present their ideas to another group.

Analysis

Allow Ss a little time to reflect and then ask them to discuss the questions with their group. Ask Ss to consider what they found easy and difficult about participating in a meeting.

What do you say?

Ask Ss to work in pairs and decide which phrases are used to agree or disagree. You may wish to highlight the use of *but* (*That's a good point, but ...*) (see Language focus below). Check answers around the class. Model how to say the phrases and ask the class to repeat. Then ask pairs to take turns giving an opinion about the subjects. One S should give an opinion and their partner responds by saying whether they agree or not and giving their own opinion.

| 1 A | 2 D | 3 D | 4 A | 5 D | 6 D | 7 A | 8 A |

Language focus: Use of *but*

But can be used when we do not want to say directly *I disagree*. It softens statements and allows the user to disagree indirectly, e.g.:

I think we should extend the deadline.
- *Yes, **but** that could cause problems for the Production department.*
- *That's a good point, **but** it could cause problems ...*
- *I see your point, **but** it could cause problems ...*
- *I agree, **but** it could cause problems ...*

Task 3

Ss have a meeting to discuss which community project their company will help. Tell Ss that they work for a company that wants to support a local community project. Ask Ss if they know of any companies that support charity or community projects.

Step 1: Give Ss time to read though the information on page 103 individually and prepare their ideas. Then ask Ss to work in pairs to discuss the advantages and disadvantages of each project.

Step 2: Ask Ss to work in groups of four and discuss which project their company should support. Say that all members of the group are responsible for asking for and giving opinions. Encourage Ss to use phrases to agree and disagree with each other's opinion. At the end of the meeting, ask Ss to tell the class which project they chose and why. If Ss have different ideas, start a class discussion about the three projects.

Analysis

Allow Ss a little time to reflect and then ask them to discuss the questions with their group.

Self-assessment

Allow Ss a few minutes to think about what they have achieved from the unit and tick the boxes. Suggest what Ss can do to gain further practice.

CD-ROM

INTELLIGENT BUSINESS (PRE-INTERMEDIATE) TEACHER'S BOOK: SKILLS BOOK

Writing 2: Emails

UNIT OBJECTIVES

Skills: Request information
Reply to a request

It is important to consider the following in relation to writing emails (and to most types of writing):
- The person who will read the email (Does the language need to be formal or informal? Are contractions and informal vocabulary appropriate? Is the information being communicated in an appropriate way? Is it too direct? Does the email need to be friendlier or more polite? What is the reader's knowledge of the subject?)
- The purpose (What is the aim of this communication, e.g. giving or requesting information, asking someone to do something, etc.? What do you want it to achieve?)
- Structure (What is the best way to organise the information? How should you sequence the points?)
- Accuracy (grammar, spelling, punctuation).

It is also useful to consider whether an email or other forms of business correspondence are the best means of communication (e.g. Would it be more appropriate to do this face-to-face or by telephone?) It is advisable to make notes before writing and to check the points above before sending.

Cultural attitudes may have an impact on the following:
- Formality of language
- Acceptable levels of directness or politeness (e.g. for requests and offers)
- How quickly an email should be replied to
- Acceptable length for an email.

Style guide, Emails, page 6
Style guide, General rules, page 3
Teacher's book, Writing preparation framework, page 188
Teacher's book, Writing feedback framework, page 189

What do you think?

Before asking Ss to open their books, introduce the topic, emails, by asking Ss how many emails they get a day/week. How many do they write? Does the class think that emails are a positive or negative part of work life?

Ask Ss to open their books and read the two emails. Ask Ss to identify which email is more formal. What language helped them decide? Which email is from someone Emir knows? What helped Ss to decide? Which email is closer in style to those that your Ss receive/write? You can use the examples to point out that the style of emails can vary depending on who the reader is (see Language focus below). Draw attention to how the information is organised in both emails (Email B uses paragraphs). You may also wish to contrast the briefer style and use of direct questions in Email A with the longer expressions and more indirect questions used in Email B.

Email B is more formal.
Email A is from someone that Emir knows.

Language focus:
Formal and informal emails

Some emails are like business letters and begin with *Dear* (*Dear Emir*, if you have had previous contact with the person; *Dear Mr Mahoud* if the relationship is more formal). When we know the person we are writing to, we can use *Hello* or *Hi* or just the person's name (*Emir*).

Depending on who is going to read the email, it may or may not use contractions and informal vocabulary. Email B uses a contraction, but the tone of the email is more formal. It uses less direct questions (*I'd like to know if it is possible ...* rather than *Can I ... ?*) and is organised into paragraphs, whereas Email A is briefer and more like a note in style.

Best wishes is a little less formal than *Regards* or *Kind regards*, which are both semi-formal (the latter two phrases can be used in formal or informal emails). These three examples of signing off an email are all more informal than *Yours sincerely* or *Yours faithfully*, which are normally used in business letters.

Task 1

To introduce the task, ask Ss to guess what type of brochure Emma and Edward were referring to in What do you think? (It could be an office supplies or electronic equipment brochure.) Tell Ss that they are going to write an email to Emir asking for information about a laptop. Elicit possible questions that Ss would ask about a laptop. Ask Ss to decide what style of email they want to write to Emir (formal or informal). Then ask Ss to use the prompts to ask questions about the laptop. If Ss would prefer to make up questions of their own, encourage them to do so. As Ss finish, ask them to check their email for accuracy (grammar, spelling, punctuation). Then Ss could compare emails with a partner and comment on similarities/differences in style. If appropriate for your class, encourage Ss to help correct their partner's email where necessary.

> **Suggested answer**
> **Informal**
> Hi Emir
> Can you send me some information about the laptop computer on page 12 of your brochure? How heavy is it? How long does the battery last?
> Thanks.
> Best wishes
> (student's name)
>
> **Formal**
> Dear Emir
> Could you send me some information about the laptop computer on page 12 of your brochure?
> I'd like to know how heavy it is. Also, how long does the battery last?
> Thank you for your help.
> Regards
> (student's name)

What do you write?

Ask Ss to work in pairs and complete Emir's reply to Emma. Check Ss' answers. Ask Ss: *Is Emir's reply formal or informal?* Focus on how Emir structures his reply, he:

- thanks Emma for her email
- answers her questions (and adds his own opinion, e.g. *It's also very good quality*)
- offers further help (*Let me know if you have any other questions*).

Elicit the phrase that Emir uses to end his email (*Kind regards*).

1 Hi	2 Thanks	3 information
4 can	5 ideal	6 quality
7 Let me know	8 regards	

Task 2

Ask Ss to read the email. Tell Ss that it is from a customer that they do not know well. Elicit any information that they can remember about the mobile phone in Unit 4, Listening 2. You may also wish to review the language for describing products and giving opinions from that lesson. Ask Ss to summarise what Adam wants. Then refer Ss to the audioscript for Unit 4, Listening 2 on page 107. Elicit key information about the product (it can be used to text and take photos underwater, it's made of metal with a special plastic cover). Ask Ss to organise the information for their reply as shown in What do you write? Get Ss to compare emails with a partner.

> **Suggested answer**
> Dear Adam
> Thank you for your email.
> Here is the information you requested on the mobile phone on page 12 of the catalogue.
> It is designed for use underwater and you can use it to text or take photos. It is made of metal and has a special plastic cover. It is also very stylish.
> Let me know if you have any other questions.
> Kind regards
> (student's name)

> **Optional activity**
> If you wish to integrate further practice in writing emails with a review of describing products, you could ask Ss to do the following for homework:
> Write a short reply to this market research email:
> *Please describe the last large product that you bought. We would like to know what it was made of, any special features that it had and your opinion of it.*

INTELLIGENT BUSINESS (PRE-INTERMEDIATE) TEACHER'S BOOK: SKILLS BOOK

Unit 7: Make appointments by phone

UNIT OBJECTIVES	
Skills:	Say dates and times
	Make an appointment
	Change an appointment
Language:	Future forms
Culture at work:	Attitudes to arrangements

In Unit 2, Ss looked at language for getting through on the phone and taking messages. This unit extends telephone language by introducing phrases for making and changing appointments. When making appointments by phone it is useful to do the following:
- Say who you are and why you want to arrange an appointment
- Repeat key information at the end of the call to confirm that it is correct (e.g. dates and times).

Cultural attitudes may affect:
- Language used to request/change an appointment (direct or indirect)
- Flexibility (if it is acceptable to change an appointment at a later date)
- The amount of small talk expected at the start and end of a telephone call.

What do you think?

The aim of the question is to get Ss to think about how structured their day is. Do they have a lot of free time or is every moment accounted for? Do they need to check the time regularly because they have to be in certain places at certain times? Discuss the question with the whole class. Include information about yourself. If Ss accidentally leave their watch at home, would they feel freer or more anxious? Can Ss imagine not looking at a watch or clock all day? Do any Ss never wear a watch? Ask Ss to look at their diaries and compare how much free time they have with a partner.

What do you say? 1 **1**

Ask Ss: *What is the time now?* Practise how to say the times 1–6. Then ask Ss to match the times with the correct watch. Check answers around the class. You may wish to elicit what part of the day *am/pm* indicates (*am* – after midnight; *pm* – after midday). At this stage, only one style of telling the time has been introduced; however, your students may also know other ways to say the times on the watches (e.g. a *seven thirty*, b *seven forty-five*, c *seven thirty-five*, d *seven ten*, e *eight fifteen*, f *eight*). You could sketch a clock face on the board and draw different times, eliciting answers from the class.

| 1 b | 2 a | 3 c | 4 f | 5 e | 6 d |

What do you say? 1 **2**

The aim of the activity is to contrast how we write times and dates and how we say them. Ask Ss to complete the sentence and dictate it back to you while you write it on the board to check. Draw Ss' attention to the use of *the* before the date when spoken. You could point out that this is used in British English (in American English it is possible to say *Tuesday 14th October* without *the* or *of*). If you would like to spend a short time practising prepositions of time, use the Language focus and Optional activity on page 141.

I'll see you **on** Tuesday **the** 14th **of** October **at** 4pm.

What do you say? 1 **3**

Draw Ss' attention to the diary for April. Spend a short time checking that Ss can say ordinal numbers for dates (*twelfth, twenty-first, thirtieth*, etc.). After Ss have read the information, ask them to point to the start date for the activity (Monday 19th April). Demonstrate the activity by saying *If today is Monday the 19th, what was the day and date yesterday?* (Sunday the 18th) *What is the day and date tomorrow?* (Tuesday the 20th). Then ask Ss to match the phrases with the dates on the calendar. Elicit answers. You could ask Ss to work with a partner and use the expressions to ask about more dates.

1 Saturday 17th	2 Monday 12th
3 Wednesday 21st	4 Thursday 22nd
5 Tuesday 27th	

140

UNIT 7

Language focus: Prepositions of time

at	9:30
	the weekend
	night
on	19th November
	Friday(s)
	Wednesday morning
in	2007
	January
	the morning (afternoon/evening)
	(the) summer

No preposition is used before the following expressions:
this afternoon/week, etc.
next Thursday/month, etc.
last year/December, etc.
tonight

Optional activity
Photocopiable resource 7.1 (page 176)
You could take this opportunity to review prepositions of time by doing a card sort. Ss work in pairs. Photocopy and cut up one set of cards for each pair. Ask Ss to shuffle the cards and group the time expressions under the appropriate heading: *in*, *on*, *at* or *no preposition*. Check answers (as on the worksheet before it is cut up) with the class.

Task 1

The aim of the task is to practise dates and times. Task 2 will introduce more expressions for making an appointment. However, if Ss know other expressions, they should feel free to use them in this activity.

Step 1: Show the class your diary and say three dates and times that were important for you this year. When you read the dates and times out, do not say why they are/were important. Ask the class to suggest reasons. After a few suggestions have been made, tell the class why the dates are/were important to you. Then ask Ss to look at their diaries (if they have them) and note three dates/times that are/were important for them this year. If Ss don't have diaries, they can make a note of dates/times they can remember, e.g. birthdays, their last holiday or meeting, an important project, their last English lesson, etc. Ss take turns to say the dates/times and why they are/were important.

Step 2: Ss work in the same pairs. Tell Ss that they are going to arrange a meeting with their partner next week. Check that Ss understand how long they should allow for the meeting (three hours). Say the phrases with the class and check understanding. Ask Ss to use these phrases or others that they know to take turns suggesting dates or times for the meeting.

Analysis

Allow Ss a moment to reflect on the questions individually and then start a group discussion. Ask each pair to say what time and date they decided on for their meeting. Find out if any Ss used other phrases to suggest times/dates.

Listening 1

Explain that Ss are going to hear Tom Davis telephone Adriana to arrange an appointment.

Ensure that Ss understand what information they are listening for (the day, date and time of the appointment). Ss listen and note down the information. Then ask Ss to read sentences 1–8. Play the recording again while Ss correct one mistake in each sentence. Go over the sentences and practise saying the correct version. Ask Ss which sentence(s) can be used to: ask for an appointment (2), suggest dates or times (3, 6, 7), say that the date is not suitable (5), ask the other person to suggest a date (4) and confirm the date and time (8).

Ask Ss to dictate the correct sentences to you as you write them on the board. You could take this opportunity to review the present continuous for future forms (see Language focus below). You could also ask Ss to read the audioscript of the conversation, on page 108, with a partner.

---

1 1:30 Thursday the 30th

2
1 What can I **do** for you?
2 I'd like to **arrange** an appointment.
3 Are you **free** at the end of the month?
4 What date's **good** for you?
5 I'm **afraid** I'm busy on the 28th.
6 How **about** Wednesday the 29th?
7 Let's **say** around 9 o'clock.
8 OK, I'll **see** you at 1:30 on Thursday the 30th.

Skills Book, Grammar reference: Future forms, page 89

Language focus:
Present continuous for future arrangements

We often use the present continuous when we are making or talking about firm arrangements in the future:
I'm meeting a client next week.
I'm visiting China at the end of the month.

Both *going to* and the present continuous can be used to talk about things that are already planned or decided. The present continuous is often used when a fixed arrangement has been decided (e.g. with a time and date).

141

INTELLIGENT BUSINESS (PRE-INTERMEDIATE) TEACHER'S BOOK: SKILLS BOOK

Task 2

Ss are going to role-play a telephone conversation to make an appointment. Ask Ss to work in pairs. Each partner looks at the diary for either A or B on the relevant page at the back of the book. If your class wish to write the conversation first or make notes of useful phrases, allow them to do so. When they role-play the conversation, encourage Ss to do it at least once without reading from notes. When Ss are ready to have the telephone conversation, ask them to sit back-to-back. Circulate and note any language points that you may need to review with the class.

Analysis

Ask Ss to consider the questions individually and then discuss with their partner.

What do you say? 2 1

Introduce the topic by asking Ss to imagine that they made an appointment to visit a client. Now they discover that their CEO wants to send them to an important international conference in Hawaii. It means that they won't be able to make the appointment with their client. What would Ss do? Elicit what Ss would say to the client. Then ask Ss to complete the sentences for changing appointments. Ask Ss to practice saying the phrase. Remind Ss to use upward intonation at the end of the second sentence. Elicit the long form of *something's* (*something has*).

> I'm **afraid** something's **come** up. Is **it** possible to **change** our **appointment**?

What do you say? 2 2

Ask Ss to look at more specific phrases for changing appointments by matching each sentence with the calendar that it describes. Make sure Ss are clear about the difference between *cancel* (the appointment will not take place) and *postpone* (the appointment will take place at a later date).

> 1 b   2 c   3 a

Skills Book, Good business practice, Telephoning, Making and changing appointments, page 80

Optional activity
Photocopiable resource 2.1 (page 175)
You may wish to photocopy the Telephone preparation worksheet and give one to each S, to help them plan the call and note useful phrases.

Listening 2

See if Ss can remember the day, date and time of Tom and Adriana's appointment from Listening 1 (Thursday the 30th 1:30). Tell Ss that they are going to hear another telephone conversation between Tom and Adriana. This time Tom wants to change the appointment. Play the recording for Ss to answer the questions. Ask Ss to compare their answers with a partner. Play it again for Ss to check. Then ask Ss to turn to the audioscript on page 108 and practise the conversation in pairs.

> 1 brings forward (from 30th to 29th)
> 2 Wednesday the 29th at 9:30

Culture at work

Ask Ss if they would feel comfortable telephoning someone to change an appointment. Has anyone changed or cancelled an appointment with them recently? How did they feel? Go over the information in the Culture at work box and check understanding. Ask Ss to discuss the different attitudes to arrangements. Then ask Ss to complete their own culture profile about attitudes to arrangements on page 82. (Ss identify and mark with a cross where they believe their culture is situated on the line ranging from Flexible to Fixed.)

Task 3

Ss use the same diaries used in Task 2. Ss cross out two appointments to create more free time in the diary. The client phones the relocations consultant to change the appointment. Give Ss time to prepare phrases. When they feel confident, ask Ss to sit back-to-back and role-play the telephone conversation. Then ask Ss to change roles and role-play the conversation again.

Analysis

Allow Ss a little time to reflect and then ask them to discuss the questions with their partner. Ask Ss to say the new date of their appointment(s) and elicit what phrases Ss used to change appointments.

Self-assessment

Allow Ss a few minutes to think about what they have achieved from the unit and tick the boxes. Suggest what Ss can do to gain further practice.

CD-ROM

Unit 8: Show round a new colleague

UNIT OBJECTIVES	
Skills:	Show someone round Explain how to do something Give advice and explain procedures
Language:	The imperative
Culture at work:	Attitude to procedures

When explaining procedures or telling someone how to do something, it is a good idea to do the following:
- Consider the level of knowledge of the person that you are explaining things to (check that you are not giving information that they already know)
- Tell the person if information is particularly important
- Do not overload the listener with unnecessary detail
- Pause occasionally to allow the listener to ask questions or to check that the listener has understood key points
- Follow up verbal instructions with a written summary.

Cultural attitudes may have an impact on the following aspects of explaining how to do things:
- Use of language (direct or indirect)
- The amount of detail that is given
- Fixed and flexible ideas to procedures (see Culture at work, page 41 of Skills Book).

What do you think?

Before opening books, ask Ss if they can remember their first day in a new job. How did they feel? What information did they need? Did the company have any procedures to help them settle in? Ask Ss to open their books and draw their attention to the photo. Ask Ss what they think the person pointing might be doing (showing the other person round). Go through the list with the class and clarify any unfamiliar vocabulary (e.g. *induction programme*, *procedures*, *full-day*). Ask Ss to look at the list individually and tick the ideas that they agree with; then start a group discussion.

Listening 1

Before Ss listen, explain that they are going to hear part of a conversation where an assistant from Human Resources shows round a new employee. They will be walking around the outside of the building. Draw Ss' attention to the map and check that Ss know where to start. Play the recording once and ask Ss to simply follow the speakers as they move around the map. Play it again and ask Ss to complete the map using the words on the left. Ask Ss to compare their map with a partner.

a car park	b warehouse	c canteen
d Production area	e Finance Manager's office	
f Sales and Marketing		

> **Optional activity**
> **Photocopiable resource 8.1 (page 179)**
> To introduce vocabulary for different areas in a company, you could write on the board:
>
> *Inside*   *Outside*
>
> Ask Ss to brainstorm areas that they might see inside or outside a company and write the ideas under the appropriate heading (e.g. Inside: reception; Outside: a car park, etc.). Ask Ss to work in pairs. Photocopy and cut up one set of cards for each pair. Ask Ss to shuffle the cards and match the area with the description. Check answers (as on the sheet before it is cut up) with the class.

What do you say? 1

Ss focus on the directions used in the listening exercise. Ask Ss to decide what preposition is needed to complete three of the directions and say which direction does not need a preposition.

> The preposition *on* completes 1, 3 and 4.
> *turn right* does not need a preposition.

What do you say? 2

Refer Ss to their completed map and ask them to say if sentences 1–4 are true or false. Ask Ss to correct any false information verbally. Elicit the words used to describe where things are (*behind*, *past*, *opposite*, *between*). Name two or three objects in the room that you are in and ask Ss to use the prepositions to say where they are.

> 1 T   2 F (*on the right*)   3 F (*next to*)   4 T

INTELLIGENT BUSINESS (PRE-INTERMEDIATE) TEACHER'S BOOK: SKILLS BOOK

> **Optional activity**
> Ask Ss to work in pairs and use the map on page 38 to ask their partner questions (e.g. *Is the car park next to the loading bay?*). Their partner responds (e.g. *No, the car park is opposite reception*). Your class may prefer to write questions first. Look out of the window of the building that you are in and ask Ss to point out landmarks and say how to get to them and where they are in relation to other buildings.

Task 1

Ask Ss to dictate how to get from the entrance of the building to the room that you are currently in. Write the information on the board. Now ask Ss to imagine that they are showing a new student to the room. Are there any other areas that they would point out to Ss on the way? Ask Ss to work individually and draw a large map of their own company/department or another building that they know. The map can show the outside of a plant or the inside of a building. Then ask Ss to work in pairs. Each S uses the map to 'show' their partner round the building and point out important areas. If Ss do not wish to draw a map of their own, they can use the map on page 39. Remind Ss that they do not have to explain every area, only the ones that they think are most important.

> **Optional activity**
> To extend Ss' use of directions, tell the class that a new Production Manager is starting work in the company shown on the map on page 39. Ss will not be available to show him round when he first arrives but they will leave written information in reception about where to find important areas. Ask Ss to look at the map and choose six areas that the manager might need to know about on his first day. Ss write sentences saying where the areas are located (e.g. *The Packing department is between Purchasing and the warehouse.*). If Ss need extra help deciding on areas, you could write the following on the board:
>
> 1 *His office is located in the warehouse.*
> 2 *He needs to go to the Human Resources department to sign documents.*
> 3 *He has a meeting with department heads at 11am.*
> 4 *He is having lunch at 12:30.*
> 5 *He needs to collect stationery from the store room.*
> 6 *The CEO wants him to go to his office after lunch.*

Listening 2

To introduce the topic, ask Ss what things they would find it useful to know about on their first day in a new job. Ask Ss if they use vending machines at work for food or drink. Can Ss explain what you do to get drink or food from the machines? Explain that Ss are going to hear Sylvia show Alberto round the department. First, Sylvia explains how to use the drinks machine. Ask Ss to listen and number the instructions in the correct order. Pause the recording after Sylvia says *Shall I go over that again?* Elicit answers around the class and ask Ss to read the instructions in the correct order. Then Ss listen to the rest of the conversation and complete Sylvia's explanations. Get Ss to compare their answers with a partner before checking answers around the class. Finally, ask Ss to match the expressions with the uses. This is a good point at which to review the language for instructions (see Language focus below).

Skills Book, Grammar reference: The imperative, page 90

> 1
> d f a e b c
>
> 2
> 1 tea 2 forget 3 good 4 sure 5 to call
>
> 3
> 1 c 2 a 3 b

Language focus: Instructions

We often use the imperative when giving instructions. This form is useful for communicating important or urgent information, but if over-used can make the speaker sound aggressive or too direct. It may be a good idea to ask Ss to compare the direct imperatives used in the exercise with the conversation in the audioscript (pages 108–9). Here, the linking words *and* and *then* are used to soften the directness of the imperative. Tone of voice can also help to soften the imperative.

Listening 2 exercise 3 draws attention to the importance of responding when someone is giving instructions. If we explain something and the other person does not respond, then it is difficult to know if the person has understood the instructions or not. As well as the responses used in the listening, the listener can also show attention and understanding by body language (e.g. nodding).

Task 2

Choose an object in the room you are in (e.g. a CD player) and ask Ss to explain how to turn it on and off. This role-play gives Ss a chance to use the language for giving and listening to instructions presented in Listening 2. Tell Ss that they are going to take turns explaining how to do something. Ask Ss to work in pairs. Ask one S in each pair to read information for Student A and the other for Student B. If your class is confident, ask Ss to work individually and prepare phrases for the role-play. If your Ss need more support, you could divide the class into two groups (A and B) and ask groups to work together to prepare the instructions for either entering and exiting a building or using a food vending machine. When Ss have prepared their instructions and are confident, ask them to take turns explaining their information to their partner. When Ss are listening to instructions, encourage them to use body language and expressions from Listening 2 to show that they understand, need to ask for clarification or are not sure.

Culture at work

Introduce the topic by asking Ss for examples of procedures that they have at work. Do most people follow these procedures? Ask Ss to read the information and discuss with a partner. Can Ss think of advantages and disadvantages in working for a company that has too many or too few procedures for doing things? Ask Ss to complete their own culture profile about Attitude to procedures on page 82. (Ss identify and mark with a cross where they believe their culture is situated on the line ranging from More fixed to Less fixed.) Ask Ss to work in small groups and identify any procedures that they think are essential (e.g. having a procedure to evacuate a building in case of fire). Get Ss to compare ideas around the class.

Task 3

Introduce the topic of procedures by writing on the board:

Starting English classes at (name of your school)

Start by asking Ss: *When somebody decides to learn English, do they just arrive at the lesson? What steps do they have to take before starting lessons?*

If your Ss need more support, ask questions to find out what procedures they completed to arrange English lessons (e.g. for Ss whose company arranges lessons, ask: *Who do employees need to speak to in order to arrange English language training? Do you need to complete any forms or documents?* For Ss who are self-funding, ask: *Who did you speak to when you contacted the school? What did they ask you to do? What forms or documents did you need to complete? Did you have to do an English test?*).

Step 1: Ss role-play giving information to a new colleague. Ask Ss to work in pairs. In the first role-play, Student B is the colleague from the Sydney office and uses the prompts on page 99 to prepare questions to ask. They can write the questions but should just refer to them, not read them out, during the role-play. Student A uses the information on page 96 to respond. When listening to Student A's advice, Student B should use expressions from the lesson to show that they understand and ask for clarification where necessary. Before attempting the second role-play, you could ask Ss to pause for a moment and consider the Analysis questions. Then ask

Ss to prepare for the second situation. This time Student A is the colleague from the Sydney office.

Step 2: Ask Ss to brainstorm different types of procedures that they have in their company, college or another company that they know (e.g. procedures for booking holidays, claiming expenses, complaining about a colleague, etc.). Give Ss time to prepare and encourage them to write notes to refer to when explaining the procedure. Then Ss take turns to explain the procedure to their partner. Remind Ss that when they are listening they should use expressions to show that they understand, or ask for clarification when necessary. When explaining procedures, Ss should check their partner understands.

For more practice, ask Ss to change partners and explain the procedure again.

Analysis

Allow Ss a little time to think about the questions individually and then start a group discussion. Give your own feedback. Spend time going over any problem areas and highlighting any good uses of language that you heard.

Self-assessment

Allow Ss a few minutes to think about what they have achieved from the unit and tick the boxes. Suggest what Ss can do to gain further practice.

CD-ROM

Optional activity
Photocopiable resource 8.2 (page 179)

This is a *Find someone who ...* exercise, where Ss can review the language from the lesson. It can be done at the end of this lesson or at the beginning of the next, as a warmer. Photocopy the sheet and give one to each S in the class. Note that there are two blank spaces at the bottom of the sheet where Ss/T can add their own questions. Ss mingle and ask another S a question before moving on. When they find someone who can do one of the items on their sheet, they should write their name next to it. For small classes or one-to-ones, Ss can take turns to ask questions (with the trainer taking part if necessary). Have a brief feedback session, asking Ss to do some of the things in the list.

INTELLIGENT BUSINESS (PRE-INTERMEDIATE) TEACHER'S BOOK: SKILLS BOOK

Unit 9: Make suggestions

UNIT OBJECTIVES	
Skills:	Make suggestions
	Respond to suggestions
	Make a choice
Language:	Modal verbs part 2
Culture at work:	Showing reactions

This unit extends the skills for meetings introduced in Units 1 and 6. In this unit, Ss focus on making and responding to suggestions. Ss also look at the language for making a choice and coming to a decision. When making suggestions, it is useful to do the following:
- Make sure you have everyone's attention
- Speak clearly and confidently
- Keep your suggestion short and to the point
- Listen carefully to the suggestions of other participants before replying.

Cultural attitudes may affect the following aspects of making and responding to suggestions:
- Language (how direct or indirect the suggestion should be)
- Interpreting responses (e.g. in some cultures nodding may not signal agreement)
- Attitudes to silence (whether some form of response is required after a person makes a suggestion).

What do you think? 1

Introduce the topic of the meeting, making suggestions, by asking Ss if their company asks staff to make suggestions on any topics. If so, how does the company find out what employees think? Do Ss attend meetings where they are expected to make suggestions? Ask Ss to work in pairs and discuss the methods of asking for suggestions. Encourage Ss to explain the advantages and disadvantages of the methods. See if Ss have any other ideas for gathering suggestions.

Skills Book, Good business practice, Meetings, Making and responding to suggestions, page 77

Suggested answers
Have a suggestion box:
Advantage: Easier for staff to say what they really think.
Disadvantage: Staff might not respond.
Send an email:
Advantage: Gives staff time to think.
Disadvantage: Staff might not respond.
Call a meeting:
Advantage: Staff are more likely to contribute ideas.
Disadvantage: Takes more time.

Listening 1

Ask Ss to read the question. Then get Ss to suggest what free gifts might be suggested in the recording. Play the recording for Ss to say how many ideas they heard. Then elicit what the suggestions were (a business card holder, a celebration party, a travel alarm clock, a pen).

four

Listening 2

Ask Ss to listen again and match the two halves of the sentences. Ask Ss to compare their answers with a partner. Check answers around the class. Say the sentences and ask Ss to repeat. You may wish to point out the levels of formality in the sentences (see Language focus on page 147).

1 f   2 e   3 c   4 b   5 d   6 a

Skills Book, Grammar reference: Modal verbs part 2, page 86

146

Language focus: Making suggestions

We often use *could* or *should* to make suggestions:
We could/should arrange a celebration party.

If we want to make the suggestion more indirect, we can put words before the modal verb, e.g.:
Perhaps/Maybe we could have a party for clients.
I think we should give customers a pen.

To express necessity in suggestions we can use *need to* and to express lack of necessity *don't need to / don't have to*:
We need to ask the manager.
We don't need to / don't have to ask the manager.

It is also possible to make suggestions without using modal verbs:
Why not … ? (+ infinitive without *to*)
How about … ? (+ noun or + verb + *-ing*)
What about … ? (+ noun or + verb + *-ing*)
These three are all less formal and are often used by native speakers when discussing ideas either in meetings or in informal discussions.

Task 1

Ask Ss if they have had a free gift from a company. What was the gift? Were they pleased with it? Why? / Why not? See if Ss can remember the four ideas from the meeting in Listening (a business card holder, a celebration party, a travel alarm clock, a pen). Ask Ss to say what suggestions they thought were good / not good and encourage them to give reasons why. Tell Ss that they work for Vantage Travel and they are going to continue the meeting.

Step 1: Ask Ss to work individually and think of another gift idea for Vantage Travel customers. Circulate and help where necessary. Give Ss time to think of an idea; if a S is having problems thinking of a gift, ask questions such as: *What could the company give clients that would help them when they go on business to other countries where they don't know the language?* (e.g. an electronic translator) *What could Vantage Travel give customers to help them pack?* (e.g. wash bags, holdalls and other types of bag) *Where could clients put their money* (a wallet/purse) *or keep their travel documents?* (a document holder). Encourage Ss to think about phrases to use to make their suggestion in the meeting in Step 2.

Step 2: Ss work in groups of four to continue the meeting at Vantage Travel. Rather than simply saying their idea, encourage Ss to use a phrase to make their suggestion. They can use language from the listening or other phrases that they know to present their idea.

> **Optional activity**
> To extend the meeting, ask Ss to decide which gift idea they will give to clients. Ask each group to present their idea(s) to the class.

Analysis

Give Ss time to consider their performance individually and then start a group discussion. Ask for examples of language that Ss used to suggest their ideas.

Culture at work

Ask Ss to work with their books closed. Get Ss to suggest ways that people can show if they agree or disagree with something that someone suggests (e.g. verbally, through body language, through facial expressions). Encourage Ss to demonstrate body language that shows that they agree with something. Then ask Ss to demonstrate how they would show that they completely disagree with something. Get Ss to open books and read through the information. Clarify any unfamiliar vocabulary. Ss discuss the ideas in pairs or small groups; encourage Ss to give examples from their own experience. Ask them to think about which statements about showing reactions apply to their own culture and complete their own culture profile on page 82. (Ss identify and mark with a cross where they believe their culture is situated on the line ranging from Visible response to Neutral response.)

Skills Book, Culture profile, page 82

What do you say? 1

Tell Ss that you are going to play the listening again, and ask Ss to tick the responses they hear. Ask Ss to compare their answers with a partner. Then ask Ss to identify which responses in the list you use if you think something is a good idea (*Brilliant! / That's a good idea / I like that*), which phrases are more neutral (*That's a possibility / That's an interesting idea*) and which you use if you aren't sure or don't like an idea (*I'm not sure about that / No, I don't think that would work*). You may wish to explain that the meaning of the neutral responses can change depending on the situation (see Language focus on page 148). Say the responses and ask Ss to repeat.

2, 4, 5, 7

Language focus: Neutral responses

The meaning of neutral responses can change depending on how they are said. For example: *That's a possibility* or *That's an interesting idea* can be said positively or more tentatively depending on whether the person saying them likes the suggestion that they are responding to.

Optional activity
Photocopiable resource 9.1 (page 180)

This activity gives Ss an opportunity to practise responding to suggestions. Ask Ss to work with a partner. Photocopy and cut up one set of cards for each pair. Ss take it in turns to turn over a card and read the suggestion to their partner. Their partner responds, using phrases from What do you say? 1 or any other phrases that they know.

Alternatively, you could ask Ss to work in pairs / small groups and use the sheet as a board game. Give each pair/group a copy of the sheet (don't cut it up). Each S has a coin or something similar as a counter. They start on the bottom right square and move round the board to the top left square. They take it in turns to flip a coin to see how many squares to move (heads = one square, tails = two squares). As they land on each square, Ss read the suggestion and their partner(s) respond(s).

What do you think? 2

Tell the class some of the things that are on your *to do* list this week (include things from work and home). Ask Ss to work individually and note some things that are on their own *to do* list this week. Ask Ss to work in pairs and discuss the questions with their partner.

Task 2

Read the information about Perfect Concierge with the whole class. Clarify any unfamiliar vocabulary. Ask Ss if they think there would be a market for this sort of company in their country. Who do they think would use this service?

Step 1: Tell Ss that they are going to add another service to Perfect Concierge's list. Ask Ss to read through the list of services again. Ss work individually and think of another service to add to Perfect Concierge's list. If your class need more support, you could brainstorm suggestions around the class first. Then ask Ss to work in groups of three and hold the meeting. Ss make their suggestions and listen to suggestions from other people in their group. Encourage Ss to respond to suggestions.

Step 2: Tell Ss that Perfect Concierge is going to have another meeting to discus ways to promote the company. Brainstorm different ways to advertise and promote a company (magazines, TV, radio, internet, etc.). Ask Ss to work in groups of four. Ss read the information on their role card. If Ss would like to use a suggestion of their own rather than the one on the role card, encourage them to do so. Encourage Ss to think about what phrases they will use to present their suggestion in the meeting. Ss should also respond to the other suggestions that they hear. Ask groups to decide on which method of promotion they think the company should use.

Analysis

Allow Ss a little time to reflect and then start a group discussion. Ask Ss to give examples of phrases that they used to make and respond to suggestions.

What do you say? 2

Ask Ss to work in pairs and complete the expressions. Read the phrases and ask the class to repeat.

| 1 make | 2 is | 3 Does | 4 come | 5 go | 6 agree |

Task 3

Tell Ss that they are going to continue the meeting at Perfect Concierge and are going to discuss how to celebrate the launch of the company.

Step 1: Split the class into four groups (A, B, C and D) and ask each group to read their information. If Ss need support, they can discuss ideas with their group. Otherwise they can work individually and add one or two ideas to their role card.

Step 2: Ask Ss to work in groups of four (each group comprising a S from Group A, B, C and D). Tell Ss to decide which of the ideas on their card they want to suggest at the meeting. Everyone in the group should make and respond to suggestions. Give Ss a time limit for their meeting (ten minutes) and tell Ss that all participants are responsible for encouraging the group to come to a decision and make a choice about which idea to choose. Remind Ss to use phrases from What do you say? 2. When the meetings have concluded, ask groups to present their choice to the rest of the class.

Analysis

Allow Ss a little time to reflect and then ask them to discuss the questions with their group.

Self-assessment

Allow Ss a few minutes to think about what they have achieved from the unit and tick the boxes. Suggest what Ss can do to gain further practice.

CD-ROM

Writing 3: Memos

UNIT OBJECTIVES	
Skills:	Structure a memo
	Explain a procedure
Language:	Future forms
	The imperative

Memos are used within companies to communicate information to individual members of staff or to groups of employees. The style of memos is usually neither very formal nor very informal. Instead, most are written in a neutral style. The following may be useful to consider when writing memos:
- At the top of the memo there is usually information about who the memo is from and to
- A subject heading is usually included
- A memo is usually clearly structured, with the most important point included in the first paragraph
- It is not necessary to sign a memo, but the writer can put his/her initials at the bottom
- A memo is an official company document, so grammar, spelling and punctuation should all be correct.

Cultural attitudes may have an impact on the following:
- The formality of language
- The type of information included
- The number of memos sent and received.

Style guide, Memos, page 16
Style guide, General rules, page 3
Teacher's book, Writing preparation framework, page 188
Teacher's book, Writing feedback framework, page 189

What do you think? 1

Ask Ss how often they write or receive memos in their job. Ask Ss to work in pairs and complete the advice about writing memos. Tell Ss that the advice is for writing memos in English. Check answers around the class and use the advice to start a class discussion about the style of memos. Ask Ss what style is usually used for memos in their country. It would be useful to point out that this is a guideline for memos that are going to be read by a number of people. *Formal* means *neutral* rather than a very formal style. When a memo is only being sent to one person, and it is a colleague you know well, then the language may be more informal and contractions may be used. You could also tell Ss that short sentences and simple vocabulary are useful for clear writing.

1 formal	2 no	3 short	4 simple	5 clear

What do you think? 2

Ask Ss to read the memo and look at the descriptions 1–6. Check Ss' understanding. Ask Ss to match the descriptions with the parts of the memo a–f. Ask Ss if this is similar to the style and structure of memos in their country.

a 4	b 6	c 2	d 3	f 5

Task 1

Tell Ss that they are going to write a memo. Ask Ss to read the information and ask check questions, e.g. *What is your name?* (Lee Stone) *Who are you writing to?* (all staff) *What is the subject?* (company car park) *What is the most important information?* (the company car park will be closed 15th–19th August). Ask Ss what friendly phrase Lee Stone uses on page 46 to end his memo (*Thank you for your cooperation*). This would be a good point at which to review/introduce language for giving reasons (see Language focus on page 150). Ask Ss to write the memo and compare their answer with their partner. Check answers around the class or collect the memos in for marking.

Suggested answer
To: All staff
From: Lee Stone
Subject: Company car park
Please note that the company car park will be closed from 15th–19th August.
This is to carry out urgent repairs in the car park and create extra parking spaces.
Staff can use the public car park in King Street while the company car park is closed.
Thank you for your cooperation.

INTELLIGENT BUSINESS (PRE-INTERMEDIATE) TEACHER'S BOOK: SKILLS BOOK

> **Language focus: Giving reasons**
>
> In memos, we sometimes need to explain why we are doing something. We can do this in a number of ways, e.g.:
> This is **because we need to** carry out repairs.
> This is **so that we can** carry out repairs.
> This is **to** carry out repairs.

What do you write?

Tell Ss that they are going to complete a memo about changes to claiming expenses. Ask Ss to predict what information might be in the memo. Draw Ss' attention to the example. Ask Ss to work individually to order the phrases and complete the sentences. Then Ss compare their answer with a partner. Check answers around the class. Ask Ss to read the memo again and say if they think the changes are a good idea. Why? / Why not?

> 2 Staff will no longer put in expenses claims every month.
> 3 Instead all staff will have a company credit card.
> 4 You can use it like a normal credit card.
> 5 All credit card receipts should be signed by your department manager.
> 6 The finance department will pay the credit card bill each month.

Skills book, Grammar reference: Future forms, page 89
Skills book, Grammar reference: The imperative, page 90

Task 2

This consolidates the language for explaining procedures from Unit 8. You may wish to review any phrases from the unit that you may think will be useful to your class. Go over the notes with Ss and check understanding. Ask Ss to write a memo to staff about the change in procedures. Check answers with the class.

> **Suggested answer**
> To: All staff
> From: (student's name)
> Subject: Changes to ordering stationery
> The procedures for ordering stationery will change from next month. Staff will no longer order their own stationery. Instead, Liz Harris will coordinate orders. You need to collect an order form from Liz and complete the form. Orders placed by 4pm on Thursday will arrive on Monday.
> Thank you for your cooperation.

Unit 10: Present information

UNIT OBJECTIVES	
Skills:	Check visual aids
	Talk about trends
	Describe graphs
Language:	Present perfect
Culture at work:	How much explanation?

This unit extends presentation skills by looking at how to describe visual aids. When using visual aids, it is useful to consider the following:
- The audience (How much do they know about the subject that you are presenting?)
- The subject (What type of visual aids will present the information most effectively?)
- The location (How big is the venue? What equipment is available? How will people be seated?)
- Language (Is the presentation in the audience's first language? Does the presentation contain any difficult vocabulary or technical words that the audience might not understand?).

Cultural attitudes may have an impact on the following aspects:
- How much information and explanation is included (See Culture at work, page 50.)
- If background colour or illustrations are used in visual aids, they may have a different meaning in some cultures than in your own
- Some cultures prefer fact-based presentations, while others concentrate more on how stylishly the information is presented.

What do you say? 1 **1**

The aim of this exercise is to make Ss aware that they can describe an object even if they do not know the exact word for it. Write *visual aids* on the board and ask Ss to brainstorm different types of visual aids that you can use in a presentation. Check Ss' understanding of the objects mentioned in 1–4 and a–d. If any vocabulary is unfamiliar, encourage Ss to use a dictionary to check. Ask Ss to match the descriptions and objects individually and then compare answers with a partner. Check answers with the class.

1 d	2 b	3 a	4 c

What do you say? 1 **2**

Point to one or two objects in the room and ask the class to help you describe what each is used for. Then ask Ss to work in pairs and take turns to describe the objects pictured. As a variation, Ss could describe one of the objects without using its name and their partner then points to the picture they think is being described. Ask Ss to describe objects to you while you write the description on the board. Encourage the class to think of variations to describe each object.

Possible descriptions
Photocopier: It's a machine for copying documents.
Whiteboard: It's a thing for writing messages on.
Microphone: It's something that you use to make your voice louder.
DVD player: It's a machine for showing DVDs.

Language focus:
Describing what something is used for

We do not always know the exact name of an object, particularly a piece of equipment, so we may need to describe it. Draw Ss' attention to the form of the verb after *for* in exercise 1 phrases 1–3 (the *-ing* form) and the possible addition of *with*:
*things **for** writing on a flipchart **(with)***

It is also possible to say:
*things **to write** on a flipchart **(with)***

Note that we could use *that* in phrase 4:
*something **that** you use to make a lead longer*

(See also Unit 4 Language focus: Description.)

What do you think?

Ask Ss to say what equipment was described in What do you say? 1. Start a discussion with the class about equipment that they have used in presentations. Have Ss used Powerpoint presentations or interactive whiteboards? Ask Ss to say what equipment was used in the last presentation they went to. Read the checklist with the class and check understanding. Then ask Ss to work individually and tick the things that they think are important to do before a presentation. Ask Ss to compare their list with a partner. You could ask pairs to prioritise their answers. Ask Ss to read the information in Good business practice, Presentations, Using visual aids. You could have a discussion with the class to see if they agree/disagree with the information. This would also be a good opportunity to introduce the present perfect (see Grammar reference, and Language focus below). Ask Ss to take turns asking the questions with a partner and encourage their partner to respond using *Yes, I have / No, I haven't*.

> The answers would depend on the particular situation. While there are no right/wrong answers, it is important to check that:
> - there are enough chairs (for the audience)
> - there are marker pens (if using a flipchart)
> - all the equipment you need is in the room
> - the electricity is working (if you are using electrical equipment).

Skills Book, Good business practice, Presentations, Using visual aids, page 78

Language focus: The present perfect

We can use the present perfect to talk about things which took place at some time in the past and which affect the present situation.

Question
Have you checked that there are enough chairs?

Response:
Yes, I have / No I haven't.

Positive
He has checked that there are enough chairs.
(so I don't need to check them again now)

Negative
He hasn't checked that there are enough chairs.
(so I have to check them now)

Skills Book, Grammar reference: Present perfect, page 91

Task 1

Ask Ss to close their books. Introduce the topic by writing on the board:

_____ we finish__ Unit 9?

Ask Ss to complete the question (**Have** we finish**ed** Unit 9?). Elicit the answer (*Yes, we have*). Ask Ss: *Have we finished unit 10?* and elicit the answer (*No, we haven't*). Ask Ss to look at the checklist in What do you think? and see if Ss can suggest any other things that are important to check before a presentation. Tell Ss that they are going to have two conversations asking and answering questions about a checklist for a presentation. Ask Ss to work in pairs. Give Ss time to prepare for conversation 1. If your class needs more support, divide the class into two groups (A and B) to prepare together.

When Ss are confident, they role-play the conversation. Circulate and note any areas to review at a later date. When Ss have finished, ask them to prepare and role-play conversation 2, again preparing in A/B groups if this is appropriate.

What do you say? 2

Ask Ss to complete the exercise in pairs. You could then write on the board:

Going up   Going down   Staying the same

Ask Ss to read out each verb and say which column it should go in.

| 1 GD | 2 GD | 3 SS | 4 GU | 5 GD | 6 GU | 7 GU |

Task 2

Divide the class into two groups. Ask Group A to look at the sales figures on page 50 and Group B to look at the sales figures on page 100. Give Ss time to prepare their description (in writing or verbally). When Ss are confident, ask them to work in A/B pairs. Then Ss take it in turns to describe the trends in their sales figures. The S who is listening should look at their partner's figures to check they are describing the trends accurately.

> **Suggested answers**
> **Student A**
> Sales increased/rose between 2000 and 2001. They dropped/fell/decreased in 2002 but rose/increased again in 2003. They remained steady in 2004 and then reached a peak in 2005.
>
> **Student B**
> Sales dropped/fell/decreased between January and February. They remained steady until March. Then they increased/rose in April and reached a peak in May. Sales dropped in June.

Analysis

Give Ss a few moments to think about the questions individually and then ask Ss to discuss the questions with their partner. Elicit some of the phrases that Ss used to describe trends.

Culture at work

Read the information with the class and check Ss' understanding. Ask Ss to think about the last presentation that they attended (or gave). How much explanation was given? Then ask Ss to discuss the information with a partner, encouraging Ss to give examples from presentations that they have attended. Ask Ss to complete their own culture profile about how much explanation on page 82. (Ss identify and mark with a cross where they believe their culture is situated

UNIT 10

on the line ranging from A little to A lot.) Can Ss think of any types of presentation where each of the two styles might be useful?

Listening

Tell Ss that they are going to listen to a radio presentation about share prices. Before listening, ask Ss to look at the list of items, and check understanding. Then Ss listen and tick the shares that they hear. Ss listen again and match the words with the meanings. Ask Ss if they know any other adverbs with similar meanings (e.g. *sharply, rapidly*). You may wish to ask Ss to look at the audioscript on page 109 and identify the verbs used with each adverb (see Language focus below).

1
oil, transport, energy, IT

2
1 c   2 d   3 a   4 b

Language focus: Adverbs

These sentences from the listening contain adverbs of manner (adverbs that say **how** something happens or is done). Note that these adverbs often come at the end of a clause:
*Oil prices have risen **dramatically**.*
*Shares have fallen **substantially**.*
*Charges have increased **slightly**.*
*IT shares continue to rise **gradually**.*

Note, too, the position of the adverb between the auxiliary and the main verb in the last sentence:
*I predict that they will **slowly** increase in value over the next two or three months.*

Optional activity
Photocopiable resource 10.1 (page 180)
Yoou may wish to photocopy the graph grid. Give one to each S to help them prepare their graphs in Task 3.

Task 3

There are a number of ways that this exercise can be used:

- Ss can use information about their own company or a company that they know well
- If your class has access to the internet, Ss could research information about the trends of a company
- Ss can use their imagination and invent information about a company.
- Ss can choose what trends to focus on (profits, sales, etc.).

Language focus: Past simple and present perfect

It may sometimes be necessary to use the past simple or the present perfect when presenting figures. Ss may find the distinction confusing, so it may be useful to point out the following: if the figures describe a finished event that happened at a definite time in the past, the past simple should be used, e.g. *Profits fell in 2003.*

However, the present perfect should be used when the figures describe recent events:
Our costs have increased in the last three months.
or when the event started in the past and continues to the present:
These figures show that sales have remained steady since July. (and they still remain steady)
Point out the use of the present perfect in the listening and that Ss should use the present perfect in Task 3.

Step 1: Give Ss time to prepare and draw a graph. Circulate and help where necessary. Encourage Ss to think about what phrases they will use to describe their graph.

Step 2: Ask Ss to work in pairs and describe their graph to their partner. For more practice, get Ss to change partners and describe their graph again.

Analysis

Allow Ss a little time to think about the questions individually and then ask them to discuss with their partner. Elicit phrases that Ss used to describe their graph.

Self-assessment

Allow Ss a few minutes to think about what they have achieved from the unit and tick the boxes. Suggest what Ss can do to gain further practice.

CD-ROM

INTELLIGENT BUSINESS (PRE-INTERMEDIATE) TEACHER'S BOOK: SKILLS BOOK

Unit 11: Present an argument

UNIT OBJECTIVES	
Skills:	Ask questions
	Clarify information
	Put arguments for and against
Language:	Passive verbs
Culture at work:	Responding in conversation

This unit extends the skills for meetings introduced in Units 1, 6 and 9. Although putting arguments for and against are particularly appropriate for meetings and discussions, the other skills included in this unit (asking questions and clarifying information) can be used in a number of business contexts.

When presenting an argument, it is useful to do the following:
- Consider advantages and disadvantages, so that you can anticipate any points that might be raised
- Explain reasons, where necessary
- Highlight any key information that supports your argument
- Check that your audience understands your argument and clarify information if needed.

Cultural attitudes may affect the following aspects of presenting an argument:
- How the argument should be presented (directly or indirectly)
- Body language (neutral or expressive)
- How the listener responds (attitudes to silence).

What do you say? 1

Before opening books, ask Ss: *Do you think that meetings are useful?* Elicit responses and then ask: *Why do you / don't you think that meetings are useful?* Get Ss to brainstorm any question words that they know. Ask Ss to open their books and work in pairs to complete the questions. Check answers around the class. This would be a good opportunity to review questions (See Language focus opposite). Then ask Ss to take it in turns to ask and answer the questions with a partner.

1 How many 2 How long 3 Do
4 Where 5 What

Possible answers to the questions
1 I attend two or three each week.
2 Between one and two hours.
3 I prefer morning meetings because I have more energy.
4 The chairperson usually sits at the head of the table.
5 I prefer formal meetings because they are usually more efficient.

Language focus: Questions

We often use questions in meetings to find out information or to clarify points. Write the questions that you asked the class on the board:

a) *Do you think that meetings are useful?*
b) *Why do you think that meetings are/aren't useful?*

Ask Ss to identify which question requires a *yes/no* answer (a) and which requires a longer response (b). We often use closed questions to get a general response and then follow up with an open question (as in the example above) to find out more specific information.

Ss can sometimes find subject and object questions confusing. Look at the possible questions relating to this statement:
Steve missed the meeting.
What did Steve miss? (*what* is the object of the question)
Who missed the meeting? (*who* is the subject of the question)
(**not** ~~Who did miss~~ the meeting?)

Ask Ss to discuss the difference between these two questions and say which one *who* is the subject of (a) and which it is the object of (b):
a) *Who phoned you?*
b) *Who did you phone?*

Optional activity

When Ss have completed What do you say? 1, ask the class to identify which question is closed (3). Can Ss think of an open question to find out more information? (e.g. *Why do you prefer afternoon meetings? What do you like about morning meetings?*)

154

UNIT 11

Listening 1 **1**

To introduce the topic, ask Ss to think of types of insurance that a company might need (e.g. fire, theft, buildings, contents, transport, medical, etc.). Tell Ss that they are going to listen to a conversation between a representative from an insurance company and the managing director of a sportswear company. Go through the statements and check Ss' understanding. Play the conversation while Ss decide if the statements are true or false. Check answers and ask Ss to correct the false information. This is a good opportunity to review passive verbs (see Language focus below). You could ask Ss to rewrite the passive sentences 1–5 as active sentences:

The manger turned off the heater.
The fire destroyed a new collection of sportswear.
They had to redecorate the store room.
The cleaner discovered the fire.
The manager tests the alarms twice a week.

> 1 F (The manager didn't turn off the heater.)
> 2 T   3 T   4 T
> 5 F (The alarms are tested once a week.)

Listening 1 **2**

Ss listen again and complete the questions. Check answers with the class. You may wish to draw attention to the fact that question 3 is an indirect question (see Language focus below). Say the questions, modelling the falling intonation at the end, for the Ss to repeat. Alternatively, use the recording as a model, pausing it after each question. Then get Ss to take turns asking the questions, using the information from the listening to answer.

| 1 How | 2 Where | 3 Can |
| 4 Who | 5 What | 6 Are |

Skills Book, Grammar reference: Passive verbs, page 92

Language focus: Passive verbs

Passive verbs are often used in formal reports and official documents, especially when describing a process. We use active verbs when we talk about what people or things do and passive verbs when we describe what happens to people or things. Passive verbs are formed by using the appropriate tense of the auxiliary *be*, followed by the past participle of the verb, e.g.:
Active: *The cleaner discovered the fire.*
Passive: *The fire **was discovered** by the cleaner.*

It is possible to omit the agent in passive sentences, and we usually do this if the agent isn't important. When the agent is named he/she/it is usually introduced using *by*. Both these sentences are possible; we would use the second one if we considered the agent to be unimportant:
*All the alarms are tested **by** the manager twice a week.*
All the alarms are tested twice a week.

Language focus: Indirect questions

When we want to make a question seem less direct, we can add a polite expression at the start of the question, e.g.:
Direct: *What was damaged?*
Indirect: *Can you tell me what was damaged?*

Word order in indirect questions is the same as in affirmative statements and we do not use the auxiliary *do/did*:
*Where **is** the conference room?*
*Can you tell me where the conference room **is**?*
*When **did he phone** the fire brigade?*
*Can you tell me when **he phoned** the fire brigade?*

Task 1

To introduce the task, ask Ss to read the introduction and say what equipment they think was stolen. Tell Ss that they are going to role-play a meeting between the security manager and an insurance representative. What information do Ss think the insurance representative might want?

Step 1: Ask Ss to work in pairs. Each S reads their information card on the relevant page at the back of the book and prepares three questions using the prompts. Circulate and help where necessary.

Step 2: Then Ss role-play the meeting. Ss ask their questions and use the information on their role card to answer their partner's questions.

Suggested questions
Student A
When was the office broken into?
Who called the police?
How many PCs and laptops were stolen?

Student B
Where is the claim form sent?
Which documents are required?
How long does Kingsway take to process the claim? /
How long does it take Kingsway to process the claim?

Analysis

Give Ss time to consider their performance individually and then start a group discussion. Check that Ss used falling intonation at the end of their questions.

Listening 2 **1**

Tell Ss that they are going to hear a meeting at CSG Electronics about the break-in. Read the statements with the class and clarify any unfamiliar vocabulary (e.g. *processed*, *independent assessor*). Ss listen and tick the statements that are correct. Check answers around the class and ask Ss to correct any information that is wrong (i.e. make the first and third statements negative: *... hasn't been found*; *... isn't ready ...*).

> The reports are being processed.
> The insurance company needs two reports.
> Stuart needs to make an appointment with the independent assessor.

Listening 2 **2**

Ask Ss to listen again and match the two parts of the sentences. Ask Ss to identify which sentences refer to someone asking for clarification (1, 3, 4, 5, 7) and which refer to someone clarifying what they are saying (2, 6). You may wish to ask Ss to identify the indirect questions used (5, 7). Point out that it is also possible to make a statement into a question by using rising intonation (4).

| 1 g | 2 a | 3 f | 4 b | 5 c | 6 d | 7 e |

Optional activity
Photocopiable resource 11.1 (page 181)

To consolidate the different types of questions used in the lesson, ask Ss to work in pairs / small groups. Photocopy and cut up the Market research questionnaire sheets A and B. Ask Ss to work in pairs and give A/B sheets to each pair. Tell Ss to vary the types of questions that they use (open/closed, direct/indirect). When Ss are confident, they should ask their partner the questions to complete the form.

Task 2

Ss are going to role-play a meeting between the Security Manager at CSG Electronics and the insurance assessor.

Step 1: Divide the class into two groups (A and B). Ask Ss to read their role cards at the back of the book and prepare for their meeting. Encourage Ss to think about whether they wish to use direct or indirect questions. Ss should also think about phrases that they might need to use to ask their partner to clarify information.

Step 2: Ss role-play the meeting. They ask questions and answer using the information on their role cards. Encourage Ss to ask for clarification or clarify their own information where necessary.

Analysis

Allow Ss a little time to reflect and then start a group discussion. Ask Ss to give examples of phrases that they used to give or ask for clarification.

Culture at work

You could introduce the topic by simply standing in front of the class, without saying anything. How long does it take the Ss (or yourself) to break the silence? Attitudes to silence can vary from culture to culture. The reason that it is important in a business context is that people may feel uncomfortable if they do not receive the response that they expect (if someone speaks when they did not expect a response, or is silent when they did expect a response). Ask Ss to read through the information and clarify any unfamiliar vocabulary. Encourage Ss to give examples from their own experience. Ask Ss to complete their own culture profile about responding in conversation on page 82. (Ss identify and mark with a cross where they believe their culture is situated on the line ranging from Silence OK to Silence not OK.)

Skills Book, Culture profile, page 82

What do you think?

Discuss the questions with the class. Write on the board:

Increase the amount of English homework?

Give Ss time to think of arguments for and against. Write the points they come up with on the board and then have a brief class discussion.

Skills Book, Good business practice, Meetings, Evaluating arguments, page 77

What do you say? 2

Ask Ss to work in pairs. After Ss have completed the exercise, encourage them to suggest any other phrases they know for putting arguments for and against. You could go back to the points they thought of in What do you think? and ask them to discuss the topic again, this time practising using the phrases they have just looked at.

> a) The fact is ... My view is ... because ... The main point is ... Don't you think ...
> b) Yes, but ... I understand your point, but ... On the other hand ... That's right.

Task 3

Tell Ss that they are going to have a meeting to discuss whether working hours should be increased in a company.

Step 1: Divide the class into two groups (company directors and union representatives). Ask Ss to prepare their arguments and to think about the arguments that the other group might use. Circulate and help where necessary.

Step 2: Now Ss work in groups of four and role-play the meeting. Each group should have two company directors and two union representatives. You may wish to review phrases for coming to a decision (see Unit 9, page 45). Ss put forward their arguments and ask for clarification where necessary.

Analysis

Allow Ss a little time to reflect and then ask them to discuss the questions with their group.

Self-assessment

Allow Ss a few minutes to think about what they have achieved from the unit and tick the boxes. Suggest what Ss can do to gain further practice.

CD-ROM

INTELLIGENT BUSINESS (PRE-INTERMEDIATE) TEACHER'S BOOK: SKILLS BOOK

Unit 12: Deal with problems

UNIT OBJECTIVES

Skills: Explain a problem
Discuss options
Deal with a problem
Language: Conditionals
Culture at work: Calm or expressive?

Units 2 and 7 introduced skills for getting through on the telephone and making and changing appointments. This unit builds on those skills by looking at how to deal with problems on the telephone. When dealing with problems by telephone, it is useful to consider the following:
If you need to make a complaint:
- Make sure that you are speaking to someone who can help with the problem
- Briefly explain what the problem is
- If appropriate, say what you want to happen to resolve the problem
- Remain calm and polite.

If someone telephones you with a complaint:
- Check that you are the correct person to deal with the problem
- Listen carefully and ask questions to find out exactly what the problem is
- If possible, offer a solution. Or say that you will call the person back when you have looked into the matter
- Remain calm and polite.

Cultural attitudes may affect:
- How a problem is expressed (direct or indirect)
- The expectations of the person making a complaint (whether they expect it to be dealt with immediately)
- Levels of politeness in dealing with complaints.

What do you think?

Before opening books, ask Ss if they have ever made a complaint. Have Ss ever had to deal with a complaint? How did they approach the situations? Which do Ss find more difficult – making or dealing with complaints? Ask Ss to open their books and read the strategies. The aim of the questions is to get Ss to think about the two different perspectives of making and dealing with complaints. Give Ss time to answer the questions individually and then start a class discussion to compare ideas.

Skills Book, Good business practice, Telephoning, Making and dealing with complaints, page 80

Suggested answers
a) 1, 3, 6
b) 4, 5
c) 2, 7, 8

Listening 1 **1**

Ask Ss to say what is in the picture (electronic components). Explain that Ss are going to hear a telephone conversation between Simone Tournis and Mark Lodge about a problem with an order. Draw Ss' attention to the order form and ask questions such as: *What is the order number? How many units of SC3 87 were ordered? What product number did Simone order 140 units of?* Play the recording of the telephone conversation for Ss to complete the missing information on the form. Ask Ss to compare their answers with a partner. Then play the conversation again for Ss to check. Ask Ss: *How many units did Simone order of AH6 98?* (1,200) *Why does Simone need it quickly?* (her company is working on an urgent order) *Did Mark deal with the problem in a calm and polite way?* (yes).

| AH6 98 | wrong **quantity** | arrange to **send** by courier |
| KJ7 6B | didn't **arrive** | arrive by **tomorrow** morning |

Listening 1 **2**

Ask individual Ss to read out phrases 1–12 and ask the class if they can remember who said each one, Simone or Mark, or if they can work it out from context. Play the recording again for Ss to note who said each phrase. Check answers with the class. You could ask Ss to work in pairs and read the audioscript of the conversation on page 110.

1 S 2 S 3 M 4 M 5 M 6 S 7 S 8 M
9 M 10 M 11 S 12 M

Optional activity
Photocopiable resource 12.1 (page 182)
You may wish to photocopy the Telephone phrases sheet containing useful expressions and give a copy to each S to help them prepare their conversations for Task 1.

Task 1

To introduce the topic, write on the board:

Make a complaint   Deal with a complaint

Ask Ss to suggest stages of a telephone call when a person is making a complaint (e.g. say who you are, explain the problem, say what you want to happen, end the call politely) and dealing with a complaint (e.g. ask questions to find out what the problem is, apologise/sympathise, say what you will do, end the call politely). Write suggestions under the appropriate heading. Ss will now role-play two telephone calls where they explain and deal with problems on the telephone. Ask Ss to work in pairs, turn to the relevant page at the back of the book and prepare phrases for conversation 1. Refer Ss to the phrases in Listening 1 and/or give Ss a photocopy of the Telephone phrases (Photocopiable resource 12.1, page 182). When Ss are confident, ask them to sit back-to-back and role-play the telephone conversation. Then get Ss to prepare and role-play conversation 2.

Analysis

Allow Ss a moment to reflect on the questions individually and then ask them to discuss the questions with their partner. Ask Ss for examples of phrases that they used for explaining the problem in their conversation.

What do you say? 1

Ss work with books closed. Ask: *What sort of catalogues have you received recently? How often do you buy products by mail order?* Read out the first two sentences of the rubric and ask Ss: *How many extra catalogues has the client been charged for?* (500) *What options do you think the sales assistant will suggest?* Ask Ss to open their books. Check Ss understand they have to order what the sales assistant says and draw their attention to the opening sentence (f). Ss work individually and put the sentences in the correct order. Check answers.

a 5	b 4	c 2	d 6	e 3
or a 6	b 5	c 2	d 4	e 3

What do you say? 2

Ask Ss what they think of the two options. Ss imagine that they are the client and choose a sentence to respond. (Either option is suitable so there is no right or wrong answer.) This is a good opportunity to look at the language for discussing options (see Language focus opposite).

What do you say? 3

Ask Ss to work in pairs and prepare a telephone conversation between the client and the sales assistant at GMH Printing. Circulate and help. Then ask Ss to sit back-to-back and role-play the telephone call.

Possible conversation

Client:	I have a problem with my order. I ordered 2,000 catalogues but I've received, and been charged for, 2,500.
Sales assistant:	(sentences a–f)
Client:	The best solution is if … (a or b).
Sales assistant:	Certainly, I'll arrange that for you.
Client:	Thanks for your help.
Sales assistant:	Glad to be of help.

Language focus: Talking about options

When we discuss options, we can use conditional sentences (conditional 1) to talk about possible results of an action, e.g. *If I arrange a refund, I'll have to charge full price on your next order.*

When there are two possible options, we can list them:
*You can **either** order online **or** visit our store.*

The following phrases are useful when saying which option we prefer:
The best solution is if (you refund the money).
I think it's better/best if (I visit the store).
I think I'll (order online).

Skills Book, Grammar reference: Conditionals, page 93

Optional activity

You could present the class with one or two other situations where they need to suggest options and decide on which they prefer. This could be done with the whole class or in small groups, e.g.:

1 You bought a plane ticket (refundable) and now the date of your business trip has changed. What two options might the travel agent offer? Which option will you choose?
(Suggestions: refund the price of the ticket or change the date of the flight.)

2 You need to discuss business with a colleague in another country. It is not possible for either of you to travel. Suggest options for how to have your discussion. Which option will you choose?
(Suggestions: by telephone, video conference, email, etc.)

See if Ss can think of any other situations and suggest options for them.

Task 2

Before starting Task 2, ensure that Ss feel confident with the language for talking about options (see Language focus on page 159 and Grammar reference on page 93 for a review of conditionals). In Step 1 Ss focus on accuracy and in Step 2 communication is the most important factor.

Step 1: Ask Ss to read the situation and then work in pairs and write the telephone conversation. Encourage Ss to refer to the Useful phrases. Circulate and help, encouraging Ss to self-correct where needed. It may be useful to note any common errors and have a feedback session to review key language after the task has finished.

Step 2: Ss role-play the conversation between the manager and the customer. It would be useful if Ss read their conversation once together and then role-played the conversation again without referring to their written dialogue. They could take turns playing the part of the customer and the manager. Ask one or two pairs to role-play the telephone conversation to the class and compare the different phrases and language that pairs used.

Analysis

Ask Ss to consider the questions individually and then discuss with the class. Encourage Ss to give reasons for the option that they chose.

Culture at work

Ss work with books closed. Ask Ss how they would feel if someone made a complaint and was obviously angry. How would they handle the situation? Have Ss ever shown anger or annoyance when making a complaint? How did the other person react? On the board write:

Calm *Expressive*

Read out the points for calm/expressive in the box in jumbled order and ask Ss to say which column they think the attitude goes in. Ss open books and discuss the statements in pairs / small groups. Encourage Ss to use examples from their own experience. Then ask Ss to complete their own culture profile about being calm or expressive on page 82. (Ss identify and mark with a cross where they believe their culture is situated on the line ranging from Calm to Expressive.)

Listening 2

To introduce the listening, ask Ss to suggest positive and negative adjectives to describe how a person can deal with a complaint (e.g. *polite, friendly, helpful/rude, impolite, unhelpful, unfriendly,* etc.). Tell Ss that they are going to listen to a telephone conversation between a shop owner (a customer) and a supplier. Play the conversation for Ss to answer the questions. Play the conversation again and ask Ss to suggest how the supplier could handle the situation better. Draw Ss' attention to the tone that the supplier uses

(uninterested and unhelpful). How would Ss feel if they were making a complaint and someone spoke like this?

| 1 c | 2 b | 3 a | 4 b |

Task 3

Tell Ss that they are going to rewrite the conversation in Listening 2 to make it more polite, so that the problem is resolved and the customer is satisfied. It may be useful to ask Ss first to read the audioscript on pages 110–111 with a partner, taking turns to be the unhelpful supplier.

Step 1: Ss work in pairs to rewrite the conversation, referring to the audioscript on pages 110–111. Check that Ss understand the aims for the shop owner and supplier.

Step 2: When Ss are confident, ask them to role-play the conversation. They can practise the conversation once using their notes, and then a second time without notes.

Listening 3

Play the polite version of the conversation. Ask Ss to tick any of the phrases in their own dialogue that the shop owner and supplier use. Have a short discussion highlighting similarities and differences between the recording and Ss' own dialogues. Draw Ss' attention to the difference in the tone of voice that the supplier uses in the polite version compared with the original version.

Analysis

Allow Ss a little time to reflect and then start a class discussion.

Self-assessment

Allow Ss a few minutes to think about what they have achieved from the unit and tick the boxes. Suggest what Ss can do to gain further practice.

CD-ROM

Writing 4: Letters

UNIT OBJECTIVES	
Skills:	Make a complaint
	Respond to a complaint
Language:	Conditionals

Letters are usually sent to people outside the company, so the style tends to be formal or neutral. The following may be important when writing letters:
- The reader (Is it someone that the writer knows and has communicated with on previous occasions?)
- Formality (in most business letters, contractions are not used, but the level of formality in vocabulary and phrases can vary depending on the sender's relationship to the reader)
- The purpose of the letter (Is the aim clear?)
- Accuracy (grammar, spelling, punctuation).

Cultural attitudes may have an impact on the following:
- The formality of language and expression used
- Layout of the letter
- Standard phrases for opening and closing the letter
- Use of titles in the greeting or signature line.

- Style guide, Letters, page 10
- Style guide, General rules, page 3
- Teacher's book, Writing preparation framework, page 188
- Teacher's book, Writing feedback framework, page 189

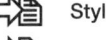

What do you think? 1

Before opening books, ask Ss how often they write or receive business letters in their job. In pairs / small groups, ask Ss to describe how a letter is usually structured in their country (e.g. Where is the address/date placed on the page? What phrases are used to start and end a letter in their own language?). Ask Ss to open their books. Explain that the letter refers to the British style of layout, etc. Ask Ss to number the items in the order that they appear in a letter and compare answers with a partner. Check answers with the class.

| a 3 | b 5 | c 2 | d 4 | e 1 | f 6 |

What do you think? 2

Ask Ss to match the parts of the letter a–f with the examples 1–6. You may wish to point out differences in openings and closings depending on whether we know the name of the person that we are writing to or not (see Language focus below). Check answers and discuss any differences in style with that used in Ss' own countries.

| 1 b | 2 c | 3 a | 4 f | 5 e | 6 d |

Language focus: Beginning and ending letters

Titles: **Male** **Female**
Mr Ms, Mrs, Miss

(*Ms* – pronounced /mɪz/ – can be used for both married and unmarried females, or if the recipient's marital status is unknown. It is generally preferred to *Miss*.)

When we know the name of the person that we are writing to, formal British English letters normally:

Start   **End**
Dear Kjeld,   Yours sincerely,
Dear Mr Larson,

When we do not know the name of the person:
Start   **End**
Dear Sir or Madam, Yours faithfully,
Dear Sir,
Dear Madam,
Dear Sirs,

Informal letters:
Start   **End**
Dear Jo,   Regards,
                    Kind regards,
                    Best wishes,

What do you write?

Draw Ss' attention to the email. Ask check questions such as: *Who is the email from/to? What is the problem? What does 'asap' stand for?* (as soon as possible) *How does Mary start/end the email? What are the differences between phrases used to start/end a letter?* Elicit other differences between the style of an email and a business letter (an email is often more informal and more direct). Go through the Useful phrases and ask Ss where these might go in the letter (beginning, middle, end). Check that Ss understand that they should use Mr Larson's address in the margin and their own name/address (not Mary Howard's) and today's date to complete the letter. Ask Ss to rewrite the email in the style of a letter.

INTELLIGENT BUSINESS (PRE-INTERMEDIATE) TEACHER'S BOOK: SKILLS BOOK

> **Suggested answer**
>
> (S's own address)
>
> Mr Larson
> Customer Services Department
> Lang and Turner
> Coleford
> Gloucester
> (today's date)
>
> Dear Mr Larson,
>
> **Customer service complaint**
> I am writing to complain because I phoned the Sales department today to ask for information about a product and the sales assistant was impolite and unhelpful. Could you arrange for a supervisor to contact me to discuss this as soon as possible?
> Thank you for your help with this matter.
> Yours sincerely,
> (S's name)

Task 1

Tell Ss that they stayed in a hotel on business and were unhappy with their room. They are going to write a letter of complaint to the manager. Instruct Ss to use their own name and address and today's date. Tell Ss to use the same structure as in the previous activity. After Ss have finished their letter, ask them to compare with a partner. Encourage peer correction before giving your feedback.

> **Suggested answer**
>
> (S's own address)
>
> Hotel Marina
> Marine Parade
> Brighton
> Sussex
> (today's date)
>
> Dear Mr Newton,
> I am writing to complain because I stayed at the Hotel Marina last week on business and was unhappy with my room. My room was small and noisy. When I booked I requested a large, quiet room.
> Could you arrange a reduction in the room rate for my next booking?
> Thank you for your help with this matter.
> Yours sincerely,
> (S's name)

What do you think? 2

Ask Ss to read the three letters and answer the questions. You could use this to highlight differences between formal and informal letters (see Language focus on page 161). Draw Ss'

attention to letter B. Ask Ss to identify the phrase that refers to something placed in the envelope with the letter (*Please find enclosed*) and offers further assistance (*Please contact me if you need any further help with this*). This would be a good opportunity to look at conditional instructions (see Language focus below).

1 C   2 A
3 B (it uses the same formal style as the letter of complaint)

> **Language focus: Conditional instructions**
>
> The simplest form of the conditional (*if* + present tense + imperative) is used for situations where we ask someone to do something in particular circumstances. It is often used to offer assistance in letters:
> *Let me know if I can be of further assistance.*
> *Please write again if you need more information.*
> *Please contact me if you would like me to clarify anything.*

Skills book, Grammar reference: Conditionals, page 93

Task 2

Ss are now going to write a letter to reply to Mary Howard's complaint (What do you write? page 60). In this letter, Ss do not need to include the sender's or recipient's address, or a signature. Refer Ss to What do you think? 2, letter B, for phrases to apologise, refer to enclosed documents and offer further assistance. If Ss know any other suitable phrases, encourage their use. You could ask Ss to write the letter for homework and then compare with a partner at the start of the next lesson, before handing it in for feedback.

> **Suggested answer**
>
> Dear Ms Howard,
> I am sorry to hear that you did not receive polite and helpful service when you telephoned our Sales department. The supervisor has discussed the matter with the sales assistant.
> Please find enclosed the information that you requested.
> Please contact me if you need any further help with this matter.
> I apologise for any inconvenience.
> Yours sincerely,

Skills book, Grammar reference: Conditionals, page 93

Unit 13: Run a meeeting

UNIT OBJECTIVES	
Skills:	Manage time
	Keep to the point
	Close the meeting
Language:	Adjectives and adverbs
Culture at work:	Attitudes to time in meetings

This unit extends the skills for meetings introduced in Units 1, 6, 9 and 11. When running a meeting, it is useful to do the following:
- Make sure participants are clear about the aims and objectives of the meeting
- Be aware of time management issues (e.g. try to ensure that the meeting starts and finishes on schedule and estimate the amount of time allocated to each agenda point)
- Keep to the agenda and avoid unnecessary digressions
- Summarise the discussion and clarify any action points.

Cultural attitudes may affect the following aspects of presenting an argument:
- Expectations about the role and function of the chairperson
- Attitudes to time (e.g. punctuality, digressions, fixed start and end times, etc.) and agendas (flexible, fixed or no agenda)
- Style of the meeting (e.g. formal/informal; how much participation is encouraged).

What do you think?

Before opening books, ask the class to think about the last meeting they went to. Ask: *Did it start and finish on time? How long did it last? How did the chairperson organise time?* Open books and ask Ss to work in pairs. Read through the questions with the class and check Ss' understanding. Ask Ss to discuss the questions and encourage pairs to report back their ideas to the rest of the class. You can extend the discussion by asking Ss to think of positive and negative factors in attending a meeting where:

a) The chairperson controls the structure of the meeting and the time spent on each agenda point.
b) Structure of the meeting and management of time are flexible.

AOB is usually discussed at the end of the meeting.

Listening 1 **1**

Focus Ss on the picture and ask what sort of place they think it shows (a health spa). Have Ss visited a spa? Where was it located? Did they enjoy it? Draw Ss' attention to the agenda. Can Ss think of any other points that might need to be discussed about opening the spa? Tell Ss that they are going to listen to a meeting about the opening of a new spa complex. Play the recording once and ask Ss: *How many people speak at the meeting?* (four). Play it again for Ss to listen and tick the topics that are discussed in the meeting. Elicit what topic is mentioned in the meeting but is not on the agenda.

Interviewing staff
Uniforms for spa staff
Press release

Extra topic: opening party

Listening 1 **2**

Ss listen again and tick the phrases that they hear. You may wish to practise saying each of the phrases with the class. Tone of voice is important when saying phrases such as these as it is easy to sound aggressive. The tone should remain neutral. You may also wish to draw Ss' attention to the use of adjectives and adverbs (see Language focus on page 164). Play the recording again and ask Ss: *What phrase does the chairperson use when he does not want to discuss a topic?* (Not at the moment) *When does he offer to talk about it?* (after the meeting). Can Ss think of any other phrases to use to say when they do not want to discuss a topic in a meeting? (e.g. *Can we talk about that later? Let's discuss that after the meeting. We don't have time to go into that just now,* etc.)

1, 2, 4, 5, 6

Skills Book, Grammar reference: Adjectives and adverbs, page 94

INTELLIGENT BUSINESS (PRE-INTERMEDIATE) TEACHER'S BOOK: SKILLS BOOK

> ### Language focus: Adjectives and adverbs
>
> We often use adjectives and adverbs when we talk about time:
> *I want to make a quick point.* (adjective)
> *She made her point quickly.* (adverb)
>
> Regular adjectives change form when they become adverbs, generally by adding *-ly*, but some do not change, e.g.:
> *He was early/late for the meeting.* (adjective)
> *The meeting started early/late.* (adverb)
>
> Some have irregular forms, e.g.:
> *It was a good meeting.* (adjective)
> *The meeting went well.* (adverb)
>
> Adverbs of frequency (*usually, often, always, never*, etc.) are normally placed before the main verb, apart from when used with *be*:
> *We **usually finish** meetings on time.*
> *We **are usually** on time for meetings.*

> **Optional activity**
> **Photocopiable resource 13.1 (page 183)**
> If you think that your class may have difficulties thinking of their own ideas for Task 1, photocopy and cut up the role cards and give one to each S in the group of four.

Task 1

Tell Ss that they are going to role-play the last five minutes of a meeting. Ask Ss to read the information and the agenda and check Ss' understanding. Give Ss about five minutes to work individually and look at the agenda and note their ideas. (If your class need more support, they can use the role cards from photocopiable resource 13.1 on page 183.) When Ss are ready, ask them to work in groups of four and role-play the last five minutes of the meeting. The objective is to discuss the three remaining agenda points before the meeting ends. Point out that everyone in the group is equally responsible for managing time. Tell Ss when the five minutes are up. Check how well Ss were able to manage time. Which agenda points did they find it easy or difficult to move on from?

Analysis

Give Ss time to consider their performance individually and then start a group discussion. Ask Ss to say what phrases their group used to manage time.

What do you say?

This exercise focuses on phrases for keeping to the point, returning to the point and moving on to a new topic. Go through the phrases and check Ss' understanding. Ask Ss to work in pairs and match the phrases with the headings. Encourage them to suggest any other phrases they know for each of the headings.

> **a** 1, 3   **b** 2, 5   **c** 4, 6

Culture at work

Ask Ss to read the information about the two attitudes to time in meetings. Encourage Ss to give examples from meetings that they have attended. How do Ss think someone who is used to a relaxed style of meeting would feel if they attended a very structured meeting (and vice versa)? Ask Ss to think about which statements about attitudes to work apply to their own culture and complete the culture profile on page 82. (Ss identify and mark with a cross where they believe their culture is situated on the line ranging from Relaxed to Structured.)

Skills Book, Culture profile, page 82

Task 2

To introduce the topic, ask Ss how they feel when people do not keep to the agenda topics in meetings. Ss are going to use role cards to role-play a staff meeting, looking at three items on an agenda. Read the agenda points and check Ss' understanding. Encourage Ss to use the phrases from Listening 1 and What do you say? when managing time and keeping to the agenda in their meeting.

Step 1: Ss work in groups of three and look at their role cards at the back of the book to prepare for the meeting. Ss look at the agenda points and note ideas to introduce in the meeting. Make sure that Ss realise that on each agenda card there is one agenda point where they will need to manage time and one agenda point where they will try to introduce something that is not on the agenda. Encourage Ss to prepare any phrases that will be useful for introducing their points, managing time and keeping to the agenda. Circulate, helping where necessary.

Step 2: Make sure that Ss realise that the time limit for each agenda question is three minutes and that there is no chairperson, so each member of the group is responsible for managing time and keeping to the agenda. How did Ss feel when group members tried to move away from the agenda point?

UNIT 13

Analysis

Allow Ss a little time to reflect and then start a group discussion. Ask Ss to give examples of phrases that they used to keep to the point. How did Ss make the meeting return to the point when necessary?

Listening 2 [1]

Tell Ss that they are going to hear the closing comments from four different meetings. Draw Ss' attention to the four different types of meeting (a–d) and ask Ss which of these types of meetings they have attended. Which type of meeting do they think will be the least structured (d)? Play the recording of the four meetings and ask Ss to match each with one of the meeting types a–d. Check answers with the class. Encourage Ss to say what information helped them to choose their answers.

| 1 b | 2 c | 3 d | 4 a |

Listening 2 [2]

Play the recording again for Ss to choose the correct words in italics to complete the phrases from the listening. Check answers with the class. Ask Ss which phrases can be used to:

a) Ask if there are any other items to discuss (AOB) (1, 5)
b) Close the meeting (2, 3, 6)
c) Thank participants (4)

Say the phrases and ask Ss to repeat; then ask Ss to take turns saying the phrases with a partner.

| 1 anything | 2 stop | 3 good |
| 4 for | 5 everything | 6 there |

Task 3

Ask Ss to close their books. Ask Ss what they do to keep cool when the weather is very hot. What products do they buy to help them keep cool at work and at home? Check that Ss understand solar energy. Ask the class to think of things that can be powered by solar energy.

Ask Ss to open their books and look at the photo. What is it? (a fan) Ask Ss to read the information and then ask Ss check questions, e.g. *What type of meeting is this?* (an emergency meeting) *What does this company produce?* (the Solafan) *Why is the product selling quickly?* (there has been a heat-wave) *What is the problem?* (the company might not be able to meet production demands). Explain that although this meeting will have a chairperson, the other members of the group are given responsibility for different aspects of managing time or keeping to the agenda. This role-play consolidates meetings skills and language from Units 6 and 9. You may wish to review any specific language areas that your class may need in order to use language and skills to the maximum benefit.

 Skills Book, Unit 6, Give your opinion, Ask for opinions, agree and disagree, pages 28–31

 Skills Book, Unit 9, Make suggestions, Respond to suggestions, Make a choice, pages 42–45

Step 1: Ask Ss to work in groups of four and assign each S a role (A–D). Give Ss time to prepare for the meeting. Role card A is the chairperson. They have general responsibility for managing time and keeping to the agenda. They have no opinion on their card, though the S can put their own ideas forward. The chairperson should begin by introducing the final agenda item and is responsible for inviting AOB (Any Other Business) and closing the meeting. Role cards B–D at the back of the book give information about the opinions that Ss will put forward, their specific area of responsibility (concerning managing time or keeping to the agenda) and the topic that they will introduce in AOB.

Step 2: When Ss feel confident, ask groups to role-play the meeting. The chairperson should begin by introducing the final agenda item. Give your class a time limit of ten to fifteen minutes to discuss the agenda item, come to a decision and deal with any other business before the chairperson closes the meeting. As groups hold their meetings, it may be useful to circulate and note any language points that it would be useful to go over with the class after the lesson.

Analysis

Allow Ss a little time to reflect individually on their performance and then start a group discussion. Discuss which roles Ss found most challenging. Ask Ss for examples of language that they used to manage time and keep to the point. Find out how individual groups closed the meeting.

Self-assessment

Allow Ss a few minutes to think about what they have achieved from the unit and tick the boxes. Suggest what Ss can do to gain further practice.

 CD-ROM

INTELLIGENT BUSINESS (PRE-INTERMEDIATE) TEACHER'S BOOK: SKILLS BOOK

Unit 14: Negotiate

UNIT OBJECTIVES	
Skills:	Present a proposal
	Accept and refuse
	Look for a creative solution
Language:	Conditionals
Culture at work:	Saying 'No' in a negotiation

This unit provides an introduction to negotiating. When negotiating, it is useful to do the following:
- Make sure proposals are well prepared
- Be clear about what you want to gain from the negotiation and what you are able to concede
- Think about how the other person will approach the negotiation
- If you reject an offer, explain why it is unacceptable
- Ask questions to gain further information where necessary
- Be open-minded if the other person proposes options that you had not previously considered.

Cultural attitudes may have an impact on negotiations in the following ways:
- The style of the negotiation (formal/informal, direct/indirect)
- The type of negotiation (team negotiation or dealing with one key person)
- Attitudes to authority (some cultures may only wish to negotiate with those who have the authority to make immediate decisions)
- Interpreting responses (body language and the significance of saying 'yes' can differ from culture to culture).

What do you think?

Begin the lesson with books closed. Write the following on the board and ask Ss to suggest letters to complete the words:

1) Present a p _ _ _ _ _ _ l
2) Accept or r _ _ _ _ e an o _ _ _ r
3) C _ _e to an a _ _ _ _ _ _ _ t

(1 proposal 2 refuse, offer 3 come, agreement)

Elicit what business situation these are all connected to (negotiating). Ask Ss to open their books and discuss the questions in pairs / small groups. After a few minutes, open it out to a class discussion. Give the class an example of a formal and informal negotiation that you have had in the past and encourage Ss to give their own examples. If Ss disagree with the view of a successful negotiation illustrated in the quotation, ask them to think of their own definition of a successful negotiation. You may wish to introduce the term *win–win* (see Optional activity below), which is used to describe a negotiation that is considered successful for both sides.

> **Optional activity**
> **Photocopiable resource 14.1 (page 183)**
> To extend the discussion about negotiations, you could photocopy the negotiations cards. Ask Ss to work in groups of three. Give each pair a set of the three negotiations cards, placed face down on the table. Also give each pair a set of the three negotiation outcome cards, placed face upwards on the table. Each S takes a negotiation card and reads it out. Ss discuss what negotiation outcome it describes (win–lose, win–win or lose–lose).

Listening Part 1

Before Ss listen, ask them to read the information about Amy Tang in the rubric and then ask check questions, e.g. *What's Amy Tang's job title? What sort of company does she work for? What does it specialise in? What does she want to happen to the deadline?* Ask Ss to say all the numbers in questions 1 and 2. Play the recording for Ss to choose the correct option. Check answers with the class.

Play the recording again for Ss to answer the questions. Ask Ss to compare their answers with a partner. You may wish to spend some time looking at how Amy structures her proposal. She:
- points out that they both want the project to move forward quickly
- clarifies what her position is
- gives background information to support her argument
- explains possible negative results if her proposal is not accepted
- says what she wants and how this would benefit the customer.

Ask Ss if they think Amy's proposal is reasonable? Should Gordon accept?

166

1

1 1 a   2 c   3 c

2
1 I know that we both want this project to move forward as quickly as possible.
2 The price of the order would increase.
3 A two-week extension and she'd guarantee the original price.

> Skills Book, Good business practice, Negotiations, Preparing for a negotiation, page 81

Listening Part 2

Ss listen to Gordon and choose the correct word in italics to complete his response. Point out that both options (position/problem; propose/suggest) are grammatically correct. Ask Ss which option they think is more formal – the words that Gordon uses or the alternatives (Gordon's choice of words is slightly more formal). Again, spend a few moments highlighting the structure of Gordon's counter-proposal. He:

- shows that he understands Amy's situation
- explains what he wants / doesn't want
- briefly puts forward an alternative proposal.

Ask Ss to work in pairs and take turns reading both versions of the response. Do Ss think that Gordon's response is reasonable? Why? / Why not?

position; propose

Listening Part 3

Ask Ss to tell their partner if they think Amy will agree to Gordon's counter-proposal (she does). Play Part 3. Ask Ss if both Amy and Gordon seem pleased with the new arrangement (yes).

You could ask Ss to turn to pages 111–112 and read the audioscript for Parts 1–3 with their partner. Highlight any phrases or vocabulary that you think may be useful for your Ss.

> **Optional activity**
> **Photocopiable resource 14.2 (page 184)**
> You may wish to photocopy the Negotiations outline for Ss to plan their negotiations. Give one to each S. Ss could also use another copy of the outline later to plan Task 2.

Task 1

Tell Ss that they are going to negotiate a problem with a deadline over the telephone. Ask Ss to suggest differences between negotiating face-to-face and on the telephone (on the telephone you cannot read the other person's body language or facial expressions; it is very important to be clear and concise;

you may need to ask questions to clarify information, etc.). Divide the class into two groups and ask all Student As and all Student Bs to read their information at the back of the book and prepare their negotiations together. Encourage Ss to use phrases from the listening to help them prepare. Then ask Ss to work in pairs and role-play the telephone negotiation back-to-back. Circulate and note any areas where Ss may need extra practice. You could ask Ss to swap roles and role-play the conversation again. This time, tell Ss that it is a face-to-face negotiation. When Ss finish, ask which type of negotiation they found easier. Why? Were both Ss happy with the outcome of the negotiation? Encourage Ss to give reasons why / why not.

Analysis

Give Ss a few minutes to think about their performance and then start a class discussion. Encourage Ss to give examples of the language that they used to present and respond to proposals.

Culture at work

Ask Ss to think about negotiations that they have had recently (at work or at home). Do Ss feel comfortable using 'no' directly? How do Ss feel if someone says 'no' to them without softening the language? Ask Ss to read through the information with a partner and give examples from their own experience, if possible. Can Ss think of any more examples of indirect ways of saying 'no' to add to those in the box? Then ask Ss to complete their own culture profile about saying 'no' in a negotiation on page 82. (Ss identify and mark with a cross where they believe their culture is situated on the line ranging from Refuse indirectly to Refuse directly.) Ask Ss if they can think of any situations that they have been in where an indirect or direct approach worked better.

What do you say? 1

Ask Ss to read the information and check understanding. Check answers with the class. You could ask Ss which phrase for disagreeing is more direct and which is more indirect (direct: *No, we can't do that*; indirect: *I'm afraid that's not possible*). Ask Ss why phrases that give you time to think might be useful (they give time to consider the proposal and also think about what phrases you need to respond). Say the phrases and ask Ss to repeat.

A: Yes, that's fine. We can accept that.
D: I'm afraid that's not possible. No, we can't do that.
G: I'll need to think about that. Can we come back to that?

Task 2

Ss are going to role-play another telephone conversation; this time an events organiser and a hotel manager negotiate the price of hotel room bookings. Divide the class into two groups (A and B). Ask Group A to look at the information for Student A and discuss how to structure their proposal and what phrases they think may be useful. Ss in Group A should consider whether they will propose a price to offer for the room rate, or whether they will ask the manager to offer a discount and consider that offer first. Group B students look at the information for Student B on page 101 and consider what discount they are willing to offer and what language they may need. Point out that Ss do not have to make the same choices as the rest of their group – this stage is about generating ideas and possible language to use in the role-play. When Ss are confident, ask them to work in A/B pairs and role-play the telephone conversation. Circulate and note any areas where Ss may need further practice. Have a feedback session, focusing on phrases and language that Ss used well. Then ask Ss to change partners and role-play the conversation again.

Analysis

Allow Ss a moment to consider their performance and then start a class discussion. Ask Ss if they can think of any ways that they would change their proposal or counter-proposal if they were doing the negotiation again.

What do you say? 2

Ask Ss to close their books. Throughout the course, Ss will have had lots of practice of brainstorming ideas, and now is a good time to examine the process in detail and focus on the steps of a brainstorming session: initially ideas are suggested without interruption or elaboration, and then the most useful ideas are evaluated and discussed at the end of the brainstorming session. Write *Brainstorming ideas* on the board and ask Ss to suggest things that people should and shouldn't do when brainstorming. What situations do Ss think that brainstorming would be useful for? (e.g. thinking of creative solutions, getting lots of ideas, looking at problems from different angles) Ask Ss to open their books and answer the questions to exercise 1 in pairs. Check answers with the class.

> 1
> Let everyone say their ideas
> Nominate someone to note all ideas
> Give short, quick ideas
> 2
> 1 B   2 E   3 E   4 B   5 E   6 B

Language focus: Conditionals

In negotiations, we often use conditional sentences to talk about the consequences of proposals and offers. We tend to use conditional 1 if we want to be direct and conditional 2 if we want to be more tentative. Compare this sentence from What do you say? 2:
If we did that, it would be a cheaper solution.
(conditional 2)
with this from What do you think? on page 66:
If you help me wash the car, I'll do the washing up.
(conditional 1)

Skills Book, Grammar reference: Conditionals, page 93

Optional activity
Tell Ss to imagine that their company has offered to pay £25,000 to a charity of the Ss' choice if Ss can raise the same amount in six months. The class can work together or in small groups. Ss brainstorm ideas on how to raise the money. Then have a brief evaluation session where Ss discuss some of the ideas in more detail.

Task 3

Ss prepare for a meeting to discuss creative ways to solve a problem with staff attendance.

Step 1: Ask Ss to work individually. Ask half the class to look at information for Student A and half to look at information for Student B. Ss look at the possible reasons for poor staff attendance, tick the two ideas that they most agree with and then add another reason of their own. Then Ss look at the ideas for the brainstorming meeting and add two more to the list. Circulate and help where needed.

Step 2: Now ask the class to work in their A/B groups (employee representatives and HR representatives). In their groups, Ss brainstorm creative ways to improve staff attendance. Remind Ss to nominate a S to note ideas.

Step 3: Ss work in groups of four (two employee representatives and two HR representatives). Ss discuss and evaluate ideas from their previous meeting and then decide which idea to recommend to the Managing Director. Ask groups to present their ideas to the class.

Analysis

Allow Ss a few minutes to think about the questions individually and then start a group discussion. Did Ss find it useful brainstorming and evaluating ideas in two stages?

Self-assessment

Allow Ss a few minutes to think about what they have achieved from the unit and tick the boxes. Suggest what Ss can do to gain further practice.

CD-ROM

Unit 15: Presentations

UNIT OBJECTIVES	
Skills:	Give reasons and explanations
	Summarise and conclude
	Deal with questions
Language:	Past simple
Culture at work:	Formal and informal presentations

Ss have looked at introducing a talk/presentation in Unit 5 and talking about trends in Unit 10. In this unit, Ss look at bringing a presentation to a close, in particular summarising and concluding and dealing with questions. When concluding a presentation, it is useful to do the following:
- Summarise key points
- Conclude the presentation
- Thank the audience for their attention
- Invite questions.

It is always a good idea when preparing a presentation to anticipate what questions the audience may ask. Then practise answering the questions clearly, giving reasons and explanations where needed.

Cultural attitudes may have an impact on the following aspects:
- The structure of the conclusion (brief or detailed summing up)
- How comfortable the audience feels about asking questions
- The style of asking and answering questions (direct or indirect).

Task 1

Before opening books, brainstorm five or six countries with Ss and write suggestions on the board. Ask a S to pick one of the countries mentioned. Tell the class that their office is going to relocate to that country. Elicit reasons why the company might have chosen that country. Then ask Ss to think of reasons for and against making the move.

Step 1: Ask the class to open their books. Draw Ss' attention to the phrases in the Useful language box. Ask Ss to work in pairs and complete the notes. Check answers with the class. Then Ss take it in turns to read the HR manager's notes as though they were presenting the reasons to an audience. This would be a good opportunity to spend some time reviewing/introducing language for giving explanations and reasons (see Language focus opposite).

1 Because of
2 so that
3 In order
4 This means that

Step 2: You can ask Ss to brainstorm ideas individually or have a brainstorming session with the whole class. Then Ss should choose one or two ideas and use any appropriate language from Step 1 to help prepare to give their decision and explanations/reasons for it. Ask Ss to work in pairs and take turns to give their decision and explanations/reasons to their partner.

Analysis

Give Ss a few moments to consider the questions individually and then start a class discussion. Elicit any of the phrases from Step 1 that Ss used to give explanations and reasons. Did Ss use any other phrases for giving explanations/reasons?

Language focus: Explanations and reasons

Draw Ss' attention to the following:
in order to ... (+ infinitive)
because of ... (+ noun)

This means that ... is used to explain consequences:
The cost of living has gone up. **This means that** *wages might increase.*
The company is relocating. **This means that** *you will need to move if you want to keep your jobs.*

So that ... can be used to explain reasons and choices:
We've updated our website **so that** *customers can order products online.*
The company will move to Slovenia **so that** *it can remain competitive.*

To give explanations and reasons we can also use *owing to* and *due to*:
Owing to *my family situation, I will not be moving to Slovenia ...* (reason)
This was due to *a rise in share prices ...* (explanation)

Sometimes when we give explanations and reasons, we may be giving information that some of the audience may already know:
As you may be aware, *because of high production costs the company will move to ...*

INTELLIGENT BUSINESS (PRE-INTERMEDIATE) TEACHER'S BOOK: SKILLS BOOK

What do you think?

Draw a seesaw on the board with *motivation* written along the middle and ask Ss if they can think of factors that can increase/decrease motivation. Read the question together and check Ss' understanding. Discuss the question with the class, encouraging Ss to expand their ideas and give reasons.

> **Optional activity**
> **Photocopiable resource 15.1 (page 184)**
> You may wish to photocopy the Motivational factors sheet and give a copy to each S. Go through the list and check Ss' understanding. Ask Ss to look at the factors and prioritise them in order of which are most important for them (1 = most important). Ask Ss to compare their ideas with a partner. There are no right or wrong answers – the aim is to focus Ss on the subject of motivation and what it means to them individually.

Listening 1 ▪ 1

Tell Ss that they are going to listen to a presentation about staff motivation. Howard Franks is summarising his main points. Ask Ss to listen and put the points in order and say which idea is not mentioned. You may wish to point out that the presentation uses different words to those in sentences a–e.

> 1 b   2 e   3 a   4 d   (c is not mentioned)

Listening 1 ▪ 2

Ss listen again and complete the summary. Some of the gaps are filled by one word and some need two words. Ask Ss to compare answers with a partner and then take turns to read the summary.

> 1 sum up   2 briefly   3 main   4 First
> 5 Second   6 Next   7 And finally

> **Optional activity**
> You could extend the vocabulary in Listening 1 by dictating the following:
> *secondly, in conclusion, also, to summarise, firstly, quickly, key*
>
> Ask Ss to look at exercise 2 again and say which gaps the words you have dictated could go in to complete the summary.
> (**1** summarise **2** quickly **3** key **4** Firstly
> **5** Secondly **6** Also **7** In conclusion)

Culture at work

Read the information with the class and check Ss' understanding. Ask Ss to think about the last presentation that they attended (or gave). What was the style of presentation – formal or informal? An informal style of presentation often focuses on making a connection with the audience, while a more formal presentation may have more distance between the presenter and the audience. You may like to point out to Ss that humour and stories should only be used in presentations if they feel comfortable using them. Humour does not always travel well across cultures. Then ask Ss to discuss the information with their partner and encourage Ss to give examples from presentations that they have attended. Ask Ss to complete their own culture profile about formal and informal presentations on page 82. (Ss identify and mark with a cross where they believe their culture is situated on the line ranging from Informal to Formal.) Have Ss attended presentations that use a mix of the two styles?

Listening 2

Tell Ss that they will hear the conclusion to two presentations. Play the two conclusions and ask Ss to say which is more formal and which is more informal, encouraging Ss to give reasons for their answers. Draw Ss' attention to the cloze phrases in exercise 2 and point out that the numbers next to each phrase indicate which conclusion (1 or 2) the sentence is from. See if Ss can guess any of the words before playing the recording again for Ss to complete the phrases. Check answers with the class. Say the phrases and ask the class to repeat.

> 1
> Conclusion 2 is more formal.
>
> 2
> **Signal the final point**
> 1 To finish
> 2 To conclude
> **Thank the audience**
> 1 Thanks for listening
> 2 Thank you for your attention
> **Invite questions**
> 1 Does anyone have any questions?
> 2 Would anyone like to ask any questions?

Task 2

This task consolidates language from Listening 1 and 2 for summarising and concluding a presentation. Tell Ss that they are going to prepare a conclusion of a presentation. Students can prepare in groups (A and B) or individually, depending on the needs of your class. In both presentations, Ss are staff trainers; however, the subject of each presentation is different.

170

Step 1: Student A looks at the information on page 72 and prepares a conclusion to a presentation about motivating teams. Student B looks at the information on page 102 and prepares a conclusion to a presentation about motivating new staff. Point out that the information under the heading *Summing up* should come in the first part of the summary and information under the heading *Concluding* should be used to close the presentation. The Useful phrases can be used by Ss to help them prepare, but Ss do not have to use them. Encourage Ss to use any other appropriate phrases that they know. In their presentations, Ss should:
- Summarise the main points
- Structure the summary (*firstly*, *secondly*, etc.)
- Thank the audience
- Invite questions.

Step 2: Now Ss work in pairs (A/B) and take turns to summarise and conclude their presentation. They can read the summary and conclusion they have prepared but encourage them just to refer to it. Ss listen to their partner's presentation and note down the main points in the conclusion. (Tell Ss that they will use the information in Writing 5.) When the presentations have finished, see if Ss can suggest any questions that they could ask about their partner's presentation.

Presentation preparation framework, page 186
Presentation feedback framework, page 187

Analysis

Give Ss a few moments to think about the questions individually, then ask them to discuss with their partner. Elicit some of the phrases that Ss used to summarise and conclude their presentation.

Listening 3 **1**

Tell Ss that they are going to listen to the conclusion to a presentation to explain problems about a recent project. Play Part 1 of the recording and ask Ss to note four questions that they could ask the speaker. If Ss wish to use other question words than those shown, they can do so. Elicit possible questions around the class.

> **Possible questions**
> (these are the ones asked in Part 2)
> Who left the team?
> Why didn't you understand the task?
> What information was confidential? / What was the confidential information?
> When was the new deadline?

Listening 3 **2**

Ss listen to Part 2, where the audience ask the speaker questions. Were any of the Ss' questions asked? Play the recording again for Ss to answer the questions. Check answers with the class.

> That's a good question.
> I'm afraid I can't answer that at the moment.
> I can't go into that now …

Task 3

In this task Ss are going to prepare a conclusion to a presentation and invite questions and attempt to answer.

Step 1: Ask Ss to look at the information about their presentation and prepare a summary/conclusion. It should follow the same structure as Task 2. This time Ss think about what questions their partner might ask and invent reasons/explanations to answer the questions.

Step 2: Ask Ss to work in pairs. As Ss listen to their partner's presentation, they should try to note one or more questions to ask at the end. Their partner should try to give explanations and reasons when they answer the questions.

Analysis

Allow Ss a little time to think about the questions individually and then ask them to discuss with their partner. Elicit questions that Ss asked and their partner's answer.

Self-assessment

Allow Ss a few minutes to think about what they have achieved from the unit and tick the boxes. Suggest what Ss can do to gain further practice.

CD-ROM

Writing 5: Short reports

UNIT OBJECTIVES	
Skills:	Summarise points
	Make recommendations
Language:	Adjectives and adverbs

Companies often have their own individual style and format for reports. The style and structure of the report may vary in level of formality according to its purpose and who will read it. When writing reports it is useful to consider the following:
- The reader (How much knowledge do they have of the subject discussed in the report?)
- The purpose of the report (Is the aim clear?)
- Accuracy (grammar, spelling, punctuation).

Cultural attitudes may have an impact on the following:
- The formality of language and expression used
- Structure and layout.

Style guide, Reports, page 18
Style guide, General rules, page 3
Teacher's book, Writing preparation framework, page 188
Teacher's book, Writing feedback framework, page 189

What do you think?

Before starting the exercise, ask Ss to think about the last report that they read (or wrote) in their own language. How long/short was it? What was the structure? Then ask Ss to match the parts of the report with the descriptions. Ask Ss to compare their answers with a partner and then check with the whole class.

| 1 d | 2 e | 3 a | 4 c | 5 b | 6 f |

What do you write? 1

Draw Ss' attention to the examples. Ask Ss to identify examples of short sentences (*Keep costs down*) and simple vocabulary (*Keep customers happy*), and to point to the bullet points (in the first example). It may be useful to point out that simple vocabulary does not mean simplifying ideas, it is simply making sure that information is presented in a clear and easy to read form. Ask Ss to rewrite the paragraph, leaving out any unnecessary or complex words and structuring the information so that it is clear and easy to read. Ask Ss to compare answers with a partner. Ask a S to dictate their paragraph to you and write it on the board. Check possible variations with the class.

Suggested answer
To summarise, here are the most important points from the training seminar on time management:
- Note down everything that you need to do
- Prioritise tasks
- Set deadlines.

(or number the points 1–3 instead of using bullet points)

Language focus: Punctuation

We can use a colon to introduce information that is presented in the form of a list:
... from the training seminar on time management:
- *Note down everything that you need to do*
- *Prioritise tasks*
- *Set deadlines.*

Task 1

Tell Ss that they are going to use information from their partner's presentation in Unit 15, Task 2. If Ss do not have details of their partner's presentation, they can use information about their own presentation to include in their report. If they didn't do Unit 15, Task 2, they should use the information from either page 72 or page 102. Refer Ss to What do you write? 1 to help them structure their summary. Give Ss time to prepare and write their summary. Ask Ss to compare their summary with a partner. Encourage peer correction. You may wish to collect in answers and give more detailed feedback using the Writing feedback framework.

Suggested answer
(for the presentation on motivating teams)

To summarise, the main points of the presentation on motivating teams were:
- Groups need to have a good team leader
- Listen to the team's concerns and help with any problems
- Involve teams in decision-making.

The speaker concluded that a motivated team produces better results.

(for the presentation on motivating new staff)
To summarise, the main points of the presentation on motivating staff were:
- Welcome new staff from day one
- Take time to get to know new employees
- Make sure new staff get the training they need.

The speaker concluded that new employees will respect you if you respect them.

What do you write? 2

Remind Ss that reports can be in various styles and that a continuous paragraph, as in this exercise, is an acceptable alternative to bulleted or numbered lists. Ask Ss to work in pairs and complete the conclusions and recommendations using the words provided. Point out that each word can be used only once (in case Ss try to say both *It would be a good idea ...* and *It would be good if this ...*). Check answers with the class. Ask Ss if they agree with the opinions in the conclusion. Do Ss already do any of these things? Elicit: a phrase to introduce recommendations (*here are my recommendations on ...*); two phrases for making suggestions (*It would be a good idea to ... It would be better if ...*); a word to signal another point (*also*).

1 recommendations	2 efficiently	3 moment
4 unnecessary	5 good	6 Also
7 Finally	8 better	

Skills book, Grammar reference: Adjectives and adverbs, page 94

Task 2

Ss are now going to write a conclusion to a report about English language training in their company. To help Ss prepare, ask them to work in pairs / small groups and discuss ways to continue improving their English in the future. Compare ideas around the class. This would be a good point at which to look at ways that Ss can consolidate their work on the course and continue the progress that they have made (see Suggestions box below). Photocopy and give each S a Writing preparation framework sheet. Ask Ss to write the conclusion to the report. Circulate and help Ss where necessary. Ask Ss to compare their report with a partner and encourage peer correction. If appropriate for your class, you could stick the conclusions on the wall and ask Ss to circulate and read.

Suggested answer
In conclusion, here are my recommendations on how to continue improving my English in the future. It would be a good idea to use the Skills Book and CD-ROM to review any areas that need more practice. Also, I will sometimes try to read English magazines and newspapers. Finally, I have made good progress and it would be a good idea to continue with another course of language training to help me continue to improve my English.

Suggestions for continuing to make progress in English:
- Make regular visits to www.intelligent-business.org
- Use the *Intelligent Business* CD-ROM to review areas where you need more practice
- Look again at the *Intelligent Business* Skills Book and review any areas where you need more practice
- Read English magazines or newspapers (especially on subjects that interest you)
- Listen to English radio and watch English TV programmes as much as possible
- Consolidate the skills learnt on the course by taking opportunities to speak English at work or at home (e.g. when visitors come to your company or when you are on holiday).

Photocopiable resource 1.1: Talking about jobs

Student A

1 Ask your partner questions to complete the information about Howard.

Howard works as an _____ for a company called _____ . It is a _____ company. In his job, Howard _____ _____ exhibitions. He is responsible for _____ exhibitions in the _____ and East Anglia region.

2 Read the information about Amanda. Then answer your partner's questions.

Amanda works as an **administrator** for a company called **YTC**. The company **develops** new **drugs** for the **medical** industry. In her job, Amanda is responsible for **updating** the company database and **sending** information about the company's developments to medical journals.

Student B

1 Read the information about Howard. Then answer your partner's questions.

Howard works as an **events organiser** for a company called **PJD**. It is a **multinational** company. In his job, Howard **organises trade** exhibitions. He is responsible for **planning** exhibitions in the **Cambridge** and East Anglia region.

2 Ask your partner questions to complete the information about Amanda.

Amanda works as an _____ for a company called _____ . The company _____ new _____ for the _____ industry. In her job, Amanda is responsible for _____ the company database and _____ information about the company's developments to medical journals.

Photocopiable resource 2.1: Telephone preparation

1 **Start the call**
   a Say who you are: _____

> **Useful phrases**
> **Telephoning someone you do not know well:** *This is (June Shen). / My name's (June Shen).*
> **You know the person you are calling:** *It's (June) here.*
> **You answer the telephone:** *Speaking. / June Shen (speaking).*
>
> **Tip!**
> - If you are phoning someone you do not know well, it's a good idea to say your full name and company name. *This is James MacDonald, from Branco.*
> - If you are phoning someone for the first time, check that you can spell your name and company if necessary. *Would you like me to spell that?*

   b Who do you want to speak to? _____

> **Useful phrases**
> *Can I speak to / I'd like to speak to (James MacDonald), please.*
>
> **Tip!**
> - Check that you know the person's full name (and job title / company name if necessary).
> - Can you pronounce and spell his/her name?
> - What will you do if the person isn't available? *(Can I leave a message? / I'll call back later.)*

   c Reason for the call: _____

> **Useful phrases**
> *I'm calling **to** (check some information).*   *Can you tell me / give me ... ?*
> *I'm calling **because** (I'd like to check some information).*   *I'd like to check/ask/arrange/have/get ...*

2 **Main part of the call**
   Note important phrases/questions/details you need for this call: _____
   _____
   _____

> **Tip!**
> - Check that your phrases and questions are correct before making the call.
> - Can you say/spell any difficult technical words, reference details or place names?

3 **End the call**
   Polite/Friendly phrase to end the call: _____

> **Useful phrases**   less formal ◄────► more formal
> **Thanking someone:** *Thanks for your help. / Thank you very much.*
> **Responding to thanks:** *No problem. / Glad to help. / It's a pleasure. / You're welcome.*

Analysis   Date: _____
What I did well: _____
What I need to practise for the next call: _____

Photocopiable resource 3.1: Card activity (small talk)

Learning a language	A model of car I like / don't like	My journey to work or class today	An interesting TV programme I saw recently	The internet
A food I don't like	A sport I like to play/watch	House prices in my country	A recent holiday or business trip	Why I have / don't have a pet
A film I enjoyed / didn't enjoy	My favourite restaurant	My home town	One of my hobbies or interests	Something I like about my job/studies

Photocopiable resource 7.1: Card activity (prepositions of time)

in	on	at	no preposition
2006	Friday	11:45	next week
June	Mondays and Tuesdays	the weekend	last month
the winter	20th February 2002	night	this Friday
the evening	Saturday 26th August	8:30 this morning	tonight
September 2008	Thursday afternoon	3:30 on Tuesday	next Monday

PHOTOCOPIABLE RESOURCES

Photocopiable resource 4.1: Describing products

1 Put the vocabulary into the correct column. You can use a dictionary to help you.

| wood | round | large | triangular | glass | curved | small | leather | straight | wool | wide |
| metal | square | tiny | long | rectangular | high | plastic | | | | |

Material	Shape	Size
wood	round	large

2 Tell the other people in your group about a product that you bought recently. Include information about the material, shape and size.

3 As a group, choose one of the products that you discussed in question 2. Work together to write a short description of the product. Read the description to another group, without naming the object. Can they guess what it is from your description? Answer any questions the group asks you.

4 Now listen to another group describe a product. Ask questions to get more information about what it looks like and what it is used for. Ask for the group's opinion of the product.

Photocopiable resource 4.1: Answer key

Material	Shape	Size
wood	round	large
glass	triangular	small
leather	curved	wide
wool	straight	tiny
metal	square	long
plastic	rectangular	high

PHOTOCOPIABLE © Pearson Education Limited 2006 177

Photocopiable resource 5.1: Talk preparation

Part 1
Prepare the phrases you will need to do the following:

1 Greet the audience:

2 Introduce yourself:

3 Introduce the subject of your talk:

4 Key points you will cover in your talk (remember to include sequencing language):

5 End your talk and thank the audience:
And to conclude …
Thank you for your attention. / Thank you for listening.

Part 2
When you are listening to your partners' talks, note the following:

	Talk 1	Talk 2
Subject of the talk:	_____	_____
Key points the talk covered:	_____	_____
	_____	_____

Tick the things that the speaker did:

	Talk 1	Talk 2
Greeted the audience	☐	☐
Smiled	☐	☐
Introduced himself/herself	☐	☐
Structured the talk clearly	☐	☐
Spoke clearly	☐	☐
Looked up from their notes	☐	☐
Thanked the audience	☐	☐

PHOTOCOPIABLE RESOURCES

Photocopiable resource 8.1: Card activity (places in a company)

Purchasing department	buys things for the company	**Sales and Marketing**	sells products or services and promotes the company
Canteen	where staff can eat	**Production area**	where products are manufactured
Warehouse	place for storing stock or products	**Human Resources department**	employs staff and helps with career development and training
Finance department	where the invoices and accounts are done	**Reception**	where visitors wait when they arrive at a company

Photocopiable resource 8.2: Find someone who ...

Find someone who ...	Name of person
can tell you how to get to the nearest post office	
thinks procedures are important	
can tell you the procedure for opening a bank account	
can name five departments in a company	
can explain how to text a message on a mobile phone	
can think of two things to do to help a colleague who is new to the company	
can tell you where to go to make photocopies	
can tell you how to make a cup of coffee	

PHOTOCOPIABLE © Pearson Education Limited 2006

179

Photocopiable resource 9.1: Card activity (respond to suggestions)

How about asking for extra homework today?	We should all travel to work by public transport to save energy.	We need to cut costs. Why not reduce employees' salaries by 10%?	Why not invest all our money in internet shares?!
We could finish early and go for a coffee!	Why not ask the company to send the English class to England for two weeks?	I think we should get a salary bonus when we complete our English course.	We have some visitors from Australia. You could come to dinner tonight and practice your English!
We could give staff an extra week of paid holiday every year.	Why not have a box in our English lessons and every time we don't speak English we put money in it?	Perhaps we could speak English together every day for half an hour.	We have an important deadline to meet. Perhaps you could work this weekend.

Photocopiable resource 10.1: Graph grid

Useful phrases	
Introducing visuals	*As you can see … / As the graph shows … / As the figures show …*
Describing trends	*fall decrease drop increase rise remain steady reach a peak slightly gradually substantially sharply dramatically*

Photocopiable resource 11.1: Market research questionnaire

Student A	Student B
Ask your partner questions to complete the leisure insurance questionnaire. Use open and closed, and direct and indirect questions.	**Ask your partner questions to complete the travel insurance questionnaire. Use open and closed, and direct and indirect questions.**

Student A

Name: _____

Place of birth: _____

Company: _____

Sports/leisure activities he/she does:
_____

Times per month:
once ☐   twice ☐   three + ☐

Smoker ☐   Non-smoker ☐

Experience of any of these during leisure activities?
Injury ☐
Illness ☐
Theft ☐
Loss of personal property ☐

Give details:

Student B

Name: _____

Job/studies: _____

Number of holidays taken each year:
_____

Last holiday:
Date: _____

Location: _____

Duration: _____

Experience of any of these on holiday?
Accident ☐
Illness ☐
Theft ☐
Loss of personal property ☐

Give details:

Photocopiable resource 12.1: Telephone phrases (complaints)

Making a complaint	Dealing with a complaint
Explain the problem *I wonder if you can help me …* *I've got a problem with …* *The problem is …* *It's the wrong logo/colour/quantity.* *The logo/colour/quantity is wrong.* *I bought … from your company but …* **Say what you want to happen** *I'd like you to (print new copies / replace the plants).* *I'd like / I need (new copies / new plants)* *… today / by the end of the week / as soon as possible …* *Because …* **End the call politely** *Thank you. / Thanks for your help.*	**Find out what the problem is** *What can I do for you?* *How can I help?* *Could you tell me what the problem is?* **Apologise/Sympathise** *I'm sorry to hear that.* *I'm very sorry about that …* *I (can) see the problem …* **Say what you will do** *Certainly, I'll …* *I'll arrange to …* *I'll deal with it (immediately / right now).* *I'll arrange that for you.* **End the call politely** *No problem.* *Glad to be of help.*
Phrases for call 1	**Phrases for call 2**

PHOTOCOPIABLE FRAMEWORKS

Photocopiable resource 13.1: Agenda suggestions

Student A
Staff reward scheme: Give all employees a salary bonus.
Reception: Paint the reception area in bright colours.
Paternity leave: Introduce it to staff who have worked for the company for more than a year.

Student B
Staff reward scheme: Offer staff the opportunity to invest in a company share scheme (if staff buy 50 shares, the company will give them 100).
Reception: Buy a large aquarium with exotic fish.
Paternity leave: No, it will cost the company too much money.

Student C
Staff reward scheme: Buy a box at the theatre so that staff can attend plays, concerts and operas free.
Reception: Have a photo exhibition in reception, featuring photographs by staff or of staff members.
Paternity leave: Introduce it to all staff, but with maximum leave of three months.

Student D
Staff reward scheme: Have a party for all staff members and their families.
Reception: Have a small multimedia area in reception, giving information about company history and current projects.
Paternity leave: Need to do more research into this topic and discuss in more detail at the next meeting.

Photocopiable resource 14.1: Card activity (negotiations)

Negotiation card

Carl tries to negotiate a salary increase with his boss. His boss explains that the company is unable to increase salaries at present. He wants to give Carl more responsibility. Carl agrees that he will accept more responsibility if they will review his salary in three months. His boss refuses to guarantee that Carl's pay will be reviewed on a fixed date, but says that no future review will be possible unless Carl agrees to accept more responsibility. Carl accepts but is not happy.

Negotiation card

Carl tries to negotiate a salary increase with his boss. His boss explains that the company is unable to increase salaries at present. However, he tells Carl that he is pleased with his work. He suggests giving Carl a temporary promotion that will include more responsibility. He promises to review Carl's request in three months' time. If he performs well in his new role, the manager will recommend a salary increase. Carl accepts.

Negotiation card

Carl tries to negotiate a salary increase with his boss. His boss refuses. Carl resigns and gets another job, which he does not enjoy as much. His boss employs a new member of staff but the new person does not have Carl's experience and needs lots of supervision.

**Negotiation outcome:
Win–Lose**

**Negotiation outcome:
Win–Win**

**Negotiation outcome:
Lose–Lose**

PHOTOCOPIABLE © Pearson Education Limited 2006

Photocopiable resource 14.2: Negotiations outline

Aim of the negotiation	What you want to offer	What you think your partner will offer
Useful phrases *If you ... , I'll ...* *If we ... , could you ... ?* *I can understand your position but ...* *I suggest that ...*	What you will accept	What you think your partner will accept

Photocopiable resource 15.1: Motivational factors

Look at these factors that can affect motivation. Put them in order to show what motivates you most (1 = motivates most, 12 = motivates least).

Motivational factors

- ☐ Learning new skills
- ☐ Status
- ☐ Financial reward
- ☐ Competition
- ☐ Job security
- ☐ Knowing that people listen to your ideas and suggestions
- ☐ Praise
- ☐ Fear
- ☐ Being able to discuss concerns
- ☐ A happy working environment
- ☐ Achieving results / Hitting targets
- ☐ Possibility of promotion

PHOTOCOPIABLE RESOURCES

Frameworks

Seven photocopiable framework sheets are provided for task preparation and feedback.

1 Presentation preparation framework
Give a photocopy of the framework to Ss when they are preparing for a longer presentation. The first section focuses the presenter on the audience and the purpose of the presentation. The second section encourages the presenter to plan a clear structure and to think of key language. The final section provides space to note down additional useful phrases.

2 Presentation feedback framework
This framework may be used by teachers giving feedback on Ss, and also by Ss giving peer feedback. It acts as a reminder that accuracy is not the key feature of a presentation in a second language; clear structure and signposting, and interesting content and delivery are often more important.

3 Writing preparation framework
This framework helps Ss to structure and plan their writing. It is particularly useful for the Write it up section of the Dilemma at the end of each Coursebook unit. The Teacher's notes for the Dilemma guide you through the framework in relation to a particular genre and refer you to the relevant pages of the Style guide.

4 Writing feedback framework
This framework may also be used to give feedback from the teacher or from peers. Once again, it reminds those giving feedback that accuracy is one element of communication only; clear structure, arguments and layout, and clear and appropriate language are equally important.

5 Skills feedback framework
This framework is similar to the presentation feedback above – but usable in a greater range of situations. Circle the skill practised (e.g. telephoning).

6 Accuracy feedback sheet
Use this sheet to give feedback following a variety of tasks. Accuracy feedback can relate to vocabulary and pronunciation as well as grammar. Start with specific positive feedback. Then focus on error correction. Finally, encourage Ss to focus on what is achievable. If Ss are too ambitious, they are likely to fail; therefore, ask them to monitor no more than three language points. When they feel confident, they can tick off these points and identify three more specific areas for improvement.

7 Vocabulary record sheet
Remind Ss that noting down a word means more than just recording its meaning. This sheet has three frameworks for Ss to record vocabulary. The first is a standard word diagram (or spider diagram) usable for recording vocabulary related to a central concept. It is also usable to indicate collocations in relation to the central word. In the final framework, Ss write a vocabulary item in the centre and different information about the item in each petal, e.g. petal 1 = meaning, petal 2 = pronunciation, petal 3 = formal/informal, petal 4 = other comments.

Presentation preparation framework

Student:	Date:
Title of presentation:	

Who is my presentation aimed at?	
What am I trying to achieve in my presentation?	

Stage	Key points	Key language
Introduction		
Body		
Conclusion		

Signposting and linking phrases	
Phrases for referring to visuals	

Presentation feedback framework

Student:
Date:
Title of presentation:

Content
- Purpose?
- Interest?
- Appropriateness?

Structure
- Structure?
- Organisation?
- Signposting?

Grammar
- Accuracy?
- Appropriateness?

Vocabulary
- Accuracy?
- Appropriateness?
- Pronunciation?

Delivery
- Pronunciation?
- Chunking?
- Projection?
- Eye contact?
- Body language?

Other comments

Writing preparation framework

Student:		Date:
Lesson focus:		

Type of writing e.g. formal/informal letter/report/memo?	
Who am I writing to?	
Purpose	
Target reader	
Structure and organisation • Is there a typical structure and layout that I can follow? • What sections should I divide my document into?	
Style • Formal/informal/neutral style? • Tone? (polite/friendly/helpful)	
Useful phrases	
Checks Have I checked my writing for: • logical structure? • clarity of ideas? • accuracy of language?	

Writing feedback framework

Student:		**Date:**
Lesson focus:		

Planning
- Clarity of purpose?
- Achievement of objectives?
- Appropriateness for target reader?

Layout
- Appropriatenes of layout? e.g. formal/informal letter/report/memo
- Clarity of layout? (paragraphs, headings, white space, bullets)

Organisation and clarity
- Clear points?
- Organisation?
- Support for main points?
- Sentence length?
- Conciseness?
- Communication of ideas?

Language
- Accuracy?
- Range?
- Appropriateness? (formality / tone)

Other comments

Skills feedback framework

Student:		Date:
Skill (*circle as appropriate*): Socialising/Meeting/Negotiating/Telephoning Other (*please specify*)		

Communication • Task achievement? • Comprehension? • Responding? • Checking and clarifying? • Showing interest? • Turn-taking? • Fluency? • Effectiveness?	
Pronunciation • Sounds? • Stress and intonation?	
Grammar • Accuracy? • Range? • Appropriateness?	
Vocabulary • Accuracy? • Range? • Appropriateness?	
Other comments • Cultural awareness?	

Accuracy feedback sheet

Student:		Date:
Lesson focus:		

What you did well

What you did less well

What you said/wrote	What you should have said/written

Action plan

List no more than three specific points (identified on this feedback sheet) that you are going to focus on and monitor when speaking and writing

1

2

3

INTELLIGENT BUSINESS (UPPER INTERMEDIATE) TEACHER'S BOOK

Vocabulary record sheet

Student:

Date:

Lesson focus:

- Use some or all of the ways suggested below to record key vocabulary.
- Remenber that knowing a word or phrase is more than just knowing its meaning.

Noun	Verb	Adjective	Adverb